AFRICAN VOICES
AFRICAN VISIONS

Edited by
Olugbenga Adesida
Arunma Oteh

THE NORDIC AFRICA INSTITUTE

Indexing terms

Political development
Future studies
Development potential
Africa

Cover photo: Eric Roxfelt/PHOENIX
ISBN 91-7106-472-9
Printed in Sweden by Elanders Gotab, Stockholm 2001

Contents

Foreword

Adebayo Olukoshi

One recurring theme in the search for a viable path for the revival of the fortunes of African countries has been the need for a well-crafted vision that could underpin both policy and politics in the quest for development. The question of a vision, whether local, national or even regional, has been made ever-more imperative by the demise of economic planning regimes and the attempt to promote market policies in their place but without paying attention to the hopes and aspirations that were often integral to the goals of national and regional planning.

A first step in redressing the vision deficit of the 1980s and 1990s was taken when the United Nations Development Programme (UNDP) introduced its African long-term perspective project, out of which emerged various attempts at formulating different national visions up to the year 2020. It is against this background, and within the context of the search in various bilateral donor communities for a new framework for development co-operation, that this book was commissioned with support from the Swedish International Development Cooperation Agency (Sida) and the Nordic Africa Institute (NAI). The book, co-ordinated and edited by Olugbenga Adesida and Arunma Oteh, was aimed at capturing the visions which a younger generation of Africans hold of their communities, countries, continent and, indeed, of the world. Being closely involved in the implementation of the project, I was most delighted at the enthusiastic response which the call for papers generated and it is out of the numerous submissions which were made by young Africans from different walks of life that the editors selected the essays which now constitute this volume.

Reading through the essays in this book, and the combination of hopes and aspirations which they convey, gives the reader reasons to be optimistic about the future of Africa, and particularly the creative potential which the younger generation of Africans is likely to bring to bear on the development of the continent. Drawn as they are from different parts of Africa and different disciplinary and professional backgrounds, the contributors are united by their common faith in the future of the continent, even if the details of their assessment point to differing perspectives on the path to the reconstruction of the foundations of the continent ready for greatness.

I should like to take this opportunity to thank Adesida and Oteh for the selfless work which they put into the realisation of this project. The Nordic Africa Institute, and especially its director, Lennart Wohlgemuth, and Sida should also be thanked for the strong support which they extended to the project. I have no doubt that readers will find this volume to be a useful window into the thinking of a younger generation of Africans about the possible, even alternative future directions that are available to their countries and continent.

Preface

Like many other Africans, we tend to talk about the ills of Africa. We are sure many people will understand the usual "armchair discussion and analysis" of what went wrong that we Africans usually start once a few of us get together. During one of these armchair discussions, we decided to do something about the ills of Africa. As you can guess, our decision was not to start a revolution, join a guerrilla movement or quit our jobs and become volunteers. The simple idea, which was the origin of this book, was how could we get young Africans to begin a dialogue, to reflect together and generate ideas on the way forward for Africa. This was in December 1995 and since then we have been engaged in the exciting, challenging, demanding and rewarding activity of trying to organize a global dialogue among Africans on the future of Africa. Part of the outcome of that dialogue is this book.

This idea, we believe, is timely for the simple reason that for more than 15 years now since African countries began to implement Structural Adjustment Programs (popularly known as SAPs), African intellectual capital has been mostly invested in debating their pros and cons. Despite the fact that the majority of African countries are implementing some form of adjustment, the debate rages on. While the world was making new discoveries in science and technology, the majority of the African intellectual elite were engaged in a debate that is best characterized as a dialogue between the deaf and the dumb. In fact, SAPs became an industry. Lectures, seminars and conferences were organized all over the world. Mind you, this is still going on! This is not to say it is not important to talk about SAPs, examine their implications and see how they can be improved or replaced. The problem was that while we were reacting to the international financial institutions no one was really busy trying to map out a future for the continent or design alternative strategies to transform Africa.

In fact, many will argue that since independence, African states have had neither a clear vision of the future nor effective strategies to transform their societies. We disagree because there were efforts such as the 1979 Monrovia Report on Africa in the year 2000 prepared by African scholars under the auspices of the Organization of African Unity, and the follow-up Lagos Plan of Action endorsed and signed by African Heads of State in 1980.

This book is a follow-up to these illustrious efforts. It is time that we Africans take the lead in charting our own future. We need to start defining the agenda rather than reacting to ideas proposed by external actors, whether financial institutions or donors. For about four centuries, Africa seemed to be at the receiving end of ideas. Remember the Berlin Conference of 1885 to divide Africa? How many of our forefathers (or mothers) were in attendance?

Our fear about the future is not just that Africa is facing tremendous challenges on almost all fronts. Africa can overcome these, as others have overcome similar handicaps. Our fear is centered simply on the lack of new and innovative ideas. This is the danger: the poverty of ideas and of the mind. Because it is only with ideas that we can dissolve the multiple crises facing Africa. That is why we have been very enthusiastic about this project.

By all accounts, it was a major undertaking. We invited over 500 Africans from all over the world to contribute papers. In addition, we persuaded several journals like *African Economy, Futurist, Futures Bulletin, Lettre d'Afrique de l'Ouest, PADIS Newsletter* and several Internet newsgroups (such as Kenyanet and Naijanet) and newsletters to post an invitation to all Africans to contribute papers. The only restriction was that the author must be forty years of age or under in 1996. The challenge was that each prospective author should think the unthinkable. Think long term (30 years into the future) and strategically, and prepare a paper of about 4,000 words on their vision for the future of Africa and what strategies can be put in place to realize it. A shortened version of the book proposal and guidelines for authors can be found in the Annex. We received very positive responses and inquiries, set up an office with a secretary and recruited research assistants. Due to demand, we extended the deadline for submission of papers twice!

The value of this project goes beyond this book. As far as we know, it is the first time that such an effort, which specifically targets young Africans, has been undertaken. As we all know, Africans believe in elders. In fact, we received exciting challenges from the older generation taking us to task on the age limit. We were reminded about the fact that quite a few African military dictators took power when they were under forty, and of the damage they did to their countries and the continent. We were also told that new ideas are not limited to youth. The interesting part is that we agree with the critics. Our aim is to get the young generations of Africans to begin to think about the future of the continent.

As noted earlier, this was a major undertaking. Luckily, we found an army of supporters that assisted us. A big thank you to all because without your assistance this would not have been possible.

First, we would like to thank all those who contributed papers for consideration. Your efforts made this initiative a success. Many of you will not see your paper in the book simply because we could not include all the papers.

Secondly, we would like to thank the Swedish International Development Cooperation Agency (Sida) for funding this initiative, and the Nordic Africa Institute (NAI) for agreeing to manage the funds and publish the book. Staff members of these agencies that assisted us included Gus Edgren (Sida), Dag Ehrenpreis (Sida), Lennart Wohlgemuth (NAI), Adebayo Olukoshi (NAI) and Susan Lindvall (NAI).

Thirdly, we would like to thank Jose Brito, for his support. Others that assisted us include: Jocelline Bazile-Finley, Joseph Okpaku, Alioune Sall, Sohail Inayatullah, Eddie Kariisa, Ted Gordon, Alfred Opubor, T. O. Fadayomi, Pai Obanya, Philip Spies, Mwangi wa Githinji, Morin Babalola, Egbichi Oteh, Federic Grah Mel, Rachel Nelson, Francis Etchie, Bernadette Kargougou, Allyson Brown Anoma, Pulcherie Damiba-Sanfo, and Ousmane Fofana. We also like to acknowledge the assistance of may others that are not listed here that contributed to the success of this project.

However, we will like to absolve all the people that assisted us of any responsibility. The views expressed in this book are entirely those of the authors and do not necessarily reflect the official views of any organization or institution. In addition, any errors or omissions are entirely our responsibility.

This book is just the beginning and we hope to continue the dialogue, by any means necessary. We invite you all to read this book and join us in this endeavor. Let us make our armchair debates more productive.

Olugbenga Adesida
Arunma Oteh

Africa: Visions of the Future

Olugbenga Adesida
Arunma Oteh

The world is at the threshold of the 21st century and the 3rd millennium. This basic fact is fuelling a major look at the future. In fact, it has become fashionable and almost a necessity to take stock and explore what the future holds for humanity. This is an ideal time to take stock, understand where we are, where we are coming from, and where we want to be in the future.

The need to explore future possibilities is particularly relevant for Africa given the precarious situation in which the continent finds itself today. Despite this basic fact, the African voice in the debate and dialogue about the future has been silent. As a continent, Africa is the least represented in the global debate and dialogue on the future of the world. In fact, it is difficult to identify the future of Africa as seen by Africans. In many instances, non-Africans dominate the debate over the future of Africa.

This book is partly a response to this shortcoming. It is meant to present to the world voices of young and dynamic Africans on the future. It presents the views of Africans who will be the leaders of tomorrow, on the future of their communities, countries, Africa, and to some extent, of the world. The goal is not to predict the future but to inspire and challenge a new generation of Africans to explore their desires and empower them to begin to think about the future. This is the first of such books on the future that specifically targets Africa and young Africans. In addition, it is also the first in which the overwhelming majority of contributors are not professional futurists. In a sense, it is a book by non-futurists about the future. This, in fact, makes the book unique and a vehicle to showcase authentic African voices on the future. More specifically, the objectives of this book are to:

– Share with the world, alternative visions of the future from the African perspective;

– Generate a debate in Africa, and possibly the world, about the role of the younger generations in creating a better future;

– Alert African leaders and the international community to the desires, wishes, and fears of the younger generations of Africans; and

– Promote a dialogue on the future, and ensure that Africans, particularly the young, participate in the debate.

The reasoning behind this effort is the need to ensure that Africans reclaim their future and take responsibility for their own destiny despite the doomsday scenarios of the Afropessimists. In an environment where the predominant message about the future of Africa is that the continent has no future, it is imperative that Africans take the initiative to begin to undertake serious analysis of the future possibilities unconstrained by ideological or cultural prejudice. Africans themselves need to begin to seriously examine what could be and what ought to be. If we do not, the negative images on the future of Africa might bombard the average African into a state of hopelessness. This fatalism must be avoided.

THE CRITERIA FOR SELECTION AND GUIDELINES

In putting this book together, there was a deliberate effort to reach out to young Africans. The selection criteria for contributing authors was that they had to be African and 40 years of age or below in 1996 when the project started. The objective is not to discriminate against those over 40 years of age or non-Africans. It is quite clear that age is not a predictor of intelligence or one's visionary capacity. Also, non-Africans may have good ideas on the future of Africa. What we wanted to do with this book, however, was to provide a platform for young Africans to present their views on the future of the continent. This is necessary given that the younger generations of Africans have mostly been left out in the discourse about the future even though they have more at stake.

To ensure cultural, occupational, and gender diversity, we identified a large number of experts (Africans and non-Africans) worldwide to assist in nominating potential authors. Over 500 people were nominated and all were invited to contribute essays for consideration. In addition, open invitations were published in magazines, newsletters and through newsgroups on the Internet.

Responding authors were asked to think 30 years into the future and to write from their own personal perspectives. Although contributing authors were allowed to explore any issue which they deemed important for the future of Africa, they were given the following questions as points of departure:

– What do you think about the future?

– What are your visions, hopes, fears, ambitions and goals for the future?

– What are your perceptions about the trends that will shape the world, your region, nation, and societies? Which of these trends would you like to encourage and which ones would you like to discourage?

– How do you see the future of the world, the African continent, your nation, and your community?

– What type of Africa would you like to live in?

– How can your vision of the future be attained?

– What role do you see yourself playing not only in your country but in the world of the future?

THE ESSAYS

In addition to the introduction and conclusion, this book contains 14 essays on the future of Africa. The essays are neither academic nor research papers and they should not be judged as such. They present the personal visions of the authors and ideas on how to create a desirable 21st century Africa. Most set out to review the past and the present, and to propose a holistic vision for the future and strategies to realize that vision.

Out of the 500 people individually invited, almost all responded positively even though most did not manage to write their essay. We received about 100 contributions; several essays did not have anything to do with the future, and many were just not visionary. As part of the efforts to ensure diversity in the final selection of papers, we recruited over twenty experts globally who assisted in reviewing submitted essays. Despite all the efforts, we did not realize our wish of having the widest representation possible and we bear the responsibility for the final selection. The authors of selected essays are mostly male, West African and anglophone. In fact, we knew at the outset that perfect balance or representation was impossible. As an initial effort, this is a major success, as we have authors representing both sexes and all four corners of Africa.

Although all the essays address the future of Africa, the approach used varies from author to author. In addition, the focus of the authors also differs. With regard to methods, some authors projected themselves 30 years into the future and narrated backwards how Africa arrived at their vision of the future. Others took a different approach. For example, some authors examined past and current trends and tried to project a plausible future for Africa. Others, however, after examining the trends, decided to present a normative vision of what they desire for the future. Despite the differences in approach and focus, all authors addressed the driving questions in varying degrees. What is clear is that all are optimistic that the African situation can be changed for the better in the next three decades.

For *Musa Abutudu*, the two fundamental challenges facing the African continent are the transition from authoritarianism to democracy and the transformation of the African economy. To him, the ideal vision for Africa is that of a participatory democracy which transcends the liberal democratic model. Given the multiethnic and multireligious contexts in African politics, democracy in Africa must pay attention to the national question. He recommends the consociational model of democracy based on proportional representation. Both individual and collective rights must be recognized. Effective decentralization must be undertaken to foster local initiative, widen the level of participation and to guard against the politics of exclusion and marginalization.

For this to happen, according to Abutudu, Africa must begin to "delegitimize dictators". As part of this, African organizations such as the Organization of African Unity (OAU) must take the lead by setting political standards for its members. African leaders, Abutudu warns, must not be allowed to hide under the cloak of African culture because there is nothing within "African culture that encourages murder, torture and incarcerations as a basis of governance and political control". On the contrary, African culture encourages dialogue and consensus as the basis of governance.

This vision can be realized because of encouraging social forces within the environment. They include, the struggle for democracy, justice and human rights despite the callousness of some African despots; communal agitation for collective rights and cultural identity; supportive signals from the international community; and the fact that one day dictators may be called upon to account for their sins as in the case of Malawi, South Korea and Argentina.

Coumba Diouf's essay, translated from French, presents a vision of a new Africa. He presented his vision of the future of Africa through a narrator who, in December 2025, was looking back at the past. The narrator, the President of an African country, was responding to an electronic mail message from his grandchildren and trying to explain how the new Africa came about. Diouf sees an integrated Africa with a Federation of African States (FAS) as its backbone in the year 2025. By that time, the continent is well integrated and has addressed the challenges of the last decade of the 20th century. In this future, Africa is an equal partner in the global order.

This new Africa, according to Diouf, resulted from the emergence of a positive identity and consciousness, and the development of the necessary knowledge and skills. Other important factors include the renewal of the African State through decentralization, political democracy, and an overarching emphasis on developing agriculture. The change began as an answer to the marginalization of the continent.

Analyzing the African dilemma using a strategic management perspective, *Godwin Dogbey* presents a conditional vision with two scenarios: (1) desired future and (2) probable future. The desired future captures his aspirations concerning what Africa should be like in 30 years time; while the probable future captures what he believes is likely. The future that will come to pass will depend on how Africa manages challenges such as governance, globalization, corruption, the Acquired Immune Deficiency Syndrome (AIDS) pandemic, information and communication technologies, gender inequality and environment that it is facing right now.

Assuming that most of the challenges are properly addressed, Africa, according to Dogbey, should be a transformed continent in 30 years. It should become a stable and peaceful continent with a committed people that share a common destiny. In this Africa, poverty, destitution and misery will be things of the past. What must be done is to develop agriculture, adopt technology, seize global opportunities, and both ensure that leaders and followers alike develop new attitudes and transform their institutions; and manage change actively in every facet of their activities. Without a decisive turnaround, change and commitment, the likely future is that of modest growth with social ills such as unemployment and the threat of instability persisting.

Admore Kambudzi, on the other hand, focused primarily on political renewal in Africa. He argues that political renewal must be seen as an ongoing process to rebuild collapsed systems of governance, administration, and public conduct. It must be a process of recreating optimal rulers, critical subjects and responsible citizens. Political renewal in Africa has to be linked to democracy with a vibrant civil society and political pluralism. Each successive generation must, to the best of its ability, build an unencumbered political heritage. In addition, key elements of the new political landscape must be term limits for rulers, non-party based presidency, intra-party parliament in the legislature, open political succession, and ethnofederalism. Like Diouf, Kambudzi's vision of the future is anchored in the union of African nation states to form the United States of Africa. The goal of this must be the unity of African states and peoples, freedom, and prosperity.

With the numerous challenges facing Africa, according to *Geoff Kiangi*, there seems to be no hope for the future. To him, the challenges facing Africa today are indicative that a transformation is needed to give people (Africans) the means to shape their own lives and future. Africa must have a compelling vision of the future that will galvanize the people into action. The elements of this vision must include peace, dignity, fulfillment and decency. Key strategies proposed by Kiangi to make this future a reality include: an emphasis on developing science and technological culture and capabilities, demobilizing the military and getting them out of politics, the provision of appropriate education that equips young people for the future, strengthening democracy and making the legal system effective. In addition to these are the need for responsible leadership and the ability to take advantage of opportunities provided by information and communications technology.

Given the multifaceted nature of the problems facing Africa today, attempting to project a brighter future for Africa, according to *Comfort Lamptey*, "seems like a trivial exercise in day dreaming". However, Lamptey notes that Africans have both good reason and the responsibility to envision a bright and hopeful future for future generations. Looking beyond the gloomy realities, she envisions an African continent that has successfully risen out of its present difficulties and transformed itself in 30 years time. Her approach, similar to that of Diouf, is to present her vision of the future using three different stories. Each story, looking backward from the year 2025, presented the perspectives of the narrators on what they perceive as the critical elements that led to Africa's development success on the world stage. The key lesson from the three accounts is the fact that "Africans alone hold the key to their future destiny". The driving forces that make her vision 2025 a reality were individual responsibility, the emergence of a strong and committed breed of leaders, and strong strategic partnerships between Africans and the African Diaspora.

Barbara Mbire-Barungi argues that the road to a brighter future for Africa must be based on the merging or blending of the old cultural ways of life with the modern. According to Mbire-Barungi, the creation of sound governance structures that combine the old and new ways is a prerequisite for Africa's transformation. In this new Africa, there must be a greater recognition and use of Africa's ethnic diversity; and democratic principles based on effective universal participation must guide the political arena. In addition, she argues that indigenization is crucial for the future development of Africa. Indigenization in the sense that rather than searching for "answers in orthodox structural transformation of the agrarian economy into an industrialized one, it is more fruitful to encourage and innovate where necessary our home grown enterprises, modes of production, and intermediate technology that suit the conditions in Africa".

Lawrence Mukuka dreams of a future of empowerment, advancement and economic development. For the individual household, this should translate into food security, home ownership, and freedom. To make this new vision a reality Africa must focus on agricultural development, as it holds the key to rapid economic development and transformation. In addition, the experience industry (tourism) should be developed to take advantage of global opportunities.

Chika Nwobi sees information technology and globalization as the two key factors that will shape the future. However, he worries that Africa will be forever left behind if the current trends and problems facing the continent continue. Writing about the enormity of the challenge facing Africa, he says: "I have never heard of a man who needs a flashlight to check whether the sun has risen". To him, corruption and tribalism are the two key evils derailing the dream for a better Africa. In addition, African "leaders are constantly engaged in political wars of control" to maintain power. With this, he says: "they see themselves as carrying an elephant on their heads. You and I know that he who is carrying elephants on his head and is yet trying to pick up worms with his feet is either foolish or very strong. It is therefore not surprising to see that our leaders think it foolish to busy themselves with developing education and technological research which are mere worms in their eyes".

Despite Nwobi's fears about the future, he believes that Africans can create in three decades what it took the Americans twenty decades to accomplish. The key lies in admirable leaders who can fight the culture of corruption and expel this demon from themselves and the body politic. As he writes: "when the bath water is poured directly on the head, it will trickle or flow down and sanitize the rest of the body".

Levi Obijiofor's vision for Africa is anchored in unity without which, he says, "the foundation of the future transformation of Africa would be laid on soggy soil". Like Mbire-Barungi, Obijiofor believes that Africa must go back to its roots and build upon key characteristics such as group solidarity, respect for elders, age grades, and others for the transformation of the continent. This, to him, is necessary as the solution to Africa's problems lies in home-grown solutions. He argues for the need to empower women and integrate them into society in such a way that all their potential can be utilized. He suggests that it is time for women to begin to lead Africa. As he says: "It is my considered opinion that African male leaders have failed Africa and that women should be given the opportunity to lead the continent out of its predicament". In addition, Obijiofor stressed the need for Africans to decolonize their minds and rid themselves of the colonial mentality.

Bolanle Olaniran believes that the innovative use of technology holds the key to the current African crisis and is the way to create a desirable future with an improved quality of life and standard of living. He presented an image of the future which is technology driven. For Africa to be able to compete in this future world, it must develop its scientific and technological capacity by investing in education and knowledge, alliances and partnering, in addition to improving the political and socioeconomic environment. To Olaniran, there is an advantage in being a late starter, as the continent does not have huge investments in old technologies and infrastructure. Africa's development can be facilitated by new technologies that are generally cheaper and more advanced than their predecessors.

Coming from a crime and justice perspective, *Paul Omaji*, articulates a vision of a safe and secure continent where everyone is afforded the maximum opportunity to earn a decent living, and an equitable chance to fulfil their lawful aspirations. Without this, he fears that the "emerging culture of fear of criminal victimization or the collapse of justice in general threatens to portray Africa as a dark continent once again". Realizing the vision, he says, requires "visionary leadership in a war against crime and injustice, a philosophical shift in criminal justice, and a functional partnership against crime". A key emphasis is the need for Africa to rely more on its traditional approach to justice, which puts emphasis on community involvement, reconciliation and healing.

Hamdy Abdel Rahman argues that there is a need for an alternative paradigm and a new way of understanding for Africa to be able to overcome the current challenges. He says: "The true beginning in creating a new Africa that is desirable lies in the need to reread the history of Africa as well as its systems and cultures from an internal perspective after about four centuries of domination by external forces". For Africa to achieve a desirable future, it must transcend the pessimistic scenario that dominates its future and which "enhances the current crisis by depriving Africans of their self confidence". To Rahman, the future prospects are good if Africans can create a state which "reflects the will of the common man".

André Wessels identifies the key driving forces of the future as population growth, the revolutionary impact of science and technology on society, and shifts in people's values and ethics. To him, Africa must choose a high road scenario, a future in which Africa is closing the gap between itself and the industrialized countries. For this scenario to materialize, African countries must become winning nations. That is, they must provide quality education and train their people to become champions, have a good work ethic, a high savings ratio, use the principle of dual logic economy, have a strong sense of social justice permeating society, and a balance between economic development, environmental health and quality of life.

LOOKING TOWARDS THE FUTURE

Most of the authors believe that the current precarious situation in Africa is unacceptable. To create a better future for future generations, the authors agree unanimously that Africans must individually take responsibility for the transformation of the continent. At the root of this is the need for a new self-identity and for Africans to re-educate themselves in order to regain control over their destiny.

The authors articulated that the primary problem or challenge Africa must face head on is the political question. The consensus view is that Africa needs a set of political ideals that respond to its culture and the challenges facing the continent, while at the same time adhering to basic fundamental tenets such as human and community rights, and freedom. The need for participation, involvement of the people in the governance of their societies, and visionary leaders were underscored as fundamental to dealing with the political question. While everyone believes that the future can be much better, they all understand that the road to the desired future will be difficult, painstaking and will require immense efforts and commitment on the part of the leaders and citizens.

The desire for a better future permeated all the essays that we received. The authors desire a future that is uniquely African, with a high quality of life and standard of living. This does not mean that the authors want Africa to become like the industrialized nations. Their desire is a new Africa with an African identity that is capable of holding its own, taking care of its own problems, is multicultural, and able to compete in the global economy. The need for human-centered development, justice, environmental security, equity between generations, people and communities, food security and peace all stand out as the key elements of the desired vision for Africa.

This represents the desire of the contributing authors: a future full of hope and promise; a dream for a beautiful future for the coming generations. The overwhelming conclusion is that we, as Africans, can make this happen. From the essays, it is clear that the authors believe that the duty to create a better future for Africa must rest on the shoulders of Africans. Africans must begin to look at their own experiences, rely more on their traditional methods and ideas, and build a new African identity.

While recognizing the need to be self reliant, Africa cannot be an island on its own. It must be part of a global community. It must compete in the new knowledge-intensive world economy, build partnerships and play an important role in the global community. While Africa must keep its house in order and cure its demons, it will need the support of the West, East and all other well-wishers. What Africa needs is understanding and support, not aid. More than anything else, Africa needs the support of the international community to deal with the debt burden for moral and utilitarian reasons.

As part of the process to exorcise its own demons, Africa must begin to evolve new democratic ideals that are uniquely African and that have as their basic elements African culture and realities. A new system of governance that recognizes the multiethnic nature of African societies, group rights and social justice must be put in place. Women must be respected and allowed to take their place as leaders. Corruption and tribalism must be eradicated. Science, technology and innovation must be domesticated in Africa. Military coups must become a thing of the past, and the Organization of African Unity working in concert with the United Nations Security Council must implement an international charter against military coups that will be enforced by member states. Part of this may involve creating a standing global volunteer professional army to enforce the charter. We need new ethics to address the challenges of the future. Africa must set new ethical standards that respect life, the environment, and the rights of future generations. Last but not the least, Africa will need men and women of character and vision to make this picture of the future a reality.

CHAPTER 2

Reflections on
Early 21st Century Africa

Musa I. M. Abutudu

INTRODUCTION

Africa is a continent in crisis. Manifested economically, socially and politically, this crisis is multidimensional and has deep-seated historical roots. If current events have a bearing on the future, and indeed, necessarily condition and shape it, there may be little cause for cheers about the prospects for the future in the next few decades or so. Yet, it is essentially because the terrible conditions are not hidden, practically hitting the headlines on a daily basis in the continent and beyond, that one might take solace in the human capacity to find solutions to identifiable problems. On an even more practical note, there are basic counteracting people-centered trends initiated outside official circles which are clear indications of a determination to overcome and transcend the harsh realities of the contemporary African economic and political climate.

In attempting to visualize the future of Africa, our aspirations and expectations must be realistically projected. This, in turn, requires that all anchors be sought in the dominant trends and tendencies at various levels of development, that are at play at the global, continental and national levels.

GLOBAL TRENDS

Certain trends, often contradictory, are discernible globally and have major implications for the future of the African continent. These are essentially reflections of the post cold war international order and the neo-liberal economic framework which, since the 1980s, has increasingly assumed the status of a global economic orthodoxy.

The first relates to the phenomenon of globalization, the process of increasing interdependence and global enmeshment which occurs as money, people, images, values and ideas flow ever more swiftly and smoothly across national boundaries (Hurrel and Woods, 1995:447). This process implies a tremendous deepening of global economic interactions propelled by the revolution in telecommunications and the near triumph of the neo-liberal economic doctrine worldwide.

However, while Africa has been the subject of much of the forces on which globalization ride, especially the ubiquitous structural adjustment programs (SAPs), the instrument of recent neo-liberal intrusion into African economies, the continent's low economic productive capacity does not place it in a position to contribute meaningfully to the dynamics of this phenomenon (Ihonvbere, 1995:19; 1996:16). In fact, as far as globalization is concerned, Africa is marginal. This does not mean that the process will not affect the continent. On the contrary, it must be realized that globalization, as Hurrel and Wood suggest, is a polarizing phenomenon. Given Africa's low economic weight globally, and the rather poor prospects of significantly increasing its share of world economic production in the next three decades, there is nothing to suggest that the continent will not continue to remain at the low end of the inequalities generated by the forces of globalization.

Closely related to globalization is the idea of "the triumph of the Western idea" (Fukuyama, 1989:1). In strategic terms, Krauthammer depicted the post cold war world as the arrival of the 'unpopular moment'. This is the global political and diplomatic dominance of the United States "attended by its Western allies" (Krauthammer, 1991). From this perspective, the U.S. (Western) agenda becomes the global agenda. Such an agenda has indeed been articulated in Africa for some time. In economic policy it takes on the form of Structural Adjustment Programs (SAPs) while in politics, it is the adoption of multiparty liberal democracy. While the outcomes of these have been mixed, it is clear that the domestic forces that initiated these processes (especially the transition to democracy) will continue to be their main sources of impetus. At the same time, Western support will not come amiss as long it is are not overly-rigid and insistent as to forms.

In general, however, it is also clear that the imperialistic undertone of the 'Western idea' will not go unchallenged. Indeed, Huntington (1993) sees this challenge, "the clash of civilizations", as the dominant tendency that will shape the emerging world order. We may, therefore, reasonably expect strong protestations concerning the specificity of African culture and identity in the face of the onslaught of the 'Western idea'. While this identity should be vigorously asserted and defended, care should also be taken to ensure that African despots do not use claims of cultural identity to erect and heighten barriers against the struggle for democracy.

Finally, we must also think of how African conditions can shape the unfolding international order. Perhaps, the greatest element in this is the political condition that is characterised by ethnic violence and civil wars. These forms of localized violence will continue to focus global attention on Africa, and may contribute substantially to structuring the activities of a global organization like the United Nations and its agencies.

TRENDS IN THE AFRICAN CONTINENT

Two other major definitive moments of the African condition are discernible. Acute poverty and a high degree of material deprivation in absolute terms, and in relation to other regions of the world define the economic and social condition of the African continent. As Claude Ake (1996:1) pointed out, "three decades of preoccupation with development in Africa have yielded meager returns". Living standards have deteriorated below what they were during the first decades of independence. This is, in most cases, an irony as Tom Forrest shows with reference to Nigeria. To quote him:

> It is remarkable that from 1971 to 1992, two decades when large oil revenue became available to the government, real per capita GDP declined by 10% (Forrest, 1995:254).

Diseases once supposedly conquered in the continent are rearing their heads again. Famine has ravaged various parts of the continent, even as the debt crisis imposes burdens for which the only (im)practical solution is a mooted repudiation (Cheru, 1989) or remission (Dent, 1996). With replacement capacity practically non-existent and maintenance capability dissipated, the economic and social infrastructure put in place in the 1960s and 1970s has deteriorated seemingly beyond redemption. Contemporary Africa, then, as Callaghy and Ravenhill aptly put it, "is distinctly 'hemmed in' by its problems of decline" (Callaghy and Ravenhill, 1993:1).

The responses of African people to this state of decline are themselves interesting, not only in indicating how people are coping, but because they also constitute the trends whose consequences may determine the economic contours of the next few decades in Africa. One such response is the migration of skilled manpower to Europe, the Middle East and North America. For the unskilled and semiskilled, the desire to migrate is no less urgent, taking on even more hazardous forms. Economic crisis and structural adjustment then, have created the African economic refugee. As host countries groan under real and imagined strains resulting from this, the resolution of the crisis of the African economic refugee may, in the coming decades, become an urgent task of African diplomacy.

The more prominent and widespread coping strategies are build around the multiplication of means of livelihood (Mustapha, 1992) and novel or re-energized organizational forms that collectivize self-sustenance and self-reliance at the local level (Rahmato, 1992). While most of these efforts may actually have the effect of sustaining survival at a rather low economic level, the determination and resourcefulness exhibited in them is a cause for optimism. This is even more so as they seem to operate largely outside the constraints usually imposed on African economic operations by the structures of external dependence. At the same time, being largely informal, they appear also to mark a form of defiance against authoritarian rule in Africa.

The second moment of the African condition, then, is the crisis of governance. In most African countries, the prevailing norms of governance are largely authoritarian. Highly personal and predatory exercises of political power are prevalent (Sandbrook, 1985, 1993; Fatton, Jr., 1992; Lewis, 1996). A situation of this nature does not encourage accountability in public life. In fact, corruption becomes a major strategy and the social basis of personal rule. Huge amounts of resources are spent on the purchase of political clientele or on warding off, in the name of state security, real and imagined political enemies. Dictatorship invariably implies a sit-tight syndrome.

The politics of exclusion and marginalization become the rule as wide sectors of the population actually live out their existence more as subjects rather than citizens. As the claims of citizenship turn into the exclusive preserve of a few groups and individuals, Africa is increasingly witnessing the resurgence of sub-nationalism "among large ethnic groups heretofore incorporated into multiethnic states" (Keller, 1995:6). As Keller further notes, such domestic insecurity problems have had a tendency to spill over borders, creating regional dilemmas. Thus, "what were once thought to be mere domestic conflicts are now increasingly seen as potential source for regional insecurity" (Keller, 1996:7). This would tend to impose certain collective security obligations on African states, if the trend is to be held in check as a first line of defense. The more substantive and durable solution must be located at the level of democratic governance.

Recent attempts at democratization in Africa have generally not achieved the level of success that would give cause to be optimistic about the prospects for democracy in Africa in the near future. Some efforts at transition to democracy have been aborted at critical stages (Algeria, 1992 and Nigeria, 1993). However, the more common end product, which indeed has become the trend, is for such transitions to be manipulated into entrenching the incumbent. In other words, political transitions in Africa are being caricatured to subvert the genuine and widespread aspiration for democratic governance in Africa. This has tended to further constrict earlier promises of democratic openings. One major consequence of this is the increasing recourse to violence as the only avenue for self-expression and the assertion of identities as other options become closed.

This is precisely why Africa has, in recent times, become a continent of warlords and embryonic secessionists, with the virtual collapse of the state in countries like Somalia, Liberia and others (Zartman, 1995). The conditions of personal rule, authoritarianism and the politics of exclusion that precipitated collapse and violent protest movements are still very much around. As pointed out earlier, most of those that have trodden the path of transition to multiparty democracy in recent times only transited to reinforce incumbency. The refusal of many African regimes to genuinely democratize and engage in broad base power-sharing arrangements does not give one cause for optimism that the conditions that bred "war-lordism", disintegrative tendencies and actual state collapse will be arrested before they reach boiling point.

THE NIGERIAN CONDITION

Economic crisis, corruption and dictatorship epitomize the Nigerian condition. This has worsened in recent times by the crisis of legitimacy that has dogged the path of the military regime since the annulment of the presidential election of 1993.

The poverty problem is underscored by a level of unemployment and under-employment which the 1991 national population census put at about 70 percent. Salaried workers are increasingly unable to meet their minimum basic needs as a result of the vast erosion of their purchasing power. At the same time, the ever-present fear of retrenchment in both the public and private sectors of the economy has become a daily problem to contend with at the personal and family levels. In the midst of all this, corruption seems to have become endemic at practically all levels of public life. Indeed, in the lower levels, it is increasingly rationalized as a coping strategy, a means of survival. By rolling back the state, SAPs were expected to reduce the incidence of corruption while discouraging the premium on public office as the basis of wealth accumulation.

However, what the Nigerian military authorities came up with as SAPs has not only deepened poverty for the majority of people and practically wiped out what was once a middle class; it has also created a small class of "nouveaux riches". The ruling regime took advantage of the demand by the International Monetary Fund (IMF) and the World Bank for exchange rate liberalization and the equally strong domestic opposition to such a measure to put in place what supposedly amounted to a compromise solution – a dual exchange rate regime. The introduction of a dual exchange rate regime in a political environment that has largely become devoid of discipline and patriotism produced a situation where those with access to the state were put in a vantage position to exploit the gap between the two rates to turn themselves into millionaires, or consolidate existing wealth without making visible additions to the national product. Thus, this 'home-made' SAP touted as a strategy to address the problem of primitive accumulation in Nigeria actually reproduced the latter on an expanded scale as new forms of political patronage seemed to thrive on it. The premium on the acquisition of political power therefore grows by the day. It is now a piece of conventional wisdom that to really 'make it' in Nigeria, politics rather than productive economic engagement is the way to proceed. This does not augur well for economic development.

The inability of the state to come to grips with the problems of poverty and corruption can be attributed to the crisis of governance in Nigeria. Indeed, the use of corruption as a tool of governance seems to have gone beyond an anomaly even in the popular consciousness. In the "settlement" form it assumed during the past decade of military rule, it has almost assumed the status of a canon of governance. Coupled with the increasing incidence of brute force as a basic tool of governance during the same period, reason, dialogue and the rule of law have taken a back-seat in the affairs of state.

The dictatorship is the central problematic in contemporary Nigeria. Given its legitimacy problems, military dictatorship resorts to material inducement as a mechanism for buying support. Thus legitimized at the highest levels, it becomes practically impossible to control it at the lower levels where, as pointed out earlier, corruption is increasingly rationalized as a means of survival. Equally, dictatorships tend to overstate the security problem or misrepresent it. This does not only lead to disproportionate expenditure on security and security-related matters, but also all manner of expenditures that have nothing to do with security are rationalized within that item, thus putting them beyond the question of accountability. This overwhelming concern with security reduces the premium placed on welfare needs and productive economic activities.

The absence of dialogue and the overwhelming reliance on force and corruption marks an increasing insensitivity to the genuine aspirations and demands of marginalized groups. Such insensitivity is also displayed with respect to environmental degradation, even as affected communities organize to draw national and international attention to this problem. Smarting from what they perceive as the politics of neglect, exploitation and marginalization, several communities, especially in the oil-producing Niger Delta, are increasingly demanding the right to 'self-determination'. Similar perceptions of political exclusion among various groups nation-wide has made the notion of a confederate structure or a loose federation, a recurring theme in political discourse. Whether or not the tendency to see disintegration as an option no longer to be ruled out for resolving the national question in Nigeria will gain strength in the future will largely depend on how the problematic of military dictatorship is resolved. In fact, it will largely be resolved through the way democracy meshes with federalism.

It is remarkable, and a real cause for despair that as Nigeria approaches the 21st century, her military leaders have openly professed their admiration for the political ways of Zaire under Mobutu or Eyadema's Togo. As the culture of intolerance, viciousness and praise singing takes hold, the incumbent military regime perfects plans to transfer power to itself, rationalizing this as the 'African model' of transition to democracy.

The prevailing order of authoritarian rule becomes even more ominous when viewed against the backdrop of the kind of socialization it imparts to the youth. The militarization of politics and society also finds expression in the militarization of Nigerian youth. The culture of violence is becoming widespread among Nigerian youths. In university campuses across the country, secret cults whose language is violence and intimidation are numerous. It will not be out of place to suggest that given the current trend of cult-induced violence may become a leading cause of death among undergraduates in Nigerian universities. Students and teachers alike are exposed to the danger of cultism, which to a large measure appears to have grown rapidly in recent times in response to the vacuum created by the crackdown on legitimate, organized associational fora of political expression by students. In spite of the noise and alarm expressed at this trend by various sectors of society, there is no solution in sight. Thus, even as authoritarian rule takes its toll directly on academic freedom, the culture of intolerance and violence it breeds among the youth has created a situation of terrorism from below in Nigerian campuses. Along with the terrorism from above (state terrorism), the Nigerian campuses are practically under siege.

The contemporary Nigerian condition, then, is obviously a catalogue of woes. At first impression, there is not much ground for optimism about the future. However, there are social forces within the contemporary situation which are suggestive of counteracting tendencies. There is the struggle for democracy and human rights being waged by various forces and at various levels of Nigerian society. While these forces are harassed daily and their leaders either incarcerated or in exile, the fact remains that these have consistently articulated an alternative vision for the country. At the same time, various communities are contesting and energetically asserting claims to collective rights and cultural identity. Given the intensity of these struggles, the authoritarian regime has often been put on the defensive and forced to make concessions, or become less vicious. Such concessions may be further compelled by signals emanating from the international community. Although weak, sanctions and international public opinion have become distinct signs of disapproval against authoritarian rule in post cold war Africa. Equally, the possibility that dictators would one day be called upon to account for their violation of human rights and corrupt activities while in office (the examples of Argentina, South Korea and Malawi are standard references) are trends that, one hopes, may act as restraints on even more draconian acts by the Nigerian military rulers.

Furthermore, as the state has become increasingly irrelevant to the welfare needs of the average person, various coping strategies have been devised. One such strategy is the physical exit option, emigration. However, only a few can actually exercise this option. Also, and quite unfortunately, it has its rough edges, especially as it has become the basis of various forms of desperate action by youths, some of which do nothing to enhance the image of Nigeria or their own dignity. However, the more notable and significant efforts are in the direction of multiplying the means of livelihood and collective endeavors that emphasize local self-reliance. While these represent imaginative attempts at survival in the midst of a harsh economic climate, it is not clear that they also hold much promise in terms of providing a firm basis for expanded accumulation.

CONCLUSION: THE FUTURE FOR AFRICA

There are two major challenges facing the African continent. The first is the challenge of the transition from authoritarian rule to democracy. The other is the transformation of the African economy and social conditions, or the challenge of development.

There are two major dimensions to the vision of a democratic Africa. First is the element of participation. This is expressed by the opportunity and the capacity to play an active part in the policies shaping one's life, community and country. The other dimension relates to the kind of security that would necessarily be associated with a democratic political order. This is freedom from the uniformed or moneyed oppressor, freedom from ethnic and religious violence, and the provision of a conducive environment for local and national values to flourish. Both dimensions add up to a vision of Africa that should transform the subject created by colonialism and sustained in that unedifying position by post-colonial authoritarianism, to the status of citizen, a bearer and embodiment of definite rights and responsibilities within a political and social context. One would certainly like to see the youth of Africa nurtured under a democratic political culture, and truly experience the joy of a cultured and decent environment.

Democracy as envisaged here must transcend the liberal democratic model, even as it incorporates its best features. The majoritarian underpinnings of liberal democracy do not pay much attention to structural inequalities, exploitation, domination and cultural diversity. Given the multiethnic and multireligious contexts of African politics, democracy must pay attention to the national question in African countries. The consociational model of democracy with its attention to the proportionality element would appear to be best suited to most African countries (Ake, 1996:132). The liberalization of policy must recognize both individual and collective rights. Also, a specific element of democratization should be the decentralization of authority. The centralization and concentration of power are strong features of authoritarian rule in Africa. This does not only stifle local initiative, it also provides a framework for the politics of exclusion and marginalization. Decentralization and a greater measure of local autonomy may, therefore, provide the much-needed tonic for national integration by widening the level of participation and creating a sense of belonging.

To realize our vision of democracy, African societies must begin to take conscious step to delegitimize dictatorships. Where necessary, appropriate steps should be taken to bring past dictators to book. The OAU could play a role here. The continental body should assume a norms-creating role on political standards for its members. The "Kampala Document: Towards a Conference on Security, Stability, Development and Cooperation in Africa", 1991, initiated by the African Leadership Forum, with the endorsement of the OAU, is a good starting point. The African Charter on Human and Peoples Rights is another step in the right direction. However, these documents ought to be taken more seriously by the OAU. While this is not expected to be easy, given the fact that the supreme policy organ of that body is made up of a large number of the heads of authoritarian regimes, the increasing transnationalization of civil society could be a strong means of pressure on this point. The tendency of African leaders to defend their gross violations of individual and collective rights by vague and unsubstantiated references to 'African Culture' or the peculiar character of the African state must no longer go uncontested. There is nothing in African culture that encourages murders, torture and incarceration as a basis for governance and political control. On the contrary, there is evidence that African culture encourages dialogue and consensus among individuals and groups who are bearers of specific rights and responsibilities, as a basic norm of political practice.

Finally, African states must show a willingness to isolate those countries in the continent that are not willing to embark upon the transition to democratic governance. Non-African democracies should be encouraged to pursue similar policies. The cloak of sovereignty and non-interference in the internal affairs of states has served for too long to render African people defenseless against ruinous despots. This should no longer be entertained as Africa enters the 21st century. Sovereignty is an attribute of the people. Dictatorship and authoritarian rule constitute a first-order usurpation of that attribute. In effect, authoritarian rule is a negation of sovereignty. It becomes self-serving, therefore, to claim immunity under what one has already despoiled.

Economic development is the second challenge facing the African continent. One would like to see Africa really launched on the path of development. All too often, the African bourgeoisie either pursues 'quick' money from close association with Government, or engages in projects of short term gestation and quick returns but little or no value in terms of addition to the national product or generating substantial multipliers for sustained accumulation. Real changes are required, and these would demand a transformed African entrepreneur capable of fashioning and executing, perhaps with missionary zeal, long term visions of development. The state necessarily has to be part of this process. A democratic order capable of harnessing the energies of the people towards this end is a prerequisite.

The 'alternative economics' that have developed in recent times only sustain survival at the minimum level for the large majority of those who participate in them. What they have succeeded in doing so far is to act as a cushion, a fallback position in a situation of extreme adversity. They do not, therefore, amount to some grand formula for transforming the African economy. Formal, systematic, and economic planning and implementation remains the key. The real import of coping mechanisms found in 'alternative economics' lies in the imagination and resourcefulness they exhibit in dealing with the issue of survival in these difficult times. What is required, therefore, is to harness these energies and channel them towards the attainment of specific, economically-productive ends. These ends should be articulated within a well-defined macroeconomic framework.

Whatever the specific plan adopted in each country, certain key factors have to be taken into consideration in order to achieve the desired objectives. The first is leadership. Africa requires leaders with vision, people who can lead by example, have a sense of history, and are willing to tackle the problem of corruption head-on. Secondly, accountability must become the central canon of economic and political practice. Thirdly, it is essential that African central banks be given real autonomy. In fact, a general ethical order with an emphasis on a strict separation of public and private property is a prerequisite for Africa's economic development. Fourthly, resource allocation should be closely associated with resource generation. The negation of this has been one of the main sources of tension in a country like Nigeria where the federal government has turned other levels of government and social organizations (especially the high resource areas) into virtual economic hostages. Finally, it would not be out of place to exercise some restraints in the wholesale adoption of free market principles in economic management.

It should be obvious that a pattern of development that simultaneously creates vast inequalities and poverty in its wake does not augur well, politically speaking, for Africa. This is why the democratization of the development process is essential. This will require the democratic determination of the goals of development as well as strategies for getting there. The market-driven neoliberal economic agenda will certainly not do this. Maybe this economic framework is affordable in the advanced capitalist countries where the standard of living already achieved assures decent and acceptable incomes even when austerity programs are being implemented. In Africa, where the abysmally low incomes for the large majority of people are simply not comprehensible to those who have never seen them, the unrestricted unleashment of market forces is a recipe for further impoverishment. It may leave some where they may never be able to get up again. The political repercussions of this will undermine whatever benefits may have accrued from that policy. Furthermore, as Africa tries to free itself from authoritarian rule, the unbridled reign of the market will itself create what Mark Swilling (1991:21) calls "the privatization of authoritarianism". There will be no point replacing one type of authoritarianism with another, or fighting one and leaving the other.

REFERENCES

Ake, Claude, *Democracy and Development in Africa,* The Brookings Institution, Washington, DC., 1996.

Callaghy, Thomas, M., and John Ravenhill, "Visions, Politics and Structure: Afro-Optimism, Afro-Pessimism or Realism' in *Hemmed In: Responses to Africa's Economic Decline,* Thomas M. Callaghy and John Ravenhill, eds, Columbia University Press, New York, 1993.

Chery Fantu, *The Silent Revolution in Africa,* Zed Press, London, 1989.

Dent, M.L., "The Mechanics of Operation Jubilee 2000. Problems of Implementation: The Application to Africa". Paper prepared for the 1996 Convention of the International Studies Association, San Diego, USA, 16–20 April, 1996.

Fatton Jr., Robert, *Predatory Rule: State and Civil Society in Africa.* Lynne Rienner, Boulder, 1992.

Fukuyama, Francis, "The End of History?" *The National Interest* (16) (1989).

Huntington, Samuel P., "The Clash of Civilizations? *Foreign Affairs* (72) (1993).

Hurrel, Andrew and Nguire Woods, "Globalization and Inequality", *Millennium,* 24 (3) 447–470 (1995).

Ihonvbere, Julius O., "Africa in the 1990s and Beyond: Alternative Prescriptions and Projections", *Futures* 28 (1) 15–35 (1996).

Ihonvbere, Julius O., "Evolving Sovereignty in an Interdependent World. The Challenge of Democratization in sub-Saharan Africa". Paper prepared for the 1995 Summer Workshops in the Academic Council of the United Nations System (ACUNS) and the American Society of International Law (ASIL), the Hague, Netherlands, July 16–28, 1995.

Keller, Edmund L., "African Conflict Management and the New World Order", *Policy Paper No. 3,* Institute on Global Conflict and Cooperation, University of California, May, 1995.

Krauthammer, Charles, "The Unipolar Moment" *Foreign Affairs,* (70) 1, (1991).

Lewis, Peter, "From Prebendalism to Predation: The Political Economy of Decline in Nigeria". *The Journal of Modern African Studies,* 34 (1) 79–103 (1996).

Mustapha, A. R., "Structural Adjustment and Multiple Means of Livelihood in Nigeria", in *Authoritarianism, Democracy and Adjustment,* Gibbon P., Y. Bangura and A. Ofstad, eds., The Scandinavian Institute of African Studies, Uppsala, 1992.

Olson, Mancur, "Dictatorship, Democracy and Development, *American Political Science Review* 87 (3) 567–576 (1993).

Rahmato, Dessalegn, "Peasant Organisations in Africa: Constraints and Potential". *Working Paper 1/1991,* CODESRIA, Dakar, 1991.

Sandbrook, Richard, *The Politics of Africa's Economic Stagnation,* Cambridge University Press, Cambridge, 1985.

Sandbrook, Richard, *The Politics of Africa's Economic Recovery,* Cambridge University Press, Cambridge, 1993.

Swilling, Mark, "Socialism, Democracy and Civil Society: The Case for Associational Socialism", *Work in Progress* No. 76, 20–23, (1991).

Zartman, I.W., (ed.) *Collapsed States: The Disintegration and Restoration of Legitimate Authority.* Lynne Rienner, Boulder, 1995.

Africa Forges Ahead[1]

Coumba N. Diouf

THE NEW AFRICA

Who would have believed it? The year 2025 is drawing to a close and all the economic reviews highlight the profound changes that have taken place in the global economy. The focus of attention is the birth of the Federation of African States (FAS) as the fourth global economic pole following the Economic Union of the Americas, European Union and the Pacific Union. The Middle Eastern pole will be created in a few years time.

In this last week of December 2025, the recently completed World Trade Organization (WTO) negotiations were crowned with Africa's emergence as a leading partner in world trade. At the preparatory sessions of the Phoenix convention, Africa managed to have its position on the standardization of the application of biotechnology in soil regeneration adopted despite strong opposition from "environmentalist" Europe. Already, the invitation of FAS to the Summit of the Group of Five[2] was in recognition of the growing weight of Africa on the international scene.

Indeed, who would have believed it? Reading the greetings messages from his grandchildren on his screen, President Diogoye could not help musing: they couldn't have imagined the progress made in the last two decades. President Diogoye switched his computer from the email mode to word processing promising himself, as an end of year present, to remind his grandchildren of yesterday of where the continent was only two decades ago!

LOOKING BACK FROM THE YEAR 2025

A lot has happened in a quarter of a century! The spread of the "Somalian syndrome" to many other African countries brought Africa to the brink of collapse. Furthermore, African traditional partners, Europe followed by USA and Canada, had turned their attention to their backyard rather than cooperating with Africa, a continent whose future was questionable. With the splitting

---

[1] This chapter was translated from French to English.
[2] The Summit of Five replaced the Summit of Seven following the creation of the United Europe Republic which also included Russia.

of the ACP (Africa, Caribbean and Pacific) Group, which occurred during attempts to redefine the framework for cooperation between the then European Union and the Group, the Europeans had gradually broken away from their African partners more or less radically depending on the country concerned. This contributed to a greater marginalization of Africa which, retrospectively, proved to be a blessing.

Indeed, it all began from there. The effect of economic marginalization, coupled with the challenges of international competition created an increasing withdrawal from Africa. The consequence of this was a rapid decline in political and especially budgetary support to African states, particularly from Europe and America, which the growing involvement of Japan and other Asian countries in African economies could not offset.

This subsequently led to the hardening of political regimes, and the collapse of the rent-seeking system upon which many African states were based. A corollary of this was the increase in social violence which was initially civil in nature at the beginning of the 1990s but soon became political. The quest for individual solutions by those excluded from the integrated global market had changed qualitatively into a collective quest for solutions, taking advantage of the culture of violence of the previous years. The constraints of the macroeconomic framework had come up against the tyranny of need.

A whole generation wondered what real life was like without violence and poverty. Its members had only known unfulfilled desires under the constraints of government mismanagement and foreign interference. They had all been born in or after the second half of the 1970s and grew up under the rigors of adjustment.

On the eve of the second millennium, Africa was, more than ever, in search of its bearings. The Afro-pessimism storm had subsided but at least, it still provided greater awareness of a number of issues, and two observations can be made in this regard:

– Africa's economic weight both in terms of the creation of wealth and trade was virtually insignificant.

– The two most authoritative global futures studies of the 1990s either completely ignored or paid very little attention to what they saw as a continent without a future.[3]

And yet a quick review of history shows that this had not always been the case. This certainly calls for a detour because "you do not know where you are going if you do not know where you are coming from!"

As the cradle of humanity, Africa remained at the cutting edge of progress throughout the pre-historical period and during a greater part of antiquity.

---

[3] These were futures studies carried out by the OECD and the Central Planning Bureau of the Netherlands in the 1990s.

With the decline of Ancient Egypt, African civilization centers shifted away from the Nile valley and moved towards the hinterland in a southerly or westerly direction.

During the Middle Ages, in the time of the Great Empires, African civilization developed to a level which was comparable to that of other civilizations of the world.

It was from the 16th century onwards that the process began that was to lead to Africa's decline, namely the slave trade, colonization and globalization.

These developments over time resulted in the loss of historic perspective, and thus opened the way for short-termist political views, which accounted for the situation of Africa towards the end of the 20th century. In order to overcome this handicap, Africa had to regain its historical leadership; and a prerequisite for this was the restoration of a positive identity and consciousness that was capable of putting the continent back on track.

In fact the history of Africa is marked by a continuous struggle between two poles:

– The first is made up of advocates of a stronger relationship with forces that are foreign to the continent, who at various points in time tried to spread their influence.

– The second pole relates to the autonomous movements which tried to resist submission to foreign powers.

Africa was once more at a crossroads towards the end of the 20th century, as it had often been before. The questions that were being asked about Africa were quite negative, and it was even suggested that the continent may have rejected development all together.[4]

THE BASIS FOR CHANGE

And yet there were reasons to be hopeful, despite the fact that the future seemed bleak in view of the difficult realities.

The emergence of a positive identity and consciousness, a living synthesis of the African experience which, from its original base, committed itself to the gradual development of black people through a reassertion of historical leadership, led to three major mutations.

Firstly, the awareness of a center of action in the world helped bolster African consciousness, which then led to the formation of the FAS, and thus liberated the creative forces of Africans and rationalized their actions by taking advantage of their multiple synergies.

---

[4] Axelle Kabou. *Et Si l'Afrique Refusait le Développement?* L'Harmattan, Paris, 1991; See critique by Ibrahima Thioub, "Axelle Kabou, Et Si l'Afrique Refusait le Développement?" Université, Recherche & Développement, *USL Review*, No.1 March 1993, and that of Malick N'Diaye in *L'éthique ceddo... Tome I Le Goorgi....* Presses Universitaires de Dakar, August 1996, pp. 87–115.

Secondly, the perception of development, not as an amalgamation of the theory of backwardness and malthusianism as seen by the defunct Bretton Woods institutions, but as a process of acquiring a strategic position in structuring the forces of the future.

Thirdly and lastly, by recognizing the preponderant role of human resources and by acquiring and developing the necessary knowledge and skills necessary to satisfy the aspirations of Africans and preserve mankind.

Three actions appeared to have been determinant in this:

Firstly, an action for renewing the African State, different from the inefficient and corrupt centralized State which had existed hitherto. The State, which was based on a system of distribution of favors by those in positions of power, only managed to marginalize the people from the political arena and fuelled their interest in promoting change. The exacerbated rivalries within the ruling classes resulting from the system's limited redistribution potential called urgently for a spirit of good citizenship.

In view of their inability to respond effectively to the increasingly urgent needs of the people, and in a bid to broaden the system's redistribution base, the ruling class relinquished some of its responsibilities to the local communities while at the same time preserving effective power at the center.

This apprenticeship, albeit limited, in the exercise of power gave birth to a generation of local leaders, and especially to a return of leadership to the grassroots level. Henceforth, it was no longer a question of awaiting some "developer" to help resolve problems facing the community, but rather resolving them oneself. This movement enhanced the sense of long term strategic thinking and commitment. In addition, it prepared the ground for the abandonment of short-term manipulations exclusively geared towards the advancement of individual and special groups' interests.

Hence, the mechanisms of reproduction of "selfish" regimes were eroded to the point of isolating men who, by the excessive use of public violence, sparked off the process that was to lead to their removal from power.

The depth of the crisis and the increased marginalization which it engendered had the advantage of forcing people to rebuild from scratch. The subsequent redefinition of the rules of the political game saw the wildest dreams of the opposition movement of the 1990s come true.

Political democracy (with the culture of good governance that accompanied it) and its attendant accountability was what gave birth to a state which, given its grassroots decentralized structures, integrated, proximity with long-term strategic management. The rent-seeking state system had been replaced with an autonomous and efficient strategist-state.

The other two actions on which the ageing President Diogoye reflected with emotion for having been a key player in it, were a consequence of this profound change in the nature of the African state and its new-found legitimacy.

First among these was the intense modernization of agriculture based on the various experiences in the continent. Indeed, the absolute priority given to the rural areas had begun in the early 1970s with the creation of conditions for opening this sector to modern methods. This necessary change was conditioned by the desire to ensure food self-sufficiency and highly inspired by the experience of Ujamaa in Tanzania,[5] and others. To ensure success, the following steps were undertaken:

– Creation of functional literacy centers for enhancing the skills of the populations in order to make them actors of modernization.

– Creation of technical centers for promoting basic mechanization and providing repair services for farming equipment and (notably animal traction) and other farming tools.

– Creation of management centers to train farmers in bookkeeping as well as the preparation of various banking, fiscal and administrative documents.

– Establishment of rural mutual funds based on communal savings principles known as *tontines* in francophone West Africa.

This helped reverse the trend towards urbanization, through a vast rural settlement program made possible by the support program for improving standards of living in the rural areas. Farmers' children, who were either unemployed or underemployed in the urban areas, returned to farming, and raised children who escaped the scourge of infant mortality thanks to an improved public health system.

All this culminated in a surge in agricultural production and the multiplication of light industrial processing plants fostering agriculture-industry integration. The modernization of agriculture was a key element of what was to follow.

Lastly, it led to an organization of the State and its labor relationships geared towards the quest for international competitiveness. "Treat as equals" became the catch phrase. And instead of reinventing the wheel or following the footsteps of some big brother, it was essential to find short cuts (rapid growth paths) that would lead to new niches in the global economy. This was mainly based on two factors: lessons from the American and Japanese trade wars and the analysis of the State-Enterprise-Workers tripartite experience in Africa. The perceived role of the State as entrepreneur in the post-independence era was over, but this was not to legitimize the unbridled privatization of state enterprises and functions. The role of the State was now:

– to ensure the coherence and convergence of the national effort;

– to organize or accompany the mobilization of various stakeholders, and actual or potential resources;

---

[5] A development experiment launched by Julius Nyerere in his famous "Arusha speech".

– to analyze the state of the world together with the various social partners, particularly the University, in order to identify and study the forces of the future; and

– to create an enabling environment and push for the relevance of Africa's positions globally as well as the defence of its views.

The spirit of individualism and collective empowerment born of the past produced a bureaucracy which, by building on the inherent characteristics of Africans, reached a significant level of insularity. This protected them from multiple social pressures and it enabled them to formulate national policies based on a long-term vision and the cohesion of the African continent. Thus a link was established between the decentralized political and administrative machinery and the centralized strategic decision-making process. This was only made possible through a network of effective exchanges and consultations between the government, private sector and civil society. This intelligent utilization of its human and scientific potential catapulted Africa's economy to among the competitive economies.

These developments, it seemed to President Diogoye, were what had restored Africa's dignity and led to a brighter future. His train of thoughts was interrupted by the appearance of a message on his screen. Kenay, the son of his late friend who had become the first black Secretary of State of the United States, wanted to get in touch. He was heading a major lobbying effort for Africa and working on an Exodus program: the symbolic return through exchanges of all kinds between Africa and its Diaspora. He switched his screen from word-processing to email, dreaming...

May the force of dreams remain so that we can turn it into the ferment of tomorrow!

CHAPTER 4

Towards a Strategic Vision for a Continent in Distress

Godwin Y. Dogbey

BACKGROUND

The continent of Africa has been beset with myriad problems including political instability, poverty, high indebtedness, underdevelopment, senseless wars, corruption and the list continues. Soon after independence, many African states suffered a series of political setbacks resulting from the emergence of civilian and military dictators. The consequences of this trend of events are clear to see: Africa, a continent well endowed with both natural and human resources, is ironically (or better still paradoxically) the poorest in terms of social, economic and industrial development.

Many of the senseless wars and/or conflicts being witnessed on the continent today have roots in long years of suppression of the people by rulers who proclaimed themselves revolutionaries, redeemers and even emperors. Eventually, these self-acclaimed 'saviors' plunge their national economies into chaos of catastrophic levels. It has been alleged that some of these rulers keep a large portion of their national financial assets in private Swiss bank accounts.[1]

Debt overhang is a heavy yoke that many African countries are carrying into the twenty-first century. From the perspective of the World Bank (1994), most of the severely indebted low-income countries (SILICS) are found in Sub-Saharan Africa. For such countries, either of two key ratios is above critical levels: present value of debt to gross national product (GNP) (80 percent) and present value or debt to exports (220 percent). Using 1992 GNP per capita, such low-income countries are those with income per capita less than or equal to $675. With heavy debt, many African countries could be trapped in a continuous cycle of indebtedness, which might eventually affect the productive capacity in the respective countries. The burden of debt servicing prevents governments from making much-needed developmental investments.

In many African countries, a large mass of people lack basic human necessities such as food, potable water, shelter and clothing. One may be right in

---

[1] A recent report from Swiss banking sources estimates that the amount being held in Swiss banks on behalf of African Leaders alone is in excess of US$20 billion. This estimate, it is believed, is even conservative.

saying that there is no absence of want and fear, or freedom from persecution on the grounds of ethnicity, religion and political belief.[2] All these leave the majority of people on the continent in poverty, with children and women being the most vulnerable. The African context also suffers a dearth of key resources and the underdevelopment of the requisite resources and attitudes towards their utilization.[3]

All but five African countries[4] are at present in the lowest category of human development as defined by the United Nations Development Programme (UNDP, 1994). Approximately, half of Sub-Saharan Africa's population lives below the poverty line, and the depth of poverty is typically worse than anywhere else in the world, and increasing. Average human welfare indexes show a sluggish overall improvement through the mid-1970s and either stagnation or deterioration since then (Ndulu et al., 1996).

Of particular concern is corruption in Africa. Corruption, according to Onigu (1982), is simply the perversion of integrity or the state of affairs through bribery, favors, or moral depravity. It also involves the injection of additional but improper transactions aimed at changing the normal course of events and altering judgements and positions of trust. Little wonder, the World Bank (1989), noted that the continent's problems are rooted in a "governance crisis" which has been exacerbated by corruption, indiscipline, general incompetence and failed leadership. With heightened economic desperation, corruption has risen to unprecedented levels to the extent that it is becoming more of a rule than an exception. For example, the civil servant had either to survive by lowering standards and ethics, or remained upright and perish.[5] Rationally, he has to survive. Corruption grew even in Botswana and Tanzania, with the emergence of economic crisis. These countries, it should be noted, have had strong normative traditions against bureaucratic malfeasance. The less said about Ghana,[6] Nigeria[7] and Kenya[8] the better.

---

[2] Conflicts in Algeria, Egypt, Sudan, South Africa, Liberia, Rwanda and Somalia, just to mention a few, fit into at least one of the reasons mentioned.

[3] ISSER refers to the Institute of Statistical, Social and Economic Research of the University of Ghana. This definition of poverty is a wider concept using resources rather than income to bring home the point that standards of living depend on the total contribution of not only one but several systems of distributing resources to individuals, households and communities.

[4] The exceptions are Botswana, Gabon, Mauritius, Seychelles, South Africa, and Swaziland.

[5] The Republic of Uganda (1980–82); Report of the Public Service Salaries Review Commission, Kampala, cited in David L. Lindauer, Oey Astra Meesook and Partia Suebsaeng (1988): "Government Wage Policy in Africa: Some Findings and Policy Issues", *World Bank Observer*, Vol. 3 No. I Jan. p. 2.

[6] Corruption appears predominant among the reasons frequently given for unconstitutional changes of government in most African states. For Ghana, as an example, the downfall of the first republic under Kwame Nkrumah was attributed to corruption. The extent of corruption existing in Ghana under Nkrumah is amply documented by the more than 40 commissions or committees of enquiry that were set up after his ousting. See Herbert H. Werlin (1972): "The Roots of Corruption: The Ghanaian Enquiry"; *Journal of Modern African Studies*, Vol. 10 No. 2 pp. 251–2.

The implementation of a process of sustainable development is contingent upon the presence of several features such as prudent, rational and farsighted decision-making. It also involves the optimal use of available resources and demands a principled leadership which enjoys the people's understanding and support (Obasanjo, 1994). Corruption strikes at three elements. First, decision-making becomes irrational, short-sighted and motivated by greed and personal aggrandizement. Secondly, resources are squandered as projects are approved not on the basis of their suitability but on the returns that they may yield to decision-makers. Thirdly, a corrupt administration quickly loses confidence of its people, resulting in cynicism and apathy. Corruption, therefore, has led to the misallocation of development resources in many African States, with the attendant problems of unequal distribution of income.

The foregoing is but a bird's-eye view of the problems that beset Africa and project it as a continent in distress; travelling along the path of despair and despondency. One will be tempted to ask: Are these circumstances beyond the continent's management capacity? Has the continent any strengths and opportunities to tone down the current high tide of development crisis? What forces are working or could work against the continental efforts at finding answers and/or solutions to the problems? What strategies should be adopted to put the continent on the high road of hope and prosperity?

This paper seeks to explore these questions by analyzing within a strategic management framework some of the fundamental issues concerning the continent. The focus is on identifying the ambitions, hopes and fears of the continent against the background of global, regional and national trends. These are captured in the ambit of the usual strengths, weakness, opportunities and threats (SWOT) analysis. The following section of this chapter looks at the current global (world) trends interspersed with regional developments. This provides a useful insight into current global developments and their likely impact on the continent. Then, strategic management perspectives are analyzed to form a basis for the conclusion and recommendations as to what strategies to be adopted to curb or halt the crisis. After that a vision for the future of Africa is provided. This vision is conditional and, therefore, is divided into desired (what Africa should be) and probable (what Africa could be) based on current trends.

CURRENT WORLD TRENDS

Recent global events have pointed to the dynamism of the world in terms of economic globalization and advancements in information technology. While

---

[7] See Femi Odekunle (1982) (ed.), *Nigeria: Corruption in Development*, Ibadan University Press, for more on Nigeria.

[8] See African Leadership Forum (1994): Corruption, Democracy and Human Rights in East and Central Africa; Summary Report of Seminar of ALF in Entebbe, Republic of Uganda, 12–14 December, for Kenya's case.

the above are positive signals, there are dangers posed by desertification, global warming consequent on the depletion of the ozone layer, and an increase in the menace of diseases, especially acquired immune deficiency syndrome (AIDS), which is caused by the human immune deficiency virus (HIV).

Globalization of world economy

The global economic environment is brighter than it has been for many years and provides a favorable setting for the continued integration of developing countries (World Bank, 1995). Globalization is a change that is transforming the world economy. This change is reflected in widening and intensifying international linkages in trade and finance. It is being driven by a near-universal push towards trade and capital market liberalization, increasing internationalization of corporate production and distribution strategies, and technological change that is fast eroding barriers to the international tradability of goods, services and capital mobility. Markets for merchandise trade are expanding, more and more services are becoming tradable, and capital is flowing in increasingly diverse ways across countries and regions in search of profitable investments.

With the new opportunities in trade and external finance arising from globalization, new challenges of economic management are emerging in an increasingly open, integrated, and competitive global economy. More and more, policy makers are confronted with a new discipline, the need to maintain the confidence of markets, both domestic and, increasingly, international. Thus, sound economic policies become paramount and command a rising premium. Globalization raises the payoffs for increased competitiveness but compounds the losses from failure to act. Increasingly, it is the more efficient policy regimes that will win out.

For African countries, policies must be structured, receive political commitment and should successfully support outward-oriented growth and production patterns. Moreover, Africa should take up the special challenge of accelerating its integration into the international economic arena. Alongside, intra-regional integration should be given another vigorous push in the wake of South Africa's independence and democratization.

Information technology

Changing patterns and advancement in information technology are gradually turning the world into a global village. However, this rapid advancement and diffusion of information technology (informatics[9]) in industrialized countries

---

[9] Information technology, used interchangeably with the term informatics, is defined here broadly to involve the supply side (computer hardware and software, telecommunications equipment, and electronics based industries) as well as the demand or user side (informatics applications in all economic sectors, information services industry, electronic publishing, broadcasting, management information systems and so on).

poses new challenges for developing countries. It also raises fundamental issues for development assistance. Understanding the ongoing transformations in the industrialized economies caused by the information technology revolution is important in two respects. First, for many years, these transformations will remain a major feature of the international trade and competition that developing countries, African countries included, must face. Second, the experiences and best practices of 'front-runner' organizations in advanced economies could suggest approaches for the successful application of information technology in the developing economies.

Information now ranks equally with other development resources; human, natural, and financial. Moreover, information can accelerate and reinforce the development of these resources. Leading industrial societies recognize the importance of information for their economic health and in global competition. The success of the Japanese economy is largely attributed to the relentless pursuit and diffusion of information by government agencies, businesses, communities, and working groups.[10]

The menace of AIDS

The prevalence of AIDS and its global dimension have become a cause for concern internationally, and in Africa in particular. The dramatic and well-publicized epidemic rise in the number of AIDS cases in the United States since 1981, the onset of a similar epidemic in Europe starting in 1982–1983, and the more recent awareness of the disease as an international health concern involving all continents have generated intense interest and work by many national and international research teams in virology, immunology, clinical medicine, epidemiology, and public health (Piot et al., 1992).

Within a few years after the original description of the syndrome, its cause and basic immunological abnormalities were identified, and the modes of transmission of the causative virus documented. Control programs have been initiated in many countries, and the World Health Organization (WHO) has been charged with overseeing international efforts to combat the pandemic.

The effects of HIV are now devastating in several African countries: estimates of the number of infected people run into millions. Evidently, in many parts of the continent, HIV infection has created a major public health problem, which may have reached the same scale as malaria, diarrhoea, respiratory diseases and malnutrition. Such is the alarming, and still growing, prevalence of the disease within various regions in Côte d'Ivoire, Kenya, Malawi, Tanzania, Uganda, Zaire and Zimbabwe, that several questions are now being raised. Will AIDS have important macroeconomic effects on the stricken societies? If so, what will these effects be, and to what extent can various policies alter

---

[10] See Vogel, Ezra (1979), *Japan as Number One*, Cambridge: Harvard University Press.

them? (Cuddington, 1993). Even if prevention strategies are effective, the current high levels of HIV infection and the long incubation period for AIDS suggest that the disease's economic impact will be a major constraint on development well into the twenty-first century (World Bank, 1993).

Little progress has been made in measuring the impact of AIDS on households and most evidence tends to be anecdotal. However, several models and simulations have attempted to capture the magnitude of the epidemic's impact on income per capita. The number and complexity of the factors influencing the macro economy make accuracy impossible. What can be said is that AIDS will probably reduce the rate of growth of the Gross Domestic Product (GDP) (Over et al., 1989).

Environmental concerns and awareness

Global concerns are being expressed day in day out about the environment. In fact, environmental issues have become the focus of attention at many international fora, symposia and seminars.[11]

The safe disposal of both domestic and industrial waste has become very crucial to policies on the environment worldwide. In addition, strategies are being adopted to preserve the environment by ensuring the optimal use both of renewable and non-renewable natural resources. There is increasing awareness of damages caused by emissions (hydrocarbon and nuclear) and other effluent to biological diversity; the danger posed by ozone layer depletion is also gaining attention, and most environmental policies are being informed as such.

It has become very clear that the state of the environment has a functional relationship with growth. Growth that relies extensively on investment in externally funded infrastructure or manufacturing will have quite different environmental effects than growth that depends on immediate resource depletion through, for example, promoting natural resource exports. In the latter case, the concern would be soil erosion, loss of productive fishery and forestry stock. In the former, water and air pollution would be the chief concerns.

For Africa, a developing region, the environment becomes a very relevant factor in determining the growth path to choose. An inappropriate choice would tend to endanger both human and wildlife, thus detracting heavily from any gains that may accrue from the chosen growth trajectory.

Gender in development

In recent times, gender issues have received prominence in contemporary national and international deliberations. From the Vienna Conference on Human Rights in 1993, and the Cairo Conference on Population and Development in

---

[11] The latest grand conference on the environment was in Rio de Janeiro under the auspices of the UNDP.

September 1994, through the Copenhagen Summit for Social Development in March 1995, to the Beijing conference in September 1995, the family with an emphasis on women has been at the core of deliberations (Sackey and Dogbey, 1996).

In Africa, for example, the existence of investment gaps in the development of women, coupled with cultural and institutional factors, have restricted their access to productive resources. Gender equality is just not an ethical concept of society's obligation to treat women as equally deserving of social opportunities and welfare. On the contrary, it has a pragmatic dimension in which the potentialities of women must be harnessed as an indispensable contribution to the process of nation building (National Development Planning Commission, 1994).

Such is the importance of women in economic development that discriminating against them does not only mean underutilization of all the productive capacity of a nation but has serious implications for the social, political and economic welfare of the individuals concerned. There is no known evidence which genetically establishes a greater productive capacity for men than women. Any assertion thereof in disfavor of women is merely based on social norms, prejudices and gender stereotyping which tend to 'pigeonhole' women into jobs of lower classification than men.

International calls for gender equality, therefore, present a golden opportunity for Africa and other developing countries to incorporate the capacities of women into their economies in order to enhance total factor productivity. To a very large extent, women respond to incentives and making these available to them goes a long way towards improving their current and potential productivity.

It is heart-warming to note that some countries are making positive strides in the direction of women's emancipation. In Ghana, for example, the National Commission on Women and Development (NCWD) and the 31st December Women's Movement are playing crucial roles in helping women get access to productive resources through advancing credit, financing and technical advice to individuals as well as women's groups especially in rural Ghana.

STRATEGIC MANAGEMENT PERSPECTIVES

Much has been said about Africa's crisis which, painfully, the Organization of African Unity (OAU, 1981) also describes as:

> The effect of unfulfilled promises of global development strategies has been more sharply felt in Africa than in the other continents of the world. Indeed, rather than result in an improvement in the economic situation on the continent, successive strategies have made it stagnate and become more susceptible than other regions to the economic and social crises suffered by the industrialized countries.

It is clear, therefore, that Africa has to do its own homework well in terms of strategy formulation, implementation and evaluation on a country specific basis.[12] Strategic management will be very crucial in helping pull Africa out of the socioeconomic doldrums. In the light of this, strategic management, which is the art and science of formulating, implementing and evaluating cross-functional decisions that enable an organization to achieve its objectives, becomes very relevant (David, 1991). Unlike a corporate organization, state objectives are carved as visions, which are specific results that the nation seeks to achieve. A shared national vision helps in ensuring the success of nations by providing direction, aiding in evaluation, creating synergy, revealing priorities, and allowing the coordination of policies. It is also a basis for effective planning, organization, motivation, and control of activities.

Development planning as a strategy for accelerating economic growth is not a new concept in Africa. During colonial and post-colonial times, many governments used development plans as means of targeting and achieving important goals for their people. However, in Africa, such national development plans are so readily formulated and at almost the same time easily consigned to oblivion that planning has come to be regarded either as an exercise in futility or as something alien to the African temperament or way of doing things[13] (Hagan, 1992). This old-style national planning has been discredited for many reasons: it assumed a predictable future in an uncertain environment; it was slow and rigid in the face of change; it focussed on comprehensive blueprints; and it ignored incentives, participation, communication, capabilities and other critical factors. The solution, therefore, is to improve strategic planning, not to abandon it. The need to plan remains to understand the direction of competition, clients and markets, and resources and technologies and to think strategically about competitive advantages (Hanna et al., 1996).

To this end, an analysis of the strengths, weaknesses, opportunities and threats (SWOT) of the continent is done to shed more light onto what Africa should be doing as a way of moving forward. The SWOT analysis below gives useful insight into the hopes, ambitions and fears of Africa. In such an analysis, the strengths and weaknesses are internal to the continent while the opportunities and threats are external. Africa should work towards minimizing the weaknesses, assuming a strategic posture in dealing with the external threats and utilizing its strengths to take advantage of the opportunities.

---

[12] Strategy is about how a state/nation takes control of its own future as far as it can by establishing (i) where it wants to go (ii) identifying internal and external barriers to getting there (iii) mobilizing resources required for such an accomplishment (iv) monitoring progress towards its goals from time to time in a manner that allows corrective action when things go wrong and (v) reassessing goals from time to time but especially as their achievement time draws near.

[13] In many cases, planned resources are diverted into activities other than those anticipated in the development plans. Planning becomes ad hoc and uncertain, See the preface of Ewusi Kojo (1973): *Economic Development Planning in Ghana*: Exposition Press, New York, for more insights.

There is no pretense that this analysis is exhaustive; particularly when we are dealing with a continent with sub-regional diversities. Nevertheless, it is necessary to serve as a barometer in facilitating our understanding of where we were, where we are and where we are drifting towards.

On this score, the SWOT analysis of Africa from a very broad perspective follows:

Strengths

The continent of Africa is naturally endowed with mineral and other physical resources, and basically supplies many industrialized countries with primary products which serve as inputs in their industrial production processes. Admittedly, the continent is a stable landmass not saddled with many natural disasters such as earthquakes, volcanoes and tornadoes on the scale of other regions in the world like Asia and the Americas.

Human capacity on the continent is potentially high. This is against the background of the capabilities of African specialists, most of whom have their basic training on the continent before supplementing it with further training outside, in performing comparably and creditably well with their counterparts from other continents on the international scene.

There is emerging consensus on the state of the African crisis. Many African intellectuals are beginning to agree among themselves on the nature and character of the problems confronting the continent. This consensus in itself marks the beginning of concrete attempts to find lasting remedies to some of the numerous problems facing the continent.

The successful transition and transformation of South Africa from an apartheid regime to a participatory democratic administration and the presence of some quite well-to-do (middle-level) economies in Southwest Africa (e.g. Botswana, Gabon, Swaziland, etc.) and North Africa (e.g. Egypt, Tunisia, etc.) present opportunities to increase intra-African trade and technology sharing and transfer.

Weaknesses

The continent is witnessing political instability resulting from factors such as dictatorship, military adventurism, heightened ethnic tensions and intolerance. Some effects of this are overflows of refugees to relatively stable neighboring states. This requires large amounts of resources and effort in these adjoining states.[14] Civil disorder, therefore, is a serious problem for the region and warrants regional responses.

---

[14] The current situation in Rwanda, Burundi and the Democratic Republic of the Congo provide ample testimonies of the "domino effect" of these conflicts in neighboring nations. Similar incursions were witnessed in Côte d'Ivoire during the heat of the Liberian crisis.

Many countries throughout Africa are dependent on the export of primary products. These products are usually subject to volatile price fluctuations on the world market. Thus, many countries are left in a state of perpetual trade imbalance and, for that matter, current account difficulties.

Attainment in health and education is relatively low in Africa. These two are indicators of enhanced human development capacity. The result is that there is a dearth of highly innovative and well-trained technological skills on the continent.

Governments in Africa have played dominant roles in their respective economies. Such interventions have, in most cases, been disastrous: bureaucracy has increased with inertia, and corruption, nepotism and lack of accountability have grown to frightening heights; and morale has fallen to a low ebb. These growing problems result in inefficiency in most of the public administrative systems.

The underdeveloped, and risk–averse and inert private sector that does not readily respond to incentives abounds in Africa. This state of affairs has contributed, to some extent, to the slow economic adjustment in many African countries.[15]

The African paradigm of colonization and slavery and a call for reparation is not a healthy development. This posture reduces innovation and capacity utilization by dissipating energy in accusing people of one's woes rather than living up to the challenges of the times. Thus, a change of mindset or a dismantling of such paradigms is a sine qua non for moving forward.

Opportunities

The internationalization of the world economy (globalization) expands opportunities by increasing trade and markets. As a caveat, however, this opportunity is not offered on a silver platter; there is need for the right domestic policies and structural changes to be able to take advantage of this global change.

The successful transition and transformation of South Africa into a participatory democracy, the technical know-how in South Africa, Mauritius, Egypt and growth in Botswana all offer opportunities for increased technology sharing and intra-African trade.[16]

The emerging information revolution presents Africa with the opportunity for skills development; technology is not just hardware but also knowledge, means, and organization involved in applying science to the production of goods and services. A large part of technology involves tacit rather than codified knowl-

---

[15] The results of adjustment or economic reforms in Sub-Saharan Africa, except for some remarkable progress in a few countries, have been modest, if not disappointing, even in those countries which escaped major political instability or protracted civil strife (Elbadawi, 1996).

[16] See Elbadawi (1995) and Gunning (1995) for failed attempts at regional integration and trade policy in Africa (Sub-Saharan).

edge and the acquisition and absorption of tacit knowledge requires a minimum technological capability to assess, procure, assimilate, adapt, use or improve technology.

The recent intensification of activities by non-governmental organizations (NGOs) as alternative development agencies provides a very relevant conduit for resource mobilization for growth and development. These agencies, owing to their community-based nature, could be prime candidates or channels for use in addressing poverty alleviation issues on the continent.

There has been quite a sizeable inflow of donor assistance funds into Africa, attached conditionalities notwithstanding, which if carefully internalized through judicious and prudent use can help the continent out of the current development quagmire.

A misfortune though it was, Africa has the singular honor of having many of its people scattered throughout the world as a result of the slave trade. African-Americans and other Africans in the Diaspora can help build a bridge between Africa and the other regions of the world in terms of capital and technology transfers back to the continent.

The newly-industrialized countries of Eastern and Southeast Asia provide ample examples or lessons that Africa can learn from in terms of resource use and policy commitments to achieve desired results. South-South cooperation is a potentially rewarding relationship that Africa can foster.

Threats

Deteriorating terms of trade threaten many countries in Africa since most of their exports are in primary commodities. This leaves the continent in continual debt as the export earnings are not enough to service the accrued debts, let alone save for the future.

There is likely to be competition for aid and investable funds between Africa and Eastern Europe in the wake of the collapse of the iron curtain. In this context, it is going to be the survival of the fittest; the region that projects herself as having growth potential is more likely to win the day.

Many countries on the continent are now becoming notable as transit camps for drug pushers. This is not only dangerous for the health of the youth of the continent but disastrous when viewed in the context of its socioeconomic implications, increase in social vices such as armed robbery, prostitution, rape and above all murder.

Many of the political upheavals on the continent had their roots in playing to the gallery of external ideologies. Perhaps, with the collapse of socialism, this may no longer pose a dominant threat. Still, the emergence of a unipolar world has got its attendant threats, one of which is over-intrusion in the affairs of states.

Inadequate success in experiments with structural adjustment programs and emerging public outcry against the 'inhuman' effects of adjustments are a threat to development in Africa. These frustrations could lead to policy reversals with the consequence of sacrificing the longer-term growth prospects.

Africa is threatened by the "disguised protectionism" of the industrialized countries under the new World Trade Organization (WTO) regulations. This could further marginalize the continent.

THE FUTURE OF AFRICA: A 30-YEAR STRATEGIC VISION

A vision refers to specific results which a nation seeks to achieve in pursuing its fundamental principles of state policy, and with given resource endowments within a long-term time framework. In constructing visions, the future is the main concern though short- and medium-term action planning is usually required in the pursuance and ultimate achievement of such goals.

The vision for Africa needs to be strategic and must be informed by SWOT analysis. With this in mind, my proposed vision is conditional: two scenarios are captured. A desired future seeks to be highly optimistic and mainly addresses the question: What should Africa be in 30 years? On the other hand, the probable future, with patches of pessimism, chooses to address the question: What is Africa likely to be like in thirty years? The latter is a positive concept whilst the former is normative.

So far, we have had some insights into strengths, weakness, opportunities and threats (SWOT) on the African continent. From this perspective, we can proceed to forecast the future. It is noteworthy that anything about the future is expectational and probabilistic in nature. The future is, therefore, considered to take note of the uncertainties that characterize events.

Many of the countries in Africa gained their independence slightly more or less than thirty years ago. However, they are facing a development crisis of even greater magnitude than they faced even at independence. One can, therefore, be quick to observe that Africa is on the decline and not developing. Many factors, as already expounded, account for this trend.

Under these circumstances, what should Africa be like in thirty years? Assuming that many things go right for the continent in terms of policy analytic perspectives, political will, good governance, and taking advantage of opportunities, in thirty years Africa should be a transformed continent. What will this entail? Africa is expected to have developed its physical and human infrastructure sufficiently up to or in the neighborhood of upper middle-level income countries. The economy of the continent should move from poor, severely-indebted low income to upper middle-level income.

About the current social and political conflicts, attempts are being made to find lasting peaceful solutions to them. Good results are emerging in some instances. If we go by the history of even the developed countries, they have also gone through such turmoil and upheavals before. Let us be cautioned, however, that this is no justification for such acts now since we can learn from history without necessarily experiencing some of the historical events. Thirty years, a period almost as long as the independence of many African states is expected to see the dwindling or eradication of such conflicts. What is desired is a stable, peaceful and committed people with a common purpose.

Currently, Africa depends heavily on agricultural production. This is, however, underdeveloped due to primitive technology and skills. In thirty years, Africa, hopefully, will absorb a lot of external technology to boost agricultural production. There will, therefore, be a shift in production possibilities, technologies and patterns on the continent. One foresees a United Africa on the scale of United Europe; a people who are action-oriented and proactive in solving emerging problems. A resulting increase in intra-continental trade cannot be ruled out. It is hoped that with such integration Africa will become a force to reckon with. The region will benefit immensely from access to global markets more easily than countries could do unilaterally.

In sum, the desired vision for Africa in thirty years is for the region to move from a severely-indebted low income to an upper middle-level income where there is a real reduction in poverty, misery and destitution. It is also expected that management of the continent's resources will be efficient and effective.

To achieve this desired vision, it is expected that the region, and for that matter the individual countries will adopt the best strategic management practices. Paradigms or mindsets need to be changed, as do attitudes. There is a need for institutional transformations to make them more responsive to changing management. It is important to understand that attaining the desired future involves having to manage change in every facet of activities of a nation and/or a region.

Back to the probable, there is a seeming pessimism. Current trends point to a gloomy future for the region. This is against the background of the region's slow response to structural adjustment. If present trends persist, which is likely as a result of long lags in adjustment response, Africa in thirty years will have experienced only modest growth in its economy (if at all). All the indicators of human development (health status, nutrition and education) will not record significant changes. Unemployment is likely to persist. Recent efforts at fostering peace will lead to only slight improvement in the political stability of the region.

Declining external aid coupled with dwindling internal resource capacities are likely to preempt the efforts by many governments at enhancing the technological skills necessary to propel the continent to a higher developmental frontier.

Summarily, the likely future of Africa is that of modest growth above stagnation in all the indexes of economic, social and political developments. This is the probable path of Africa's growth trajectory judging from the fact that thirty or more years after independence developments have been rather slow. Yet, in infrastructure for example, much has been destroyed during civil wars and social conflicts. How, then, in the face of dwindling resources, can we say we can achieve the desired vision?

CONCLUDING REMARKS

Africa has been looked at from a strategic management framework. An analysis of the strengths, weaknesses, opportunities and threats of the continent reveals many interesting issues. That there are some strengths and opportunities on the continent is satisfying and gratifying. This helps to allay the fears of the pessimists who predict doom for the region. On the contrary, the existence of weaknesses and threats points to the fact that complacency, self-delusion, inertia and arrogance cannot pull the continent out of its woes.

Combined efforts and energies are required to combat the crisis within the confines of strategic management practices. Policies must be right and conform to best practices. Policy errors and reversals are not acceptable. Many mistakes have been made and these need urgent rectification or correction (in those cases where correction is feasible). Changes in management are an integral part of reaching a high level of attainment in developmental efforts in Africa.

The future of Africa, seen from both perspectives does not look too bleak. Neither the desired or the probable visions point to a downhill gallop in the prospects of the region. While the desired is highly optimistic, the probable is modest. The degree of pessimism is tolerable. This is somewhat good news for the continent. All is not lost and there is a glimmer of hope.

The road to achieving the desired future seems to be very rough and tortuous, requiring immense committed efforts on the part of governments, institutions and individuals. There is a dire need for institutional as well as attitudinal changes if ever the desires are to be met. However, current efforts and expected changes in the region in terms of structure and governance point to the existence of a silver lining on the dark clouds; and there is light at the end of the tunnel. Again, all is not lost for Africa and it can find solace and inspiration in the lines of the hymn writer:

> *Courage Africa do not stumble*
> *Though thy path be dark as night*
> *There is a star to guide the humble*
> *Trust in God and do the right.*

REFERENCES

Aryeetey, Ernest (ed.), *Planning African Growth and Development, Proceedings of the ISSER/UNDP International Conference on Planning for Growth and Development in Africa,* Held at University of Ghana, Legon, March 13–17, 1989, Assemblies of God Literature Centre Ltd. Accra.

Cuddington, John T. (1993), "Modelling the Macroeconomic Effects of AIDS with an Application to Tanzania", *World Bank Economic Review,* May, pp. 173–89.

David, Fred R. (1991), *Concepts of Strategic Management,* Third Edition, Maxwell Macmillan Publishing Company, New York.

Elbadawi, Ibrahim A. (1995), "Growth and Development in Sub-Saharan Africa: Evidence on Key Factors"; Paper Presented at XIth World Congress of the International Economic Association, Tunis, 18–22 Dec. p.14.

Elbadawi, Ibrahim A. (1996), "Consolidating Macroeconomic Stabilization and Restoring Growth in Sub-Saharan Africa" in Ndulu, Benno (ed.): *Agenda for Africa's Economic Renewal.* Transaction Publisher, New Brunswick (USA) and Oxford (UK).

Gunning, William J. (1995), "Regional Integration and Strategies for Trade Policy in Sub-Saharan Africa"; Paper presented at XIth World Congress of 'the International Economic Association, Tunis, 18–22 Dec. pp. 1–20.

Hagan, George P. (1992), "African Cultures as Parameters in Planning Process" in Aryeetey, op. cit.

Hanna, Naggy, Boyson Sandor and Gunaratne Shakuntala (1996), *The East Asian Miracle and Information Technology: Strategic Management of Technological Learning;* World Bank Discussion Papers, The World Bank, Washington D.C., p. 16.

Hanna, Naggy K. (1991), *The Information Technology Revolution and Economic Development,* World Bank, Washington D.C.

ISSER (1979), *Poverty: Its Scope, Extent and Impact on Development: A Research Proposal,* University of Ghana, Legon.

National Development Planning Commission (1994), *National Development Policy Framework: long-term Development Objectives,* Vol. 1, Accra, Ghana.

Ndulu, Benno and Nicolas Van de Walle (1996), "Africa's Economic Renewal: From Consensus to Strategy" in *Agenda for Africa's Economic Renewal,* Transaction Publishers, New Brunswick (USA) and Oxford (UK), p. 13.

OAU (1981), *Lagos Plan of Action for Economic Development of Africa 1980–2000,* International Institute of Labour Studies, Geneva.

Obasanjo, Olusegun (1994), "Welcome Address" in *Corruption, Democracy and Human Rights in East and Central Africa,* Summary Report of a seminar organized by Africa Leadership Forum in Entebbe, Republic of Uganda, p. 57.

Onigu, Otite (1982), "On the Sociological Study of Corruption", Presidential Address, in Femi Odekunle (ed.) *Nigeria: Corruption in Development,* Ibadan University Press, pp. 11–19.

Over, Mead et al. (1989), "The Direct and Indirect Cost of HIV Infection in Developing Countries: The Cases of Zaire and Tanzania", in Alan F. Fleming, Manuel Carballo, David W. FitzSimons, Michael R. Bailey and Jonathan Mann (eds). *The Global Impact of AIDS. Proceedings of the First International Conference on the Global Impact of AIDS.* New York: Alan R. Liss, Inc.

Piot, Peter et al. (1992), *Aids in Africa: A Manual for Physicians,* World Health Organization, Geneva.

Sackey, Harry A. and Godwin Y. Dogbey (1996), "Women, Inequality and Productivity: Some Reflections and Policy Implications for Ghana", forthcoming in *Greenhill Journal of Administration* (A special edition on Gender and Productivity at the Workplace).

UNDP (1994), *United Nations Human Development Report:* New York: Oxford University Press.

World Bank (1994), *Reducing the Debt Burden of Poor Countries: Framework for Action: Development in Practice,* The World Bank, Prepublication Edition, p. 7.

World Bank (1989), *Sub-Saharan African: From Crisis to Sustainable Growth;* Washington D.C., World Bank, p. 60.

World Bank (1995), *Global Economic Prospects and the Developing Countries;* A World Bank Book, The World Bank, Washington D.C., Executive Summary.

World Bank (1993), *Aids and African Development: A Publication of the Africa Region,* The World Bank pp. l–14.

CHAPTER 5

Issues and Problems
of Political Renewal in Africa

Admore M. Kambudzi

INITIAL REMARKS

Asiwaju has spoken of "artificial boundaries and conflict" (Asiwaju, 1990:15) as the most characteristic features of Africa. However, an Africa of positive heritage, peace, prosperity and excellence is the type of land that young Africans would like to see. The kind of Africa in which we aspire to live is, therefore, not difficult to imagine at all. First, let us have peace, then works of excellence in every field. Logically, prosperity and a positive heritage will follow.

The liberation of South Africa, the decline of civil wars from Mozambique, Angola to Liberia, enhanced intra-African economic cooperation, the leap forward of African personnel in international fora, especially at the United Nations, are all signs of a better future. The appointment of Kofi Annan as United Nations Secretary General at the end of 1996 is one of the clear signs of the universal renaissance of the African people. The Cold War is over, giving African countries the opportunity to concentrate more on social, economic and political problems. There are, of course, some ongoing constraints (armed conflicts, foreign debt, low technological capacity) but these are not insurmountable obstacles.

The most important transformation in Africa, which places the continent in a forward-looking position, was summarized by Julius Nyerere. As he said, "most of Africa is now free from colonial rule and only apartheid remains to collapse".[1] And, apartheid collapsed in 1994. Nyerere also assessed the situation in Africa some years after independence. He noticed our limited successes and many failures during that time. Lastly, he noted the persistent problematic issues facing a decolonized Africa. These include "real and very severe neo-colonialism", which he viewed as a "limitation on national sovereignty";[2] as well as economic backwardness and poverty. There is, therefore, no doubt that the underprivileged and deprived constitute the majority in African countries

---

[1] Nyerere, J. Cited from Goulbourne H. (ed.) *Politics and State in the Third World*, The MacMillan Press Ltd., London, 1979, p. 248.

[2] Ibid., p. 252.

today. This is a direct result of colonial rule, post-independence mis-governance and lack of economic vision.

The long-standing vision of Africa was that it would be a free, united and prosperous land. This was certainly a circumstantial vision, based on conditions within Africa before independence. Any vision of the future should be framed against the background of the prevailing conditions at any given moment. Such a vision should be guarded against distortion by the undue weight of the body of contemporary ideas. An attempt has been made here to avoid this distortion. There are two things to take note of:

THE PROBLEM OF ENVISIONING THE FUTURE OF AFRICA

I am convinced that African political renewal is a vision that can be realized. Africans have held a vision of achieving freedom from colonial rule and this has been realized to a large extent. Freedom has always been a relative and not an absolute human condition. No one can be absolutely free, but every one of us can be free from undue constraints.

Political renewal on the continent, which is a process of rebuilding collapsed systems of governance, administration and public conduct, should not be seen as an event. It is a process of recreating optimal rulers, critical subjects and responsible citizens. Once these people are on the ground and on the correct political platform, then peace, prosperity and heritage will abound on our continent.

In framing this vision of Africa, one confronts the problematic of the burdensome influence of existing ideas. For example, the collapse of the communist system and its ideology means that liberalism has triumphed. So how does one escape the need to refer to liberal intellectual authorities in the process of envisioning the future of Africa? The liberal thinker envisions an Africa integrated in a global market based on advanced technology, information and competition. The notion of globalization has already gained currency in academia, and international politics and economics. Does this conception tolerate a diverging interpretation? Thus, any work on new visions of Africa should bypass, as much as authors can afford, the influences and limits imposed by current liberal political and economic theorization.

Of course, this is not to overshadow the legacy of Marxist and neo-Marxist analysis which, by and large, suffers from declining subscription and rigor. The age of Marxist ideology belongs to the past. One can not see it otherwise.

Misinterpretation of the current situation

We have a right to envision the future. But we have no right to misinterpret the situation in which we live. The hazards from such a misinterpretation are enormous, especially the risk of creating and upholding an erroneous prescription to resolving a problem. Why should we forget that most of the political and economic mistakes of all these years of independence have their origin in misinterpretation.

According to the former Tanzanian President, Julius Nyerere, "Our mistake was in the assumption that freedom – real freedom – would necessarily and with little trouble follow political liberation from colonial rule".[3] This was a disastrous misinterpretation both of the struggle for and the management of independence. From this vagary emerged one-party rule, tyranny, dictatorship, civil war, genocide and ethnocide. As aptly noted by Obaseki (1983), these are real experiences from which we should draw lessons. In the same light, due to the gravity of the errors made, President Nyerere hopes that "lessons would be learnt from experiences so as to prevent a repeat in the future".[4]

"Why is Africa a crisis-ridden continent?"[5] asked I.W. Zartman. In searching for a response, Zartman attributes this condition to the fact that "African states are being born and shaped... and the stakes are high".[6] Zartman further observes that conflict on the continent is aggravated by the absence of rules, limits and controls in political conduct[7] which, he correctly says, could not have been easily established in this short period of independence.

Having focused on these problems of framing a vision of the future of Africa, it is now possible to propose one. But one must not bypass the starting point: a correct comprehension of the present condition of African states and peoples. Accordingly, my vision of the future of our continent will follow this assessment, especially the changes in the nature of the state in Africa within the context of liberal-inspired democratization.

DEMOCRATIZATION AND POLITICAL RENEWAL

"In a number of countries of Africa, democracy in the 1990s has been reduced to multi-partyism".[8] Without a "vibrant civil society"[9] one does not see how an effective democratization and political pluralism can take place.

The problems of the current democratization process in Africa are summarized by Ernest Wamba dia Wamba as violation of human rights, religious fundamentalism, ethnic domination, civil wars, gender domination and erosion of

---

[3] Ibid., p. 252.

[4] Ibid., p. 249.

[5] Obaseki N.O. *African Regional Security and the OAU's Role in the Next Decade*, International Peace Academy, New York, 1983.

[6] Zartman I. W. see citation 8, p. 18.

[7] Ibid., p.18.

[8] Wamba dia Wamba, E. cited from *African Journal of Political Science*, Vol. 1, No. I June 1996, p. 10.

[9] Ibid., p. 18.

national sovereignty. We should, however, seriously examine the impact of current democratization on African states since these changes have a bearing on the silent African masses. This process does not necessarily liberate these masses because of the inappropriate conditions induced within African states. Thus, the democratic state and society are still far away on the continent. But we can shorten the journey to these goals.

Post-independence leaders in Africa became infatuated and preoccupied with the security and defense of the state. "Notions of nation-building"[10] were invoked to mask these dire but nonetheless personalized, ideological needs. Thus, the army, the police, secret services and the presidential guards grew much faster and bigger than civil organizations. The paucity of human rights advocates, if not their actual absence, was self-evident.

Democratization on the continent has led to the emergence of a new topology of African states. The significance of this topology is that it places these states at different levels in terms of their disposition towards democratic political development. In the Cold War era, an ideological topology was characteristic, i.e. socialist versus non-socialist states. The present conditions of Africa are such that such a topology has significance only in retrospect. The present topology comprises the following types according to a democratic yardstick:

Self-countenanced democratic states

This category includes states which were able to embark on a democratic path of government right from independence. Regular (free) elections were held and political pluralism was provided for in the constitution. There was a political commitment to issues of human rights and development. Even in the cold war era, this category of state survived the temptation to convert the state into a police/security state.

Botswana and Senegal fall under this category. The post Cold War pressures for democratization have conveniently saved them as compared to states such as Kenya, Algeria, Benin, and Togo. In 1990, Namibia emerged as an independent state to join this group. More recently, in 1994, the emergence of a majority-ruled South Africa has further expanded the category. Both the Namibian and South African constitutions expressly recognize diversity and basic freedoms.

Non-central government states

It should be noted that the end of the Cold War unleashed tremendous energies for internal conflict. This conflict has torn apart certain states to a greater magnitude of political chaos. What marks this category is the quasi-non-existence or total absence of a firm and operational central government. Somalia

---

[10] Ibid., p. 18.

and Liberia are typical examples. The constant instability in Rwanda and Burundi makes them candidates for this category.

In this case, the processes of democratization, social, political and economic developments have been severely dislocated. Human rights violations have been rife within these states. The persistent massacres in Liberia, for about seven years, the massacres in Somalia in 1992, those in Burundi in 1994, and similarly those in Rwanda in 1994 are evidence of unprecedented human rights violation in post-independence Africa.

Military culture states

In Nigeria, Zaire and Togo, the pressures for democratization have not been effective enough to break the existing culture of military rule. In 1993, Nigeria, then under General Ibrahim Babangida, made yet another attempt to restore democratic and civilian rule. This attempt collapsed as the military put aside the democratic agenda and re-embarked the country on further military governance. In Zaire and Togo, the window-dressing arrangements towards democratization have all been aborted, as military tyrants remained entrenched in power. What is also common in this category is the deliberate, forced marginalization of the democratic and civic groups, including human rights activists. Nigeria has emerged as one of the most hostile environments for democratic and human rights movements.

Islamic states

In North Africa, the Cold War conflict has been superceded by a struggle for power and influence between quasi-civilian regimes (Egypt and Morocco) and Islamists. In Algeria, the confrontation is between the military and Islamic fundamentalists.

Journalists, human rights advocates, progressive scholars, civic leaders, civilians and foreigners have all been victims of this internal conflict in North Africa in the post Cold War era.

Emergent democratic states

Zimbabwe, and to some extent, Zambia, Kenya and Tanzania, have developed a credible democratic framework. In the latter countries, multiparty elections were held in 1992, 1993 and 1995 respectively. Since independence in 1980, Zimbabwe has held regular elections but its democratic space has not expanded enough. Tanzania has shifted from the enlightened leadership of Julius Nyerere to the democratizing tendencies of Ali Hassam Mwinyi and later, Benjamin Mkapa. Democratic development in Mozambique since the Rome Peace Accord in 1992 makes this country eligible as an emergent democratic state.

Thus, in view of this topology, it is not the entire African continent that is favorably disposed to democratic development. It is only the self-countenanced and emergent states that offer comparatively stronger opportunities for democratic, political and social development on the continent.

AFRICAN POLITICAL RENEWAL: A REALIZABLE VISION

Whenever there is vision, there is hope. It is this hope that provides the basis for all initiatives. It is rather difficult to envision the future of a continent as large as Africa with such a diverse cultural landscape. Christians and Muslims may not necessarily share a common vision of the future. Similarly, African traditionalists may hold a different vision altogether. Thus, one cannot escape confronting the question as to whether a common vision of Africa can be subject matter for meditation.

Nevertheless, there are three compelling reasons why the people of this continent could visualize and share one vision. But still, one has to advise caution since a vision may not necessarily be popular. Essentially, Africa needs a common popular vision. It is the people, the citizens of African states themselves, who must visualize the way they wish to live and desire to bestow upon subsequent generations.

Accordingly, our search should be focused on facilitating the evolution, dissemination and assimilation of a shared popular vision of Africa. This is something which can be achieved over a short period of time.

Let us come back to the reasons why Africans can easily build upon a popular vision. These are not conceptual or intellectual reasons, but reasons arising from the real life experiences of the African populations themselves. For the most part, these experiences have been bitter and those that persist to date still remain bitter.

Firstly, the colonial experience throughout the African continent has left an indelible mark on every individual African, dead or living. The colonial situation was not to our advantage, which made it a fact of life that we Africans inherited a detrimental status from this experience. The aspiration to be free and to become freer out of this defeating experience was symbolized by the decolonization campaign. To become free, and much freer implied having a vision of the future. The visions that have been instilled upon us by such notions as "Pan-Africanism", "Unity" as propounded by both continental Africans and the Diaspora represented visions of the future of Africa. I will turn later to the debate on why these visions have not been popular and have not galvanized African energies at all in forging a great continent. Africa represents the potential of a great continent of culture, lifestyle, imagination and wealth.

Secondly, political decolonization has not triggered economic and technological decolonization. There was, of course, some misconceived immediate post-independence euphoria. The Africans celebrated and ululated for only a few years after independence. Then came a long period of deprivation, disorientation and crises. "L'Afrique est mal partie"[11] wrote René Dumont. This observation is characteristic of the sad turn of events in many African countries following what Kwame Nkrumah and others called "flag independence". The prophecies of enlightened life in post-colonial Africa, as embodied in the philosophies of Leopold Senghor, Julius Nyerere, Nnamdi Azikiwe and the like, were soon to dissipate. The collapse of Nyerere's Ujamaa socioeconomic experiment in the late 1970s marked the beginning of the end for most of these prophecies. One would suggest that one of the reasons why such prophecies fell empty was because they were personalized. Ujamaa was just as much a conceptual and political tool of Nyerere as Negritude was a form of justification for Leopold Senghor's rule in post-colonial Senegal.

Vision of Pan-Africanism and unity

'Pan-Africanism' and 'Unity' have a long standing as a projected vision of the future of Africa. This is a realizable vision and the hope still remains. Although the notion of Pan-Africanism originated from the Black Diaspora (USA and the Caribbean in particular), it quickly gained a foothold on the African continent. W.E.B. Du Bois and Kwame Nkrumah were largely responsible for introducing pan-Africanism into Africa. Since then, pan-Africanism has remained a major symbol of an African vision of a future, with Africans living in dignity, self-esteem and material well-being.

"Twenty years ago, the 6th Pan African Congress convened in Dar es Salaam, Tanzania".[12] It was only, in April 1994 that the 7th Pan African Congress was again convened in Kampala, Uganda.[13] Since its inception, Horrace Campbell notes that Pan-Africanism has always been centered on the campaign to remove racism and to win political independence. Campbell also notes that one of the objectives of the 7th Congress was to "articulate a vision for the 21st century and a program of action for the Pan African Movement".[14] Today, a commonly-shared vision among Pan Africanists is to repoliticize and remobilize the African peoples at this critical stage in world history, characterized by the total re-organisation of the international political and economic system.

It should be noted that the most significant contribution of the Pan African Movement to African history is that it has sustained an optimistic view of Africa. A vision of the future and plenteous hope has always been at the center of the movement.

---

[11] See Mutiso G.C. and Rohio S. W. (eds) *Readings in African Political Thought*, Heinemann, London, 1975.

[12] Campbell, H. cited from *African Journal of Political Science*, Vol. No. 1, June 1996, p. 1

[13] Ibid., p. 1

[14] Ibid., p. 1

Yet today, we have to accept and face the challenge. The Pan African movement needs to be transformed into an economic force. Rather than remain an interface of civic advocates, activists and intellectuals, Pan-Africanism needs to be related closely to solving the economic problems of the continent and in the Diaspora.

Problems of Pan-Africanism and unity

The notions of 'pan-Africanism' and 'unity', whilst noble, have tended to remain elitist in nature. These notions have not attained grassroots stature and hereupon lies the problem. Grassroots notions and practices are by nature immediately beneficial to the ordinary people who are driven by the need to lead a normal life. Since independence, Africa has not seen any continental congress of African men and women to debate pan-Africanism and unity. The summit of the Organization of African Unity has accommodated despots and enlightened rulers at the same time.

Pan-Africanism was conceived as a global movement. Some have argued that the "horizon of Pan-Africanism was to develop into a form of internationalism and emancipatory politics".[15] Of course, unity was essentially conceived as a continental issue. Though limited in geographic scope, unity has not succeeded on the continent to date. The Great Lakes region of Africa faces a serious threat of political upheaval and dismemberment of states. Does this mean that the huge states of Africa, created by colonialists, are doomed? Maybe, if smaller and peaceful states emerge, it will be better for the African people. There is no need for African countries to become refugee states. At the moment, there are around 400,000 Rwandan refugees in Tanzania – an obviously unbearable situation. Most importantly, we need to rethink Pan-Africanism and Unity. The challenge is how to render these popular with the masses as weapons to fight against poverty and division.

CONCEPTION OF AFRICAN POLITICAL RENEWAL

Perhaps it is too parochial to work on the sole aspect of political renewal. Obviously, the scale of devastation that has been provoked on the African continent, from slavery, colonization to neo-colonial domination and exploitation, does oblige that there should be a universal renewal in Africa. Universal in that it is every aspect of African life, culture, image personality, economy, language, power, information, technology, etc., that has been damaged or disoriented in the past that needs to undergo renewal. Not least, the African person needs to be renewed. So why center on political renewal?

Simply because politics is that arena of power games and plays that has influenced and determined life from time immemorial. Slavery, colonization

---

[15] Wamba dia Wamba, op.cit.

and neo-colonial systems were first and foremost political manifestations. If we have to explain correctly why little socioeconomic progress has yet been realized on the continent since independence, we should start from politics and then proceed to other perspectives. Zaire's political situation under the long rule of Colonel Mobutu has not been propitious for the spiritual and material development of the people of Zaire. On the contrary, his rule buttressed and enriched corrupt and neo-colonial forces. One may naturally assume that once we rectify the political anomalies still persisting on the continent, a decisive part of the battle for this vision of renewal will have been won.

Firstly, political renewal should be seen and undertaken as a process whereby conditions for affordable government are recreated. Secondly, it is about bringing up new generations of rulers, subjects and citizens. Rulers who resemble earthly gods and subjects who behave like political slaves should not have a place any more on this continent. Likewise, long incumbency for rulers should be abandoned to the past, once and for all. Political genius in Africa can only be resuscitated with the regular replacement of government through popular elections. There is a need to galvanize a vigilant, self-assertive civil society. And with this, there must be institutions for effective popular participation.

Paving a new political landscape

We should recognize, as a guiding principle for African governance, development and community life, that each successive generation should build to the best of its physical and intellectual capacity a non-burdensome political heritage.

The fact that the present African generations have inherited a political culture dominated by political conflict, dictatorship and civil war (Saul, J.S., 1975, Ibingira, G. 1980, Campbell, H., 1975) is more than instructive. The political misdemeanors of the post-independence African political leadership are weighing heavily on the African people. To avoid the persistence of such problems, the following will be most essential to implement on the African continent; and this may be one of the visions to hold:

Abolition of long political incumbency

Few African presidents have given up power willingly and constitutionally. By a mistaken conception or whatever, politics had become a life profession for them. Yet a profession of politics has rarely developed in any society. Politics is a go-in, go-out arena with no experts at all. Nicollo Machiavelli, in *The Discourse,* imagined for us quite well some of the methods, including vice and mischief, of successful and pragmatic politicians.

Mobutu Sese Seko has emerged as Africa's longest- serving president (1960–1997), out of all constitutional bounds. He survived the downfalls that faced most long incumbent African presidents in the early 1990s, such as Mathew Kerekou, Siad Barre, Moussa Traore, Kenneth Kaunda and many others until recently. In Uganda, faced by years of internal political chaos, ethnocide and fratricide, the National Resistance Movement introduced a system called 'No-Party Democracy' (Khadiagala, 1995 pp. 33–47). However, this does not resolve the problem of overdue political incumbency on the continent. Even the multiparty elections that saw people like Chiluba assume power in Zambia is no solution at all. The virus of long political incumbency persists in our continent.

The solution to this problem is both civic and constitutional. On the civic side, the African political following needs a psychological revolution that will help to transform it from a culture of worshipping the president to a culture of tasking the president and subjecting him to public account and appraisal. In Malawi, we saw how the aged Kamuzu Banda was still venerated towards the 1994 multiparty elections in that country. Why still venerate him? This was a man who ruled his country to ruin and loss of pride over thirty years. So, it is essentially a question of fostering new political attitudes amongst African citizens.

From a constitutional viewpoint, binding term limits and a terminal national scrutiny may be two instruments that may be used to guarantee normal periodic political succession. Two terms of office are adequate for any president, his ministers and any parliamentary members associated with the president. At the end of these terms, the president and his ministers need to go through a national scrutiny to be exonerated from any acts of corruption, embezzlement, violation of human rights, abuse of office, and related vices. It seems that this may be one of the deterrents in African politics against abusive government.

No-party president

Our experience from the mid 1950s on this continent is that presidents and their Governments have made use of political party machinery, more than anything else, to entrench themselves in power. This has been quite upsetting for many countries in Africa, since most of the political decay that followed was related to this political set up.

There is a need to try and encourage No-Party presidents. These will be individuals who will compete openly for political votes towards a presidential office and such presidents should be accountable to both the intra-party parliament and the electorate.

The non-party presidency could go a long way in resolving the persistent confusion over the separation line between the arena of party politics and the real realm of public and national leadership. The dividing line between these two spheres has been obscured by the manipulations of post-independence presidents. Africa should be the first place in the world to abolish party-based presidents.

Intra-party parliament

Since parliament provides an open debating and legislating forum, it is most appropriate to attract party politics and representation here. This is where we need all shades of opinion before a law or a policy emerges. To sustain the inflow of such shades of opinion, parliament must embrace as much diversity as can be proportionate with the existing viable political formations. Remember that, over the past thirty-six years, Africa has gained nothing from parliaments that, in fact, masked the machinations of the ruling president and his party. So why keep an arrangement that has defeated good purpose?

Open political succession

The African people have always been surprised whenever a successor is announced. Yet political succession should not be secretive at all. More often than not, African presidential successors have been figures who had remained invisible to the nation; invisible both in their good and mischief. In such cases, rather than call the president to task over national issues, African citizens have had to learn the successor's conduct. Each time, this has been an elusive task. How many Zairians knew exactly Mobutu's inner and outward conduct? Indisputably, very few, if any.

We need a system of open political succession whereupon those individuals who aspire to higher political office should expose themselves in advance, regularly and prior to old age. What is the point of having a president who is over sixty? Nelson Mandela is an exception, since he deserved to lead South Africa from apartheid to a new democracy. Otherwise political gerontocracy should not have any place at all on the African continent.

Ethno-federalism

Africa's ethnic diversity has been appropriately harnessed neither by colonial regimes nor post-independence African regimes. Attempts have been made, but all in vain, to forge nations out of diverse ethnic communities. In Nigeria, western-style federalism was tried all the way from 1960 to its present fragile state. Except for continued territorial re-vision, from three regions in the past to the present thirty states, nothing else reflects an attachment to federalism in Nigeria. Rather, there is a constant threat of civil war and the collapse of the Nigerian state. This is one of the factors that underlines the longevity of military rule in Nigeria.

The problem is that the continent has developed escapist political systems which, rather than accommodate diversity or resolve differences, have simply enabled those in power to procrastinate and pass on the problems. The escapist political system is Africa's gravest political misfortune that we have to deal with.

In practice, African countries need political systems and constitutions which recognize the place, culture, tradition and language of every credible ethnic grouping. The cost of overshadowing such groupings remains too ghastly to contemplate: ethnocide and genocide. Rwanda and Burundi typify the costs of such negations relative to ethnic conditions.

Western-style federalism is inappropriate to African ethno-political diversity, and the answer to this problem lies in building upon ethno-federalism: a framework of multiple recognition and respect among various ethnic communities as a means of political coexistence.

FREER, PROSPEROUS AFRICA – A VISION

Colonial Africa was such a precarious place to live. Yet post-colonial Africa, so far, has been a less secure political and economic habitat. Thus, the celebrated and shared vision of the future of Africa at Kwame Nkrumah's time was the union of African countries, in the form of a "United States of Africa". This vision has not lost all its prospects. The goal of the Organization of African Unity (OAU) was, and remains, the unity of African States and peoples. There is no doubt that, even in the wider human context of Africa and the African Diaspora, "Union" among African States and "Unity" among African peoples are important goals that must be pursued.

Having focused on an earlier vision, I would like to say that times have changed; old challenges have vanished as new ones emerged. The need for a freer, prosperous Africa is today more than a common cause. The main challenge to Africa and the Africans themselves today as we struggle to renew ourselves is threefold:

Constitutional renaissance

One would agree with the views of the South African President Thabo Mbeki when he talks of the "African Renaissance". This must be seen in the constitutional realm. The basic laws (constitutions) governing African States should be prepared by Africans themselves through consultations. At the moment, the majority of African constitutions are replications of constitutions from Western Europe and North America. The resulting constitutions are neither rooted in African culture nor relevant to it. This is one of the reasons behind the incessant instability and war on the continent. Accordingly, a "new Africa" can only emerge in the process of constitutional redrafting which gives a new foundation to the African States and economy.

Restoration of community governance

The last thirty to forty years of independence have witnessed the ultra-centralization of political power and authority in a dominant party and all-powerful government. This trend has eroded the potential for initiative by individuals and communities. The result has been catastrophic: waste of resources, corruption, oppression, poverty, dehumanization, etc. This catastrophe can, of course, be offset, and one of the necessary measures is to revive and re-empower local communities, with the political center retaining simply the representative symbols.

Re-generation of indigenous intellectual production

Since the colonial era, Africa has seen an unprecedented export and import of intellectual capital. The relevance of any form of intellectual capital resides in whether such capital is generated from a local self-sustaining system because such capital serves to solve the problems of society in a given place.

It must be recalled that colonization submerged, inter-alia, indigenous intellectual production. The problem that arose, and which persists, is that foreign intellectual capital, whilst useful in certain respects, is not appropriate to solve the problems confronting Africa. African intellectuals must today go to task, not only in reflection, but in practical intellectual engagement to free the African lot from a catastrophe in the making.

Imaginably, these are some of the necessary conditions to stimulate the rise of a freer and prosperous Africa. Their realization would offset the negative consequences of colonial rule, post-colonial mis-governance and economic mismanagement. Conditions such as constitutional renaissance, restoration of community governance and the regeneration of indigenous intellectual production would eventually bring to fruition the long-cherished vision of a United States of Africa", as reflected in Nkrumah's views.

CONCLUSION

One hopes that a lot will change in Africa from now on and at least, a change that will engender more benefits than costs for Africans. Democratization in the 1990s has not really delivered us from political incertitude. Instead, with the pervasive multiparty systems, the risk of implosion has even increased today. Likewise, economic reforms have brought more stress to African populations, thus further heightening the tension and risks. Therefore, we need further substantive reforms, as I have indicated above. Political self-renewal is long overdue on the continent. The economic and political reforms, exacted on Africa from the outside are not the recipe for African success; rather, they are methods for continued distortion and foreign domination. Political renewal is the way forward for Africa and its people.

REFERENCES

Adedeji, A. (ed.) *Africa within the World*. Zed Books, London, 1993.

Asiwaju, A. I. *Artificial Boundaries*, Civiletis International, New York, 1990.

Campbell, H. *Conditions for Political Renewal in Africa*, Colloquium Paper, African Association of Political Science, Dakar, 1995.

Diamond, L., Juan, J.L. and Lipset S.M (eds) *Politics in Developing Countries: Comparing Experiences With Democracy*, Lynne Rienner Publishers, Boulder, 1990.

Goulbourne, H. (ed.) *Politics in the Third World*, The Macmillan Press, London, 1979.

Ibingira, G. *Africa: Upheavals Since Independence*, Westview, Boulder, 1980.

Khadlagala, N. *Zambezia*, No 24 Volume 12, 1995.

Martin, L. K. *Stride Toward Freedom*, Harper and Row Publishers, San Francisco, 1958.

Museveni, Y. *What is Africa's Problem*, NRM Publications, Kampala, 1992.

Mutiso, G.C. and Rohio S. W. (eds) *Readings in African Political Thought*, Heinemann, London, 1975.

Mwengo and All Africa Conference of Churches, *Civil Society, The State and African Development in the 1990s*. Central Graphic Services, Nairobi, 1993.

Obaseki, N. O. *African Regional Security and the OAU's Role in the Next Decade*, International Peace Academy, New York, 1983.

Organization of African Unity, *Resolving Conflicts in Africa – Implementation Options*, OAU Information Services Publication, Series (11), Addis Ababa, 1993.

Saul, J. S. *Labour Supplies in Southern Rhodesia*, Pinter, New York, 1975.

Yansane, A.Y. *Decolonisation in West African States With French Colonial Legacy*, Schenkman Books Inc, Vermont, 1984.

CHAPTER 6

Africa: Problems, Challenges and the Basis for Hope

Geoff E. Kiangi

INTRODUCTION

Poverty comes from "laziness", remarked one lady. "Yes, particularly in Africa", replied an elderly gentleman. This is part of a conversation I happened to hear from two visitors in Africa. They could have been tourists, or perhaps expatriates. I could not help but think of my youth and my parents. My parents worked hard. Always rising early in the morning to work in the farms, sometimes for the whole day. Yet poverty was a real threat in the family. My father spent his whole life working for a meager salary that would not adequately support his family. My parents were not unique, they were typical of all families I knew. I wonder what they would have said, hearing the above conversation. I wish the poverty problem was that simple!

Karl Marx thought differently. He regarded poverty as the evil of a society where few own the means of production, and the majority are forced to sell their human labor. This inexorably drives the society into class divisions: A class of haves (bourgeois), and a class of the have-nots (proletariat), or the poor.

The South Commission Report (1990) agrees with Karl Marx to some extent. The report states that the difference between the "haves" and the "have-nots", the rich and the poor, the developing and the developed, the South and the North, is indeed a difference in Science and Technology. If science and technology are regarded as the "means of production", then the South Commission seems to be in agreement with Marx.

Many people have grappled with the problem of poverty in Africa. And perhaps calling it a problem, or even a crisis, is an understatement. More aptly, the situation in Africa can be referred to as a catastrophe. Just to put things in perspective, a brief overview will assist to explain the Africa we are referring to. This is only a brief.

Put bluntly, if Africa were to disappear completely into oblivion, apart from a few emotional tears, the world would not flinch. Indeed, African issues hardly matter outside the limits of the continent, apart from relief and aid programs.

The contribution of Africa to world GNP is a mere 1.2 percent, and to the world trade only 1 percent (Adedeji, 1993). These values are a pittance, at best. Internal conflicts and wars ravage the continent, and present scenes of carnage beyond description. In Somalia, or what used to be the Somali nation, gun barrels are wielded and used against people too weak, too hungry and too dilapidated to chew a morsel of bread in their own mouths. Somalia still festers with civil strife even today. At one time, 5,000 Somali children were reported to be dying every day (Okigbo, 1993). In the last decade, average rates of inflation of 107, 60.9, 49.7 percent were recorded in Uganda, Zaire, and Somalia respectively. Similar rates of inflation were recorded in other Sub-Saharan countries (IMF, 1992).

As much as up to 55 percent of export earnings, the only income by which the countries can acquire all needed imports, is used to service foreign debts (Okigbo, 1993). Endemic corruption is prevalent. While the world's poorest countries are found in Africa, the world's richest presidents are also found in Africa. When it comes to beating the odds, Africa never fails to come up with surprises. Despite hunger, diseases and wars that have decimated whole communities, the overall population growth of 3.1 is the highest in the world. Such a level of population growth undermines whatever little economic growth is recorded. As we climb beyond year 2000, the economic crisis in Africa is deepening further. The disappointing rates of economic growth of 2.1 and 1.4 percent for 1991 and 1992, respectively (ECA, 1993), are completely overshadowed by population growth.

The food problem is looming large. Most countries in Africa have recorded a decline in annual growth of agriculture outputs. The proportion of the population whose average calorific intake is below the recommended FAO minimum has increased over the years, and so has the number of primary school age children unable to enroll in schools (Okigbo, 1993).

Indeed, as Adedeji (1993) reports, "The situation in Africa is one of perennial famine, recurrent economic crisis, dictatorship, blatant violations of human rights, and gross carnage wreaked by merciless warlords", and the litany continues. If this is the Africa we are referring to, is there any hope?

Where there is no hope and vision, the people perish. We are determined not to perish and so we have hope and a vision for Africa. The walk to our vision of a liberated Africa will be a difficult one. Yet we must walk that road, because the alternative is also a difficult road but one leading to self-destruction. Is our hope real, given the odds?

Africa has a great deal of potential. This potential needs to be converted into real opportunities, into programs of action, an Africa with dignity, into an Africa where programs can be turned into realizable targets, where ideas can be expressed, debated and tested.

Africa has considerable raw materials and natural resources, but it has remained an exporter of unprocessed raw materials and a market of finished products. This trend should be reversed so that Africa processes its own raw materials. Africa, strangely enough, has made great strides in education. There are some African countries where the proportion of advanced degree holders compares favorably with some developed countries. In the world scene, Africa has played a significant role in its membership in the UN. Recently, Africa has been able to place its candidate on the hottest seat of the UN, that of the Secretary General. Africa played a significant role in the group of non-aligned countries. But this does not account for all the potential. The greatest potential lies in the problems themselves. Great problems disguise great opportunities. The pearls from oysters come out of great suffering. The current problems are urging Africans to rise to the challenges. Africa is already seeing more focused strategies, albeit few now, and a public that is more determined to see leaders implementing appropriate economic reform programs. These are only a few of the emerging "pearls" of suffering in Africa. Yes, there is hope for Africa.

AFRICA'S PROBLEMS

The problems of Africa are formidable and real. So that we can face them head on, we need to understand them clearly. As we survey them, we realize how much effort we need to muster. While there is no claim that the list of problems given here is exhaustive, the coverage provides a picture of challenges.

Poverty and famine

Sub-Saharan Africa is probably the poorest part of the entire world. Grouped together with a few countries in South Asia and Latin America, these countries together are generally regarded as the world's poorest. Between 1970 and 1989, the difference in income between the richest 20 percent of countries and the poorest 20 percent increased from a ratio of 32.1 to 60.1 (Adedeji, 1993). While overall, third world countries recorded an average annual economic growth of 3.4 percent between the years 1980–1989, countries of Sub-Saharan Africa had an average negative annual decline of 1.7 percent. The economic gap between Sub-Saharan Africa and other poor countries is significantly widening (UNDP, 1992). The early 1980s can be considered as a watershed period in Africa. National budgets in many African countries failed to cope, and loans were sought from the World Bank and the International Monetary Fund (IMF). These loans have since become a crippling burden to Africa. Currently, more than half of African foreign earnings are used to service the debt. With this level of poverty, more than half of the entire population is below the FAO recommended minimum caloric intake (Okigbo, 1993).

In 1986, forty six percent of all World Food Programme emergency food aid went to Africa. This amount increased to 85 percent in 1990. It is estimated that over 30 million Africans require food aid (George, 1993).

The Global 2000 report submitted to President Jimmy Carter just before he left the White House reports, "Hunger, and disease may claim more lives especially lives of babies and young children. More of those surviving infancy may be mentally and physically handicapped by child malnutrition", (CEQS, 1980). This, the report suggests, will be the result of population explosion. Of course, the situation will be worse in Africa, where population growth is highest but food supplies are dwindling.

Wars

Wars in Africa present another problem. It is estimated that 8 million Africans live as refugees, and a further 10 million are displaced. Some of these wars are perpetrated by African leaders themselves, with instigation from former colonial masters, in what might be called surrogate colonialism. Protracted and bitter conflicts have, on several occasions, turned into serious wars over control of power within national borders. In these countries as Basil Davidson (1993) describes, the rule of the gun has altogether displaced the rule of constitutional law.

The Democratic Republic of the Congo (formerly Zaire), set the ball of tribal warfare rolling in Africa in the 1960s. This was followed by the Biafra war in Nigeria, where an estimated 2 million civilian lives were lost. With the trend set, Uganda, Angola, Mozambique, Liberia, Ethiopia, Somalia, Sudan, and recently Rwanda all followed suit. In 1996, U\$1 million a day was being spent on 42 camps to support more than a million Rwandan refugees (STI, 1996). Many think the solution is to return the refugees to their own countries, but African history shows that each repatriation provokes fresh conflicts and further exodus.

Although the causes of wars are varied, most of them are wars of secession, where a geographical section of a country demands an independent state. This was the case with the Katanga province under Moise Tshombe, which wanted independence from the then Belgian Congo. A similar situation sparked the Biafran war in Nigeria. Like the oil rich Katanga province, Biafra did not agree on the way in which the government used revenue from natural resources drawn from their particular region. In Sudan, the largely Christian south is fighting for freedom from the powerful Islamic north. In Ethiopia, the Eritreans and Tigreans mounted a secessionist struggle against what they considered the heavy-handed Ethiopian rule which, among other things, forced the Amharic language on them (McCarthy, 1994).

Many other wars in Africa are probably due to the unchecked drum-major instinct, a natural desire to be top, which some psychologists argue is the most dominant drive in all human beings. An individual wants to be above the rest, a tribe exercises tendencies to rule over others, one group wishes to dominate another group. These are all examples of the drum-major instinct. While the instinct is present in every individual, tribe and nation, it has found greater expression in Africa where the legal system is not well-developed enough to keep the negative tendencies in check. The friction and bitterness arising from this often result in bitter and protracted wars. While these wars may not always be big, the social breakdown, the insecurity and the effect on the economy are by no means small. A spirit of revenge pervades, and continual conflicts flare up. The wars in Zimbabwe, Angola, Burundi and many others fall into this category. It is noteworthy that some of the newly independent African nations have adopted a policy of national reconciliation which has worked very well. Here, the "Elder Brothers" need to learn from the young ones.

Breakdown in moral values

Man is a moral being capable of knowing right from wrong. This implies that there are certain principles and values that man ought to respect and uphold. To a large extent, this is what distinguishes man from other animals. The very existence of man means that human consciousness exists to guide in making moral decisions. This way man can make value judgments and take responsibilities. (Olsen, 1988). "Moral laws regulate the moral universe just as physical laws regulate physical universe .... Conscience is to the moral universe what gravity is to the world matter .... Conscience is the law obeying energy to [Man]" (Baldwin, 1892).

However, unlike the physical law that dictates how matter must behave, moral laws guide how man ought to behave. Herein lies the dilemma, because what man ought to do is not what man ends up doing. "The fate of the earth hangs by the thread of moral recognition", note Mantangu and Matson (1983). "Hence the more [morality] holds sway, the more [people] turn from blind choice to be guided by [objectivity]" (Abbott). But if moral laws are ignored, the very existence of man, by which moral laws distinguish from other forms of life, is in danger.

Moral excellence is, therefore, at the heart of man's very existence, and dictates his well-being. Moral values should be fixed before any other goals are set. Olsen (1988) emphasizes that

> when [moral] values are in crisis, then the material things of life will go from good to bad to worse, with catastrophic damage to the quality of human existence [and with] uncalculated destruction of the fabric of civilized society. In the financial world, we speak about bankruptcy, but economic bankruptcy is generally preceded by bankruptcy of values and moral principles.

Nowhere is this truth more evident than in Africa. Hunger, diseases, refugee problems, are all the result of wars and economic bankruptcy, which in turn are a result of moral decay. Corruption is endemic in Africa, with those at the top as the major culprits (Adedeji, 1993). Corruption affects all countries of the world. In the West, it is associated with big businesses. In the third world, and Africa particularly, the excessive concentration of economic power in the hands of government and the corporate sector, and in the hands of a few individuals, while the majority of the people are underpaid, form fertile conditions for corruption.

The major cause of all these problems in Africa is undoubtedly the problem of moral decay. We cannot hope for a better Africa without addressing the question of moral values and responsibilities. This should be our point of departure. We should grasp the bull by the horn.

Technological stagnation

The South Commission (1990) observes that "the creation, mastery, and utilization of modern science and technology are basic achievements that distinguish" the advanced North from the underdeveloped South. The inability of Africa to excel in science and technology is evident, and has a long history. This history dates back more than a thousand years. From about the 9th century, Arabs engaged in the slave trade transported slaves from East, South, Central and West Africa to the Middle East. By the 15th century, the Arabs were joined by the Europeans, who shipped slaves to America. The slaves required were youthful and strong, thus depriving Africa of its prime labor and intellect that would have developed indigenous skills. The resulting social unrest and the atmosphere of insecurity meant that people were only preoccupied with their immediate needs. Europeans were not satisfied with the slave trade alone. They needed to own Africa. Thus, the slave trade was followed by colonialism. Colonialism resulted in intellectual enslavement. Technological innovations were forcefully suppressed. One of the fears was that Africans might develop the same weaponry used to subjugate them. In some places, local artisans and craftsmen were either killed or maimed. The greatest two evils of mankind to mankind, slavery and colonialism, prevailed in Africa for centuries.

The years that followed independence (1960–1970) were years of hope. The liberated countries of Africa inherited the colonial systems of governance, and their institutions en masse. These institutions were the creations of the West with a different history and culture. They were also designed for a different purpose, that of suppression. These systems and institutions were totally inadequate to address the new hopes and aspirations of the newly independent countries. They were too bureaucratic, too complex, too unresponsive to the needs of people, and distanced leaders from the people they led.

Emerging from colonialism, there was no indigenous technological base. The few technological skills that the locals possessed were regarded as crude and out of fashion. While ignoring the local technological base, ambitious technological projects were embarked upon. The lack of the "Western" technical expertise needed to support these big technological investments created severe problems. Within a few years of operations, the industries closed in need of spare parts, roads collapsed, and hydropower plants ceased to offer a reliable supply of power. Policies on science and technology were not integrated into national development plans. Technology management, coupled with inadequate governance and policy systems, was the heart of the problem. Africa is now waking up to realize that there is a need to reappraise past experiences and map new approaches for technological advancement, a realization coming at a time when investment capital is more elusive than in the "lost decades" of the past.

THE WAY FORWARD

After identifying some of the major problems that are facing Africa, in our resolute hope and vision of a respectable Africa, this section charts some of the necessary land marks on the way to a new Africa, an Africa where human decency will once again take root, where Africans can lead lives of dignity and fulfillment. Africa needs peace, food, health care, education and millions of jobs.

Science and technology

Soon after independence, many countries attempted to rapidly develop their societies by investing in big, government-supported technological projects. These failed because of the lack of local capacity, unavailability of foreign exchange needed to purchase spare parts, and poor management. Accelerated development in science and technology is not only necessary to improve the battered economics of African countries, but also for Africa to assert its rightful place in the world arena. It is important to stress here that to realize a meaningful achievement in technological development, an integrated approach is necessary. Such an approach must address the problems of technological development in a holistic manner.

Poverty in Africa is perverse and exists on a large scale. Isolated technological solutions, although they may offer some relief, such relief is only temporary and very limited in scale. Meaningful solutions must address the two thorny problems of scale and sustainability. This means that the results should benefit a large number of people who live in abject poverty, and that any technological program must be run within the financial means of the country concerned, without depending on perpetual donations. Donations, or technical staff complements, should be regarded as temporary and unsustainable sources of relief. These ideas may sound radical and even outrageous, but they are the keys to any breakthrough in technological development. A few projects implemented in other parts of the world that adopted this philosophy are beginning to bear fruits, and of course people are excited that it is possible!

This integrated approach to technological development addresses the issues of scale and sustainability and it has the following four elements:
- specific technology interventions;
- technology management and entrepreneurship;
- financial support; and
- marketing.

Specific technology intervention is necessary to solve a particular technological problem. It is specific in nature. As a result, technology for this is imported and adopted, or developed locally. Use of this new technology results in increased productivity and, therefore, increased income. However, the realization that there is a need for such a technological intervention, and the ability to initiate and maintain the intervention, will depend on the level of technology management and entrepreneurship existing in the country. Poor technology management has been the cause of many failures of technological programs in Africa. It is through technology management that mechanisms are developed to acquire, adapt and disseminate technologies. The research infrastructure of a country, comprising of research institutions, and the way in which these link to the indigenous technological base of the country, and how research can be commercialized, all form part of technology management.

It is important to note that there is a recommended minimum amount to spend on research and development. There is a threshold amount of research that is necessary to provide a meaningful contribution to economic development. Financial institutions and the marketing of technological products have to be closely linked with the commercialization of new technologies. Financial institutions should support new technology investments, and marketing should be planned to enable the realization of increased income as a result of improved technology and improved products. Governments need to play a leading role in ensuring that all elements in the integrated approach as described above are created. The countries of the Far East which are gaining new industrial strength and are making great headway in transforming their economies, had their governments actively promoting the build-up of national capabilities to import, adapt and diffuse technologies. These governments also encouraged the growth of design and engineering capabilities, and provided the necessary capital (South Commission, 1990). Africa can follow suit.

Demobilizing and redeploying the military

The existence of military armies in Africa has been more of a bane than a boon. Military armies have drawn heavily on the countries' meager economic resources. Aristocratic and monocratic governments of Africa have tended to keep heavy armies to protect their leadership. In many instances, failure to keep the military "happy", through higher salaries and extended benefits has resulted in military coups.

To keep the military "happy" has meant excessive expenditure of public money on the military. Expenditures as high as 60 percent of GDP were reported to have been spent on the military in some African countries. We ask ourselves a question: Is it sane to spend so much on an idle horse, a white elephant at best?

The military have contributed to the number and intensity of the many wars fought in Africa. The developing countries' military expenditures in 1980 on average amounted to 25 percent of the world total, while their contribution to the world economy was about five percent. Arms imports averaged US$22 billion per year during the 1980s (South Commission, 1990). This is so despite the fact that more than half the population in these countries lives below survival level. Surely, this defies all manner of human understanding. Africa does not need such a heavy army. Often, it has been argued that an army is needed for national defense. Often, this army has been used to destroy the very nation that it is supposed to defend. In this age of globalization of the world economy, trade, and information sharing, cross border conflicts should be settled through negotiations and peaceful means, rather than through fights and "gunboat" diplomacy.

Redeploying the army should not be taken to mean disbanding it immediately, for doing so would mean increased insecurity and lawlessness. Trained soldiers turned civilians can become a great liability, if they are without engagement. The process of redeployment of the army should be done through dialogue between the military and the government where, in a gradual manner, soldiers are redeployed in development programs. This should be done through a process where soldiers are properly educated concerning the intentions of the government. Examples are available which show that the army can be deployed in a useful way. In Zambia, for example, soldiers were used to remove the water hyacinth, a weed that had invaded one of the lakes, stopping navigation and fishing activities.

The redeployment of the army does not mean doing away with the army. A small army within reasonable expenditure levels can still be kept, even if only for deterrence. Gunta Pauli (1996) identifies opportunities in using the military against environmental degradation, in building national infrastructure particularly telecommunications networks, providing early warning on aspects like environmental scares and food security, and the construction of underground facilities. Redeployment of the army could save Africa considerable amounts of money.

Appropriate education

In all African countries, educational infrastructure was grossly inadequate at the time of independence. Considerable resources were mobilized to expand education systems, and large amounts of money were spent on education soon after independence. Slogans were made to encourage the eradication of illiteracy. If performance in education were to be measured in quantitative terms, i.e. the number of graduates, African education has performed spectacularly. "Between 1960 and 1983 the number of students enrolled in African institutions at all levels quintupled to about 63 million. Enrollments increased by about 9 percent annually during the 1970s, double the rate in Asia and triple that in Latin America. At the primary level, the gross enrollment ratio rose from 36 percent in 1960 to 75 percent in 1983. At the tertiary level, the number of students enrolled in African institutions had reached 437,000 by 1983 growing from 21,000 in 1960". (World Bank, 1988).

Impressive, though these successes are, there are some hidden problems too. The South Commission (1990) reports that these efforts neglected training in the basic sciences. The Commission further reports, "The education has too often continued on the lines set in the past, and has been too academic and unsuited to the scientific, vocational, and other needs of societies in the process of modernization".

Population growth (average 3.1 percent) places significant pressure on school enrollments and school facilities. The increasing numbers have also meant a decline in quality. "Cognitive achievement among African students is low by world standards" (World Bank, 1988). Government subsidies to education are increasingly becoming inadequate, and more private schools are opening. This makes it difficult to address any existing inequalities in the provision of education, and the poor continue to be denied easy access to education.

In short, education reform today requires adjustment to increasing numbers, more financial allocations, the revitalization of existing education infrastructure to address the issue of quality, and the selective expansion of services to ensure that science-related subjects are emphasized.

The World Bank document mentions three weaknesses in Africa's Higher Education. These are: an output mix that is no longer suited to the requirements of development; poor quality of output; and excessively high costs of production.

Many countries in Africa have attempted to reform their primary and secondary education systems mainly through syllabus reviews and changes in teaching methodologies. Basic Education Reform in Namibia is one example. The reform, outlined by the Ministry of Education and Culture (MEC, 1993), addressing four issues of equity, access, relevance, and quality, is an impressive document which, if followed, will result in great achievements. Many similar efforts can be noted in other parts of Africa.

The biggest problem of African education lies in tertiary institutions. These have failed to meet the actual needs of the people. Universities are the greatest culprits: while in some African countries the rural population is as high as 90 percent of the population, engaged in what might be termed microenterprises and farming, universities continue to offer a Western type of education with marginal benefits to this sector of the population. Graduates in Theoretical Physics, Pure Mathematics, and Marx-Leninist Philosophy continue to pour out from universities, with few employment prospects, while the majority of the population are grappling with drought, micro-business, and bread-making. If universities could redirect their output and target these areas, this could benefit both the graduates and the country. Arguments have been put forward that universities should not be vocationally oriented, but rather produce people with a broader view of things, who will need retraining into specific jobs, and who can become philosophers of the country. If this argument was given for a few graduates, it would make sense. But if university training, which spends large amounts of public money, totally ignores the pressing needs of the public, then something is wrong. Universities should be challenged to link their research programs directly with the villagers and micro-entrepreneurs. The point here is not to do away with the "humanities" or "theoretical" type education, but rather to strike a balance in the output-mix of graduands.

The leadership problem

One of the greatest problems in Africa is that of leadership. Many African leaders are only a little better than dictators. There are some countries where even mentioning the possibility of another leader can warrant your arrest. Leaders centre power around themselves and rule for several decades. With the exception of a few occasions, leadership changes hands only if there is death or a coup. Plato pointed out that the best leader is the one who does not wish to lead, but has been requested to lead for a period, and who is very happy when his term ends. Unfortunately, as former President of Tanzania, Julius K. Nyerere, said, in our countries we do not have such leaders. Our leaders like to cling to power.

Perhaps the brand of leadership we have was appropriate for the independence struggle. At that time, people needed to have a single focus, no let-out was allowed until the enemy was deposed. Total commitment and unity of purpose was needed. An aristocratic and monocratic approach was necessary, to ensure secrecy in operations, and singleness of purpose. This, our leaders did well. But the times have changed, and our leaders have not changed.

There is a need for leadership that is responsive to the needs of society, that can accept and absorb criticism. Leaders that can take the divergent interests of the constituents and arrive at solutions that serve the interests of all. Leadership that can allow peaceful existence in diversity and that can recognize and seize opportunities. Above all, leadership that is people-centered. Africa is in need of such leadership. Strengthening democratic structures and the legal systems can help us to arrive at such leadership. These two aspects are discussed below.

Making the legal system effective

Many African leaders place themselves above the law. Once in power, they embezzle and squander public money, centre power around themselves, and use this to abuse the people they lead, all with impunity. "When Satan was still in heaven, he argued that angels like him are infallible, and therefore God should do away with the law". In doing so, he broke the law of God and conceived sin, proving the need for God's law. Living above the law is claiming infallibility, which we have not seen in any worldly leadership.

Through popular participation in debates, media, and public pressure Africans should demand that all their leaders respect the law. If this is achieved, basic though it may be, Africa would have made great headway in one stride. The next step would then be law, particularly focusing on the law enforcement officers themselves. These simple facts are not easy to achieve. Transparency, democracy and freedom of the press will facilitate their attainment.

Strengthening democracy

Democracy places the power in the hands of the people. It means governance by the people, comprised of leaders from amongst the people, whose goal is to benefit the people themselves. Many African countries lack true democracy beyond the ballot. Even the right of ballot is grossly abused through wholesale rigging.

While democracy is urgently needed in Africa, this does not mean that the models that the Western countries are promoting in Africa are the right ones. Africa needs to appraise and develop its own democratic structures that will allow a form of popular participation that is essential to genuine development. "The people must be able to determine the system of government, who forms their government, and in broad terms what government does in their name and on their behalf. Respect for human rights, the rule of law, and the possibility to change governments through peaceful means are among the basic constituents of a democratic policy". (South Commission, 1990).

Once people have a national democratic machinery that they have confidence in, most will be willing to give all for their country. A British soldier captured by the German soldiers in World War II remarked the following as he was led to the firing squad, "I am sorry that I have only one life to give for my country". This soldier was happy to give even his life to the country he loved. He definitely had confidence in the governance and leadership of his country.

Strengthening the legal system, widespread public debate, freedom of speech, independence of media, all these will assist in accelerating democratic forms of governance which must be created by Africans for Africans. Assistance from well meaning partners outside Africa is welcome, but outside pressure to implant democratic structures developed elsewhere undermines the very efforts that are intended to support democracy – which means allowing the people to make their own decisions.

To achieve true democracy, education is needed, education both about the democratic structures created and how they work, and education that will allow people to take responsible and well-informed decisions. Current developments in information technology can assist greatly.

Opportunities in information technology

Today, in the information age, one cannot hope for economic development in Africa without considering Information Technology (IT), which offers great opportunities and far-reaching consequences. Many analysts today assert that a country's competitiveness and economic strength, to a large extent, depend on how well it manages its information resources through computer networks and information highways. Some have attempted to colour the age in which we live by introducing the concept of Netizens, computer users who make contacts, share needs, hold conferences, and transact business through the global information super highway.

To many in Africa, this may sound like a fairy-tale, while in the developed countries it is a reality. So, while the evolving digital world and information superhighways are providing new opportunities, they also present a risk, as UNESCO rightly identified in its 150th Executive Board Session, "of exclusion of disadvantaged populations" and further marginalization of developing countries like those in Africa. Yet these same technologies which are already being used on the existing telecommunications infrastructure, offer tremendous opportunities for Africa. IT can facilitate debate and dialogue which may enhance national cohesion and unity, enable the provision of distance education in a wider and more cost-effective manner, and also allow for novel programs such as community telemedicines, and facilitate extension services.

MAKING THE VISION A REALITY

Despite the fact that poverty, hunger, wars and economic stagnation characterize Africa, today there is a vision for Africa. Based on the nobility and tragedies of the past and present, our vision for Africa is that of peace, tranquility, prosperity, true democracy, dignity and individual fulfillment. The previous section discussed the needed changes; now we will consider different paths to the vision.

Many countries wish to achieve the prosperity of the western countries but agree that they do not need to follow the development paths of the West to achieve it. Socialism spoke of a higher level than capitalism and advocated an entirely different development path. Although socialism seems to have failed, the emergence of the East Asian Tigers has confirmed that there is more than one path to development.

Western countries transformed their economies through the industrial revolution in the 19th century. Individual drive, hard work, competitiveness and resilience, coupled with scientific and technological inventions were the engine of the growth and development.

The success of the far eastern countries, on the other hand, is attributable mainly to their culture which seeks dialogue, harmony, consensus and mutual trust. This allowed the countries to develop close relationships between government and the private sector in a smart win-win partnership.

In both the western and the far eastern countries, peace, hard work and commitment to purpose were the preconditions for the great leap forward. Africa can learn from these experiences and chart its own path, which must be based on its culture and unique experiences. Whichever path is chosen, however, there is a need for peace to prevail. In this regard, adopting a policy of reconciliation and inclusiveness is the only way to achieve meaningful peace.

Once peace prevails, many options are open for the great leap forward. A country may wish to invest more in education and focus on human resource development. The education provided should be relevant to the development needs of the country. For example, self-employable graduates that can create microenterprises are urgently needed in many African countries. The educational system in these countries should be reformed to produce entrepreneurs. Properly educated and developed human resources will then act as a springboard to trigger off economic activities. This will be referred to as the human activation mode of development.

Another option would be to examine the situation of a country and invest heavily in areas with high potential and use the best-suited technologies. For example, a country may decide to excel in the food processing industry because it has great potential in agriculture. After developing a strong food industry, this becomes the engine of growth for other sectors, as well as an example to emulate. This approach is ideal for countries that are rich in natural resources, which can use this wealth to provide initial capital. This will be referred to as the technology mode of development.

Yet another route would be through strong emphasis on private enterprise and good leadership based on democracy. In such an environment, governments can build effective partnerships with the private sector that would be regarded as the real engine for development. A key role of government would be to create a conducive environment for the private sector to flourish. This will be referred to as the partnership mode of development.

Another country may try to improve all areas it deems necessary for economic development to occur. This may involve improving education, promoting business ventures, improving the quality of governance – all at once. This will be referred to as the mixed mode of development.

It is important to note that these alternative routes do not spell out exactly what should be done and what should be left out. Rather, the various modes of development stipulate where a country strategically places more emphasis. Therefore, it does not mean that once an area of focus is selected, all other areas are neglected. Thus, a country adopting a technology mode of development will still need to invest in education to develop its human resources. Likewise, the government will still need to promote partnership with industry. However, given the scarce resources, the country decides to strategize and focus on priority areas which are likely to have the greatest impact given the available resources.

Additionally, the modes of development listed here are not exhaustive, but are indicative of how to forge ahead. The philosophy is to identify an area that can allow a country to move forward with relative ease by concentrating resources on it. Once success is realised, efforts can be diverted to other sectors. If one strategy fails, the country can select another, having acquired useful lessons from its experience.

Whether a country adopts the technology, partnership, human activation or mixed mode of development, history shows that hard work and commitment are unavoidable hallmarks of success. Many African countries have generally approached development without a coherent and comprehensive strategy. In many cases, they are basically struggling to administer the effects of change, and are hardly able to plan and manage change. The different modes emphasize the need to strategize, prioritize and manage change.

CONCLUSION

The problems of Africa are formidable. Yet they are not insurmountable. Big problems often disguise big opportunities arising from the challenges they pose. As one scholar said, "Africa the most vulnerable continent is also the most resilient". The resilience of Africa throughout the many tragedies of today offers hope.

The challenges facing Africa today indicate that a transformation is needed to give people the means to shape their own lives and future. The rise of popular mass movements clamoring for change and demanding transparency in decision-making, herald the coming of a new era for Africa. Such popular movements, audible but sometimes not so visible, emerge from across different groups. They transcend tribal lines and group divisions. This suggests that an era of greater national unity, where individual differences are set aside in search of a common hope for more jobs, greater peace, a better way of life and increased security.

The discussion given here outlined the hurdles and how these can be overcome. We need to re-deploy the army for peaceful activities. We need to be more strategic as we seek greater technological capacity. We need democracy and greater involvement in decision making. We need leaders who are willing to listen, and able to play a key role in supporting the private sector to become the engine of growth and development. This is achievable if each country can identify the niches on which to concentrate, and use these as catalysts for economic growth and development. The specific niches selected should depend on the country's resource endowment, experiences, and cultural setting. No approach, however, will provide meaningful results without hard work and commitment. Furthermore, there must be an atmosphere of peace and mutual trust, respect for human values, and rewards for excellence.

REFERENCES

Abbott, *Vatican 11*, pp 213–214.

Adedeji, Adebayo, "Marginalization and Marginality: Context, Issues and Viewpoints", in *Africa Within the World: Beyond Dispossession and Dependence,* Adebayo Adedeji (ed.) Zed Books, London, UK, 1993.

Baldwin, Joseph, *Psychology Applied to the Art of Teaching,* Appleton & Co, New York, 1892, pp. 264–266.

CEQS, (The Council on Environmental Quality and State), *Global 2000 Report,* Government Printing Office, Washington D.C., 1980.

Davidson, Basil, "For Politics of Restitution", in *Africa Within the World: Beyond Dispossession and Dependence.* Adebayo Adedeji (ed.) Zed Books, London, UK, 1993.

ECA, *Economic Report,* Addis Ababa, 1993.

George, Susan, "Uses and Abuses of African Debt", in *Africa Within the World: Beyond Dispossession and Dependence,* Adebayo Adedeji (ed.) Zed Books, London, UK, 1993.

IMF, *World Economic Outlook,* World Bank, Washington D.C., 1992.

Mantangu, Ashley and Matson, Floyd, *The Dehumanization of Man,* McGraw Hill, New York, 1983.

McCarthy, Stephen, *Africa: The Challenge of Transformation*, I.B. Tauris & Co. Publishers, London, 1994.

MEC (Ministry of Education and Culture), *Towards Education For All,* Gamsberg, Macmillan, Windhoek, Namibia, 1993.

Okigbo, Pius, "The Future Haunted by The Past, in *Africa Within the World: Beyond Dispossession and Dependence,* Adebayo Adedeji (ed.) Zed Books, London, UK, 1993.

Olsen, Norskov V, *Man – the Image of God,* Review and Herald, Washington, D.C., 1988.

Pauli, Gunta, *Breakthroughs: What Business Can Offer,* Epsilon Press, Surrey, U.K, 1996.

Scott, John, *Issues Facing Christians Today,* Marshall Publishers, 1984.

South Commission, *The Challenge to the Youth,* Oxford Press, 1990.

STI, (The Straits Times Interactive) Editorial: "Africa alone can save itself", (Internet: http//www.asil.com.sg/straitstimes/pages/stopinon-htlm) Nov. 18, 1996.

UNDP, *Human Development Report,* Oxford University Press, Oxford, 1992.

World Bank, *Education in Sub-Saharan Africa: Policies for Adjustment, Revitalization, and Expansion,* World Bank, Washington D.C., 1988.

CHAPTER 7

Three Accounts of Change

Comfort Lamptey

INTRODUCTION

Given the common perception of Africa as a continent in need, a place where poverty, disease, deprivation, wars and hunger are everyday realities for the majority of people, the task of envisioning a future of hope and prosperity in this context is a challenging engagement, to say the least. For most Africans, the reality is indeed one of an uphill struggle to mitigate the worst excesses of some of the problems reflected above. Thus attempting to project an image of a brighter future at first seemed like a trivial exercise in daydreaming which could be dismissed lightly, given the seemingly permanent grip which today's problems have assumed over the continent. Furthermore, the immensity of these challenges has meant that for most Africans, a day-to-day survival approach presents the most sensible strategy for coping with life. Even at the intellectual level, many analysts seem unable to move beyond the stage of elaborating the multifaceted and multidimensional nature of the problems confronting Africa, to a level of analysis that focuses on how to transcend the current failings. The difficulties inherent in addressing this latter task becomes obvious in an undertaking of the kind reflected below. This is because one is forced to move beyond spelling out the problems and implicating guilty parties, to the stage of actually proposing strategies to overcome these problems in the midst of a gloomy reality.

HOPE FOR AFRICA

Notwithstanding the gloomy realities across much of the continent today, Africans have both good reason, and a responsibility to envision a bright and hopeful future for future generations. The three accounts which are presented in this chapter are premised on a forceful vision of hope for Africa. The vision is that of a continent which has successfully risen out of its present difficulties, and transformed itself into one of strength and might. This strength will be reflected in an Africa that will boast among other things: a self-reliant approach to development; long-term investments in developing untapped human resources

– with equal weighting to both male and female potential – that exist on the continent; economic integration along sub-regional and continent-wide levels; the establishment of strong institutions to manage and transform future conflicts through non-violent means; strategic alliances between Africans at home and those in the Diaspora, for the common goal of advancing development on the continent; the cultivation of an unflinching loyalty and commitment to the continent by all its children; and a strong unity of purpose amongst Africans at every level of society.

Realizing the vision

The accounts presented below draw on the many available opportunities and strengths to chart the transformation process on the continent. They also underscore the importance of cultivating those critical elements to sustain Africa's development which are presently weak or underdeveloped. The available strengths include a wealth of human resources – a largely young populace composed both of skilled and unskilled; a wealth of natural resources – oil, natural gases, minerals and ores, precious metals and stones, to name but a few – which would provide fuel for economic regeneration; poignant ideas expressed by important visionaries such as the late Dr Kwame Nkrumah of Ghana, and the late Cheikh Anta Diop of Senegal, whose thoughts continue to provide relevance for the cultivation of a self-reliant model of development through the economic, political and cultural integration of Africa; and a committed leadership of Africans both on the continent and in the Diaspora. These are clearly important ingredients that will facilitate the realization of the vision for a development miracle in Africa, three decades from now. Thus, the starting point of this engagement is the need to harness our strengths within Africa, as they offer the only viable means for creating a vision of a hopeful future.

The three accounts represent the voices of Africans from three different sectors – the village community, the highest position of government and a voice from the Diaspora – reflecting on what they each perceive as critical elements which have made for Africa's development success on the world stage, three to four decades from now. The common thread running through these accounts is the point that Africans alone hold the key to their future destiny. This is reinforced in the personal account that sets out the operational challenge for the next century at the individual level. That, after all, should be the starting point for every African's endeavors.

Assuming responsibility

It is midmorning in this West African village school, and a class of adolescent girls and boys listen attentively as their history teacher recounts some of the dramatic developments of the last few decades which propelled the African continent from the depths of poverty, despair, deprivation and instability, into what is now referred to worldwide as the development miracle of the 21st century.

He began by describing the most common characterization of Africa at the end of the last century, as a continent plagued by wars, diseases, poverty, underdevelopment, intolerance and corruption. At the time, many observers – both within and outside the continent – expressed little confidence and hope in the future of Africa, and for some, this situation presented an opportunity to plunder the continent of any remaining wealth and resources. In the midst of all this turmoil, it took strong will, determination and commitment on the part of those who continued to believe in the future of Africa to overcome what barely four decades ago appeared as a lost cause.

"The keyword to understanding the source of the development success in Africa today", he continued, is "Responsibility". In other words, the point at which Africans across different levels and sectors of society began to look to themselves, their communities and their continent, as the starting point for transforming the social, political and economic ills that plagued Africa in the latter part of the 20th century was the defining moment which set the ball rolling for what is now widely referred to as a development miracle".

The students listened as their teacher proceeded to elaborate on two critical levels where the exercise of responsibility facilitated positive change in Africa. Here, the first level of change described was a responsible commitment to advancing human resource development in Africa. Investing in the people of Africa opened up a very important avenue for the realization of self-reliant development. This required a wholesale attack on the disease of illiteracy, which until a few decades ago was one of the principle obstacles to development. Today, as a result of those actions, over 95 percent of young people in both rural and urban communities across the continent have obtained, at minimum, a secondary level education. The equally strong commitment to overcoming adult illiteracy from this period onwards ensured that the gains made applied equally to the older generation of Africans. Investments by African governments in education and skills development were complemented by an equally strong commitment to infrastructure development, and these achievements provided a strong foundation for the current economic success.

At a related level, the strengthening of local government structures through the devolution of power and authority provided another important avenue for investment in the people of Africa. Previous leaders had unsuccessfully employed largely authoritarian styles of leadership in their attempts to govern diverse groups and cultures within their territories. This was often characterized by an overwhelming concentration of power in the state, and often in the hands of a few individuals. The deficiencies and inadequacies of this style of governance was soon evidenced through the wide gap which emerged between ruling elites, and the majority of African citizens, whose basic needs and aspirations remained unmet. In many instances, this problem culminated in a constant struggle for the control of state power by marginalized groups, and by those who had been prevented from sharing in the privileges at the power centers. These internal pressures on the state, coupled with strong external pressures in the form of the rapid and intense global transformation processes at the end of the last century, were important factors which opened the way for the development of new power centers in Africa.

This transformation was greatly facilitated by the strong will, determination and hard work of Africans in civil society, who assumed responsibility for charting their individual destinies and those of their communities, instead of looking to the state for redemption, an approach which undoubtedly provided a strong driving force for development. All across the continent, both in rural and urban settings, a visible trend of community self-reliance in meeting vital social service needs – basic health and hygiene, education and shelter provisions became commonplace. African men and women drew on both innovative and traditional techniques and institutions to address the basic needs of their communities. It became increasingly evident to those governments which up until this point had resisted any argument in favor of devolving power to local authorities and structures, that this was both an unavoidable and necessary path to assuring the future development of countries across the continent. Today, we see that far from weakening state structures, the creation of local power centers has provided for stronger, leaner and more efficient states, better able to manage the challenges and opportunities presented at national and international levels.

At this stage, the teacher paused for a few seconds before proceeding to elaborate on what he termed the second level of responsibility. The assumption of responsibility at this level was, he said, evidenced through the vigorous pursuit of regional economic integration, particularly in the last three decades in Africa. In important terms, he described this phenomenon as having been instrumental in promoting a self-reliant approach to development in Africa, thus vindicating the views of post-independence political leaders such as Dr Kwame Nkrumah of Ghana, who back in the 1950s and 1960s, strongly advocated economic integration as the key to facilitating rapid, successful development on the continent. Whilst this vision continued to occupy priority place on the agenda of the OAU throughout the latter part of the last century, it took the emergence of the right quality of leaders in recent decades to turn the vision into reality. The investments which have been made by governments across Africa in developing intra-Africa transportation, information and communication links has greatly facilitated the ascendancy of Africa into the strong eco-

nomic power bloc it is today. Another important development which facilitated the latter process was the priority given by governments to overcoming
the practical problems created by language barriers amongst French, English
and Lusophone countries in Africa. Thus, the decision by an overwhelming
number of states to integrate all three languages within the education structures of their individual countries has derived important practical as well as
political benefits for strong partnerships and development.

Towards the end of the last century, regional economic integration was increasingly advanced through sub-regional cooperating arrangements and institutions. Over time, these sub-regional blocs have served as important avenues
for nurturing and supporting economic development within individual states.
The OAU has now come to represent an effective medium for coordinating
interactions and cooperation between the different sub-regional groupings, and
also represents the vehicle through which cooperating arrangements at the continent-wide level are pursued. In significant terms, regional economic integration has strengthened Africa's bargaining power vis-à-vis the Western multilateral lending institutions, as well as other regional economic blocs of the world.
It has boosted the growth and development of the indigenous private and industrial sectors of African countries, and provided a bulwark against shocks
on the international market place, which in past decades had persistently threatened the economies of individual African countries. Thus, through regional
economic integration, the goal of African unity, which appeared as an unattainable dream in the last century, has today been made real. The driving force
behind this success was the unity of purpose amongst African governments and
people, who realized that this strategy was necessary for lifting Africa out of
the economic doldrums which challenged the continent's development prospects throughout the last century".

In summing up, the teacher noted that although problems and obstacles to
growth will continue to challenge Africa, as it progresses from a continent of
largely middle-income to that of high-income countries, the strong foundations
that have been laid over the 40 years since the beginning of the present century
– strong states and institutions of governance; a different approach by African
leaders and peoples to resolving problems on the continent; an empowered,
highly literate and highly skilled population, an environment which fosters peace
and security; and a confident generation of younger Africans to bear the torch
of future development – will shield the continent from the shocks and uncertainties of the external environment.

At this point, the teacher paused to survey the class of confident and dedicated students whose commitment and competence provided assurance to him
that the African development miracle would be sustained well beyond the 21st
century by a future generation of Africans who understood the value of assum-

ing responsibility for their individual challenges, and those of their communities.

A QUESTION OF LEADERSHIP

Loud applause preceded the chairperson's ascent to the podium to address a hall full of delegates, gathered here at the Summit of OAU Heads of States. Barely four decades ago, the notion that Africa would boast one elected female Head of State seemed like an unattainable dream. Yet, assembled at this Summit were all ten elected female Heads of State, whose rise to political power was proof again that Africa is certainly charting an exemplary path on the stage of world development. At the start of her speech, the President paid homage to the fact that the host country where delegates were today gathered, presented the best illustration of the African development miracle, given the rapid pace at which the country had progressed from a collapsed, ungovernable and war-ravaged state, to become a middle-income economy within the space of barely three decades. "This East African state" she continued, "is today as strong as any of the other middle-income economies of Africa, and indeed the World". She attributed the key factors of this success to the emergence in Africa of a strong and committed breed of leaders, willing and able to place the interests of communities, nations and the continent at large above those of narrow, selfish pursuits. She noted that the exercise of good, responsible leadership at all levels of African societies has created an environment where, for the overwhelming majority of Africans, an unquestionable loyalty and commitment to advancing the interests of their countries and continent precedes individual actions. She underlined the importance of this principle as having provided a strong foundation on which the current successes have been built.

She continued:

> We in Africa have a lot to celebrate at this juncture of our historical development. Gone are the days when corruption, nepotism, manipulation of ethnic differences for cheap political gains, abuse and mismanagement of our wealth and resources, and suppression of healthy opposition and institutions of democracy were characteristic of our political leadership styles. We owe our victory today to those Africans – both in the Diaspora and on the continent – who through an unflinching commitment to servicing the needs of their people, even in the midst of extreme turmoil, succeeded in breaking the cycle of poverty, despair and hopelessness that was the lot of Africa. These leaders, many of whom are gathered here in this room today, skillfully blended a commitment and political obligation to advancing the interests of Africa on the one hand, with excellent managerial skills on the other, to ensure effective administration both of the scarce and the abundant resources on the continent. As good managers, the new breed of leaders have been able to design effective mechanisms to accommodate diverse group interests and priorities at all levels of the political decision-making processes.

The clearest demonstration of the great strides which have been made in this regard lies in the smooth and careful management of the transition processes in all the countries which were afflicted by violent internal conflicts in recent decades. In placing a broader definition of peace and security at the heart of the reconstruction agenda in war-torn countries, leaders presiding over these countries were able to move beyond superficial remedies to tackle the root causes of the conflicts. The key strategy pursued here, of sustaining peace through economic and political development, respect for human rights and the promotion of a culture of tolerance within and amongst all sectors of society, continues to this day to provide guidance for the actions of African governments. Leaders have been able to transcend short-term interests – fuelled by greed, fear and insecurity – which had prevented earlier generations from thoroughly addressing the source of political instability in Africa. In doing so, they have pioneered effective systems of governance to meet the realities of Africa's political landscape at both local and national levels. The emphasis today, is not on favoring the interests of one group or sector over another but is, rather, premised on the realization that the available political space and material resources within the confines of individual states, when well-managed, is sufficient to accommodate the needs and interests of all the diverse elements within society.

> The path of peace has also been furthered by the commitment of resources away from the purchase of land-mines and cheap, outdated firearms (which were nevertheless highly effective in consuming the lives of innocent victims) to investments in the development of human potential in Africa. Africa has, thus, been cleansed of the problem of small arms proliferation which was a particularly acute challenge at the end of the last century and which greatly contributed to an atmosphere of insecurity and the promotion of a culture of violence within communities. The shift in priorities away from arms purchases to investments in human development has contributed greatly to the cultivation of a highly literate and highly skilled work-force in Africa, able to compete effectively with their European and Asian counterparts.

> Credit for these achievements did not, however, derive solely from the efforts of governments, but were greatly complemented by the emergence in Africa of a strong and articulate civil society, able to hold governments to account where necessary. Civil society has, likewise, been an effective partner of government in other instances – working hand in hand to chart a common path and agenda for development in Africa. The strong role which civil society continues to play in designing and implementing community and national level development priorities, provides clear demonstration of the fact that Africa's development miracle could not have been secured without investments in the empowerment of all sectors.

As she proceeded to wind down her speech, the President reiterated that in using the opportunity presented to highlight some of the key ingredients for Africa's ongoing development successes, she sought to remind African leaders of how far the continent has come in a relatively short space of time, and to urge leaders to embrace with even greater confidence the opportunities offered by the future.

The next speaker also chose as the theme of his speech, a celebration of Africa's achievements to date. He begged to make a confession at the start of his oratory.

There was a time, "when even I did not and could not see the value of investing in half of Africa's population – our women folk. Statements calling for the empowerment of women rang hollow in my ears, and I believe equally so in those of many of my male counterparts. Today, however, history has proved right those African men and women who had the foresight to understand that full-scale development of our continent would require investments in developing the human potential both of men and women. The coming together of African men and women to transform gender relations on the basis of our distinctively African experience, provided grounds for building what today represents a strong partnership based on mutual respect. This undertaking required that we boldly move to review the cultural values and norms which defined the nature of male and female relations, and on the basis of that review, to strengthen and highlight our positive traditions, and to discard those discriminatory laws and practices which undermine the potential of women to participate as equal citizens in our communities and societies.

As a result of this effort, the African experience today provides grounds for emulation by many societies worldwide. Not only do we score the highest marks in the drive for gender parity at educational and professional levels, and at the level of participation in economic and political decision-making processes, but we stand as the only region which, through this transformation process, has strengthened our families and communities. This significant achievement was facilitated by the important lessons we derived from the shortcomings of other regions where efforts to encourage men to assume equal responsibility and ownership for the process of transforming gender relations came late in the day. Consequently, this generated difficulties for the management of conflicts arising out of efforts to negotiate new power relations between men and women, the culmination of which, in many cases, was a weakening of the family institution and ultimately of social mores and values. Africa's experience has, however, been different in this regard. In jointly committing to make development on the continent a priority, African men and women resolved to transform gender relations on the continent (which in itself is necessary for attaining the development goal) to ensure that the individual rights of men and women were preserved, whilst at the same time ensuring that this process guarantees a strong partnership between women and men at family and community levels. As a result of these gains, we stand today as an example to the rest of the world on how to build healthy, strong partnerships for change. Although we still have someway to go yet in this direction, our successes to date do, however, provide confirmation that we are on the right path.

PARTNERSHIP WITH THE DIASPORA

Strolling with their two children through a quiet park in this Western capital, the parents discuss plans for their forthcoming family visit to Africa. Years back, they made a commitment to ensure that the children maintained strong ties with the continent – irrespective of whether they chose to live there or not – through, among other things, frequent visits home like the one they were presently planning. They also take pride in recounting to the children some of the significant ways in which Africans in the Diaspora have participated in advancing the African development miracle. This, they hope, will strengthen the latter's commitment to the continent, and help to sustain Africa's development success.

In turns, the parents explain to the children, how the strategic partnership between Africans on the continent and those in the Diaspora has strengthened in recent decades. In important respects, investments in infrastructure development in African countries presented opportunities to greatly boost this partnership. At one level, this development resulted in large returns by Africans in the Diaspora back to the continent, since this investment provided for them an enabling environment within which they could introduce new and fresh ideas, technologies and methods for advancing the continent's development. A large number of those who remained in the Diaspora included second and third generation Africans who kept their obligation to the continent alive by frequently visiting their countries of origin, and in doing so were consequently able to capitalize on the numerous opportunities open for advancing Africa's development from the outside. Many undertook to invest their financial resources inside Africa. These investments extended beyond remittances to include: business ventures of all kinds, stocks and shares from the indigenous market, and investments in the development of the communications and service sectors, amongst others. This process thus provided another important avenue for the injection of funds in the continent for development purposes.

Africans in the Diaspora also exercised their responsibilities to the continent through the cultivation of strategic alliances and networks between those Africans in key international institutions outside the continent, and relevant/ counterpart institutions within Africa. This provided for an effective system of knowledge and information sharing, and served as a useful channel by which Africans in the Diaspora advised African governments and institutions on important trends and developments at the global level which had implications for Africa's development prospects. As a result, the defense and promotion of Africa's interests – whether by those within or those outside of the continent – was fortified. This process also worked to loosen the traditional ties between Africa and former colonial powers who, up until this point, continued to exert large, albeit in some cases subtle influences, over development in African countries. The move to loosen the former colonial linkages encouraged the development of a more flexible and confident approach to partnership building with the rest of the world.

As they neared the end of their walk, the parents stressed to their children, the importance of keeping alive these strategic networks and partnerships. This required that they also consider meaningful ways in which their contributions to the continent's development would be recorded, as others before them had done.

A PERSONAL CALL TO DUTY

As a young African contemplating the continent's future at the end of the 20th century, I believe that hope and strength provide the most apt characterization of Africa's fortunes in the next century. Thirty years from now, I foresee a different Africa – an Africa which, having undergone all manner of suffering, poverty, exploitation and marginalization, would rise out of the depths of its misfortunes and derive strength from this present crisis, to become a powerful force. Sitting amongst friends and family, we shall be able to recount the experiences and stages which provided the path for Africa's development and transformation: the march for liberation and the optimism of the 1950s and 1960s; the onset of the economic crisis in the 1970s; the debt burden and structural adjustment in the 1980s; the wave of 'democratization' which swept the continent in the early 1990s; regional economic integration from the late 1990s into the 21st century; a new wave of leadership with an agenda for self-reliant growth and development in the first part of the 21st century.

By the end of the third decade of the 21st century, Africa would have scored important victories for eradicating, among other things, the diseases of poverty, wars, corruption, illiteracy, AIDS and underdevelopment. In recounting my personal journey along this path, I recall the important pledge I made to myself many years back to premise my actions less on the demands of personal ambitions and narrow considerations, but rather on the political obligation which I had (and still have) to the African continent at a critical stage of its development. This has served as a cardinal principle in all my engagements both within and outside of the continent.

In concrete terms, this meant for me a determination to understand the different facets of the problems that confronted the continent, and to explore and focus my attention and energies on the opportunities and means available for overcoming these challenges. It also translated into a call to both learn and comprehend the workings of the key international decision-making systems and institutions, since this provided a basis for defending and pursuing the interests of Africa within a highly competitive and often unfriendly environment. At the same time, it provided an opportunity to identify and build strategic partnerships and alliances which promote the continent's development agenda, and also provided a chance to educate partners outside of Africa on the priorities and potential which exist in Africa.

The principle of political obligation was as important for directing my actions on the continent, as it was for those outside. At home, this required an approach of striving to transcend "short-termism" in all my actions and decisions, and often necessitated that I forego immediate gains for the sake of the longer term good and development of Africa. This process has also required the cultivation of an open-minded approach, by way of a bold reassessment of the cultural values and norms which impact negatively on the development process in Africa; to discard these elements, and move to adopt more progressive values, befitting the realities of the world of today and tomorrow. The journey along this path has in no way been an easy one, and often, the temptation to give up the struggle was great, particularly earlier on, when the same level of commitment to the continent was visibly absent from the motives of some Africans who should have known better. That a large mass of Africans both on the continent and in the Diaspora resolved to employ this approach today speaks wonders for the continent's advancement. This provided a basis on which to rebuild confidence and cultivate solidarity and partnerships amongst African countries, which in turn provided fuel for the self-reliant model of development which we have today.

I rejoice in the fact that today's development successes have been attained through hard work and the coming together of both men and women, younger and older generations of Africans, rural and urban communities, governments and civil society, and between Africans and strategic and well-meaning partners outside the continent. Throughout this entire process, the most significant lesson which I have personally drawn, is the importance of realizing that in the final analysis, the interests of Africa can best be promoted by Africans themselves. Friends of Africa – and there are many of such – can only play a facilitative role and show solidarity with the African cause. Ultimately though, we have to chart our own course. For many Africans, this lesson had to be learnt the hard way. Nevertheless, we did it, and the benefits are today clear for all to see.

CHAPTER 8

The African Development Challenge: Living the Experience

Barbara Mbire-Barungi

Three decades after the assertion of the Independence of the African Nation states, the fragile Continent reels under seemingly insoluble political, economic and ethnic problems. Yet this could merely be an evolutionary process into a future of solidarity and strength upheld by the almost perfectly interwoven African societal fabric. What follows is an attempt to provide an optimistic image at the end of the tunnel of the challenging evolutionary process that the continent is undergoing, and strategies to realize this vision of hope.

A VISION OF AFRICA

Three decades from now will be a time in the future when the traditional cultural ways of life will blend with the 'modern'. Politically, a niche for the harmonious coexistence for both traditional leaders and progressives will have been found. Sound Governance structures that combine the old and the new ways will be erected. There will also be greater awareness and recognition of our deep ethnic diversity and the need for universal democratic participation alongside preservation of the vast and diverse cultural heritage. Economic development will have quickened its pace as economic integration across the continent is strengthened. Africa thirty years from now will only survive the trials and tribulations of globalization as a united front.

The Africa of tomorrow envisages a new brand of leadership that must inspire confidence in the people they lead, especially the youth. Men and women of the stature of Kwame Nkrumah, Nnamdi Azikiwe, Jomo Kenyatta, Abdul Nasser and Leopold Senghor who this time around will lay down political and economic strategies designed to improve the quality of life throughout the continent. This calls for good governance devoid of the "African village chief" dictatorial mentality, while accepting the rule of law as a cornerstone for political stability. Culturally, we will have preserved our diverse African traditions and yet remain fused together by our African identity. The masses will have attained an acceptable standard of general education to be in a position to assert their human rights. In the economic field, the leadership will seek to build vibrant economics that must break the vicious circle of ignorance, disease, poverty that has bedeviled post independence Africa. Those at the helm of affairs will be personalities of integrity, immense dedication and responsive to the needs of the citizens. Africa will then be a continent free of illiteracy, violence and chronic problems of refugees, capable of feeding its people and with medical care that will be accessible to the majority of the inhabitants.

Caring governments will be in place in all regions giving guidance and assistance to the citizens in all aspects of their endeavor and formulating such other policies as are necessary for good governance and a conducive environment for creating prosperous, contented and stable communities. It is only with that type of trend that Africa will be in a position to take full advantage of the current knowledge revolution and be able to assume its rightful global status in the comity of nations as a politically stable and economically viable continent.

If these seemingly optimistic evolutionary processes of the political and cultural African structures are not realized as quickly as one would hope, we may have a relatively bleak future three decades from now. What we must emphasize is that to create a better future there is a need for greater awareness and the development of institutions with a greater African flavor. This will entail a mix of traditional and modernist approaches with the aim of creating more cohesive governance systems. The 1990s have already witnessed various experiments with democracy, revival and strengthening of local government structures, and greater dependence or political support from traditional leaders in several countries.

CHALLENGES AND PROBLEMS

The main challenges that Africa must address in order to make my vision of the future a reality are political, economic and human development.

Political challenge

The younger generation of today contrasts sharply with that of thirty years ago when independent nation states ruled by the African elite were established. Then, the young African visionaries were at the very least politically curious; today, the future leaders are largely apolitical and seemingly dedicated to individualism in the westernized fashion. This has created a political vacuum in many countries and only serves to further entrench the old order of partyism (KANU in Kenya, ZAPU in Zimbabwe) in some and military dictatorships in others.

Indeed, the young visionaries have something to learn from the past. When many of the African nation-states were created in the 1960s, the mood on the continent progressed from the great African dream by pioneers like Kwame

Nkrumah of Pan Africanism to the more realistic phase of Africanization where Africans felt they should be left to attend to their own affairs instead and not to those of the 'colonial masters'. As the feelings of nationalism strengthened, territorial spheres of influence were further deepened across Africa. In East Africa, for example, slogans like 'Ugandanization' were entrenched within development policy, there was consolidation of territorial power, and trade barriers were erected. Any hope of an East African Federation was totally abandoned. A major cause was the fact that none of the leaders of the three East African countries was willing to subordinate themselves to the federal power superstructure in the name of regional political union.

In reality, there was no fundamental change. It was simply a change of guard from white colonialism to African colonialism that carried forward the repressive colonial inventions which only served to pave the way for some of the worst dictatorships in the World. Examples include Idi Amin (1971–1979) of Uganda, The reign of Emperor Jean Bokassa (1966–1979) of the Central African Republic; and the dictatorship of Mobutu Sese Seko of Zaire.

The more likely political future of Africa is a move from usurped power of military dictators to popularly elected authoritarian leaders. The leadership can no longer continue to turn a deaf ear to those that they govern. An attempt has been made in several African countries to create a more democratic political environment. Local governance structures are playing a more significant role. However, at the higher echelons, absolute power remains vested in the leadership. This is best exemplified by Yoweri Museveni of Uganda, Jerry Rawlings of Ghana, and Arap Moi of Kenya.

One could argue that African leadership since pre-colonial times has been authoritarian bordering on dictatorship by nature. In the future, for as long as many African nations remain poor and lack a vibrant indigenous entrepreneurial class, "dictator politics" will thrive.

THE ECONOMIC CHALLENGE

The African dual economy

The predominantly agrarian dual structure of the African economy poses a serious challenge to the wisdom and applicability of conventional economic development theory. One cannot really confidently hope for the structural transformation of the primarily rural subsistence sector into an industrialized, urbanized economy because the informal sector is simply not a transitory phase.

Dual economic structures are a unique characteristic of the African economy featured by the coexistence of a relatively small capitalist central business enclave surrounded by a largely subsistence sector. Rather than the predicted structural transformation, Africa continues to experience the increased and persistent outburst of a shadow economy in the form of the urban informal sector since the mid 1970s. Contrary to mainstream beliefs, the informal sector is a highly structured entity whose economic relations are embedded in social relations. Structural adjustment programs have tended to dismiss the increasingly thriving informal sector as transitory. But some of us argue that the informal sector is a permanent structural feature of the labor market given that it absorbs about 75 percent of new entrants to the labor force. It is more than just a means of survival. The informal sector is an increasingly critical source of income generation and employment.

All over Africa, the period of the 1990s and beyond promises to be the urbanization era. Within a generation from now – by the year 2025 – more than half of the total population of the African continent will be living in urban centers. Since the mid 1980s, the numbers eking a living out of the urban informal sector have increased, slums and shanty towns have mushroomed to uncontrollable levels, and policy makers remain torn between hostility to and acceptance of the economic activity of indigenous traders, labor and entrepreneurs. As Akin Mabogunje descriptively puts it :

> Attempts to understand what is happening in African cities have been shrouded in controversy. Some have argued that we are witnessing the decay of urban area, arising from the premature blossoming in economies that have not fully transformed from their protocapitalist colonial mode. Others, on the other hand, have suggested that a deconstruction of colonial cities is unfolding to make way for a restructuring of urban life and conditions based on African mores and value systems.[1]

The persistent thriving of the informal sector cannot be explained simply as a manifestation of poverty. A deeper analysis reveals an element of the cultural underpinning of the society as a whole. The informal sector operations clearly depict the familial network set-up of African socioeconomic activity. It is a strong reflection of the African work ideology, which revolves around informal governing rules. It could be argued that this familiar networking is the strongest safety net for the most vulnerable groups. African bureaucrats that declare harsh policies against the informal sector activity should make the effort to understand the structural difference between the African economic system and that of the developed world. After all, the informal sector is really an adaptation to the problem of segmented markets and its existence is partially due to low domestic capital accumulation within these dual economies. It is time to move away from the old philosophy of trying to bridge the gap between the South and the North. And rather find home-grown solutions to the differently structured African economic systems.

---

[1] Akin Mabogunje, "Overview of Research Priorities in Africa", in Stren, R. (ed.). *Urban Research in the Developing World*. Toronto, 1994, p.22.

A full discussion on how the informal sector could become the engine of growth is not possible here. However, it is worth mentioning that vast research has been done on the dynamism of the urban informal sector. What is adamantly advocated for by researchers is the need to promote and strengthen the linkages that exist between the formal and informal sectors. A major literature on subcontracting between informal, small, medium and micro enterprises and formal establishments has built up over the years of investigation of the informal sector.

It should be safe to predict that the future of African economic development lies in the capitalization of indigenous entrepreneurial activity, which is centered on interpersonal exchange in small-scale production and local trade. Formal financial institutions that are able to develop innovative financial packages targeted at small operators are required to enable a more realistic transformation from informal to formal economic activity.

Governments and donors alike need to recognize the importance of developing a coherent and well-coordinated policy framework that will facilitate indigenous participation in economic development and growth. Lessons from South East Asia can be drawn upon to enable the progression of seemingly dynamic small-scale enterprises that are shunted by the poor macroeconomic policy environment in Africa. It is important to emphasize that such an initiative should be through partnership of donors and national governments.

African governments will need to be more responsive to the needs of their populations and identify priorities for the development of small scale and micro enterprises. Technical expertise from donor organizations and global networking are important in building a supportive and sustainable policy framework. The urban informal sector has come a long way since the 1970s in being formally acknowledged as a sector that has a positive implication for employment generation and poverty alleviation. However, controversy over how best to tap this potential continues to stagnate any progress. Perhaps some insightful advise can be drawn from North (1995, as cited in Nissanke and Aryeetey, 1997), who argues that adaptive rather than allocative efficiency should be the guide to policy.

Failing to see informal economic activity for what it is, 'informal', and persistent policy prescriptions of structural change from informal to formal as has been the case for the last two decades or so without any remarkable sustainable success, will only maintain the status quo. This is simply to keep the small operator marginalized and in some countries like Uganda, Kenya, and Côte d'Ivoire, trade continues and will remain foreign dominated (Asians in East Africa and Lebanese in Côte d'Ivoire) unless indigenous entrepreneurs are capitalized.

Structural adjustment

As the end of this century draws near, Africa is faced with the very daunting challenge of accelerating the economic growth momentum sparked off by structural adjustment. Most fundamental is the need to attain sustainable growth so as to ensure the urgently needed poverty reduction.

The economic crisis of the Sub-Saharan Africa (SSA) region which reached its apotheosis in the 1980s still continues to be an issue of serious global concern. The region has been wrecked by the dismal economic performance, acute decline in economic growth and consequential erosion of welfare. Africa hardly shows any major signs of socioeconomic improvement. Today, many African economies are still caught up in the vicious cycle of poverty, backwardness and poor governance.

Having said that, there seems to be a slow reversal of the decline in economic growth of SSA countries since the adoption of structural adjustment policy reforms. Africa's growth performance, however, remains poor at 1.4 percent (African Development Bank estimates, 1993). Economic growth rates stood at an annual average of 6 percent between 1965 and 1973, dropped to 2.5 percent during the period 1973–1980, and further declined to about one percent in the 1980s (World Bank, 1989). The region did witness a resurgence in economic growth in the late 1980s (an average rate of 4.3 percent during the three years 1988–90). Alas, this was short-lived and the region has once again plunged into relative economic decline since 1992.

Evidence shows that recent macroeconomic performance has been mixed despite the SAP policies of curbing domestic expenditures, reducing inflation, correcting exchange rate misalignment, boosting exports and slicing the external debt. The deep-rooted underlying structural rigidities and political instability continue to undermine any attempts to attain macroeconomic stability and growth.

In most African Countries implementing SAP, key reforms are still incomplete. Nonetheless, there has been some growth, even though GDP per capita growth remains low and well below what is needed for rapid poverty reduction and sustainable development. What, therefore, are the lessons learnt from more than a decade of structural adjustment? Which policy reforms in particular clearly have large impacts on growth? Is the continued weak economic performance due to lack of commitment to reforms or a result of the failure of the reform policies to restore sustainable growth? Or is it a consequence of the failure to address the institutional weaknesses of the African economies? The recent wave of research on African economic development seems to point to the need for a new paradigm.

This new paradigm should seek to create a better understanding of the institutional set-up of the African political economy. More recently in the literature

(Adam and O'Connell, 1998), there is an increasing focus on the role of institutions in economic development, particularly in the case of Africa. This can be interpreted as an attempt to solve the baffling mystery of Africa's persistent development tragedy despite the orthodox policy restrictions of such programs as structural adjustment, and the huge aid flows. Africa has received much more aid both per capita and relative GDP than any other continent. Paul Collier (1997) argues that Africa's slow growth suggests that aid must not have been decisive in economic performance.

I will argue that the goal of sustainable development will, for a long time, elude African governments unless national priorities are redefined. Governments need to respond first and foremost to the domestic needs of the populace. Donor aid and technical assistance should be a supplement to domestically designed development programs. What transpired in the 1990s are countries that have shown remarkable economic performance as a result of being 'aid-driven'. Uganda as a success story of IMF and World Bank structural adjustment programs is a classic example. As Paul Collier (1997) points out:

> A country such as Uganda, which is extremely poor by any standard and has an usually good policy environment, will be a recipient of aid for many years (at least a decade or so) even in the best of circumstances.

Thirty years from now sustainable development will remain a long-term goal unless drastic institutional restructuring emanating from Africa itself is undertaken.

HUMAN DEVELOPMENT

An important universal hallmark of this decade is the advocacy for human development. The "human dimension" of development has been stressed from one global summit to another. Africa, however, desperately needs to act quickly in order to attain the much-needed improvements in human development. Greater progress can be made by focusing international support and national policy on concrete targets, including poverty alleviation, employment-led growth and universal coverage of basic social services.

One of the main criticisms of structural adjustment policy reforms is the delayed action in implementing measures to alleviate the social costs of adjustment. Human development should be at the very core of the structural adjustment policy package. To achieve the urgently required poverty eradication, micro and macro policies must be integrated into the adjustment framework in addition to increased external assistance and debt relief, thereby enhancing economic growth and sustainable development.

HOPES AND STRATEGIES

The political and indeed the overall development of Africa cannot be completely divorced from our ethnicity and our traditional systems. If African nation states are to regain some autonomy and entrench an African civilization, then there will have to be an even more radical wave of innovation directed at creating stable, decentralized and democratic systems right from the grassroots to the top ruling hierarchy.

In more recent times, democratic elections have been held in Uganda, Benin, Chad, Guinea Bissau, Gabon, Ghana, Zambia, Zimbabwe, and South Africa. Political freedom in these countries may vary, and in some, may even be simply superficial, but it is a healthy sign that democratic ideals continue to sweep the African continent. Democracy hand in hand with economic adjustment are a true test of the African political economy. There is a strong message of not just the need for fundamental change but the acceptance by the populace of this change. The economic reforms under adjustment can only be reinforced by the increased political participation of the masses. In the last decade, Africa has witnessed the emergence of the new Africanization school of political thought. This school advocates the rethinking of the role of the state, the populace and the "governors/leaders" in order to redefine an African approach to democracy and development.

Greater hopes may lie in the global and regional integration of South Africa, a country that has experienced one of the most mammoth and rapid transformations in modern times. Apartheid has been dismantled peacefully. There is a joint recognition and commitment by all stakeholders of the need for political stability, social cohesion and economic progress.

Across Africa and the entire globe, there has been an explosion in community and associational groups in civil society everywhere. This is, indeed, a welcome global trend and may be the best way to tackle the 'economic and political poverty' on the African continent. Stren (1994) states that the strong expansion of civil society groups constitute new stakeholders in an expanded policy-making process that is no longer confined to formal bureaucratic and political structures based on national state systems. For the sake of illustration, the local governance system in Uganda is outlined.

The Ugandan experience

The local government system in Uganda has evolved over the past 90 years from British colonial administration to the present Resistance Council (RC[2]) system of democratic participation and representation. The RC system was introduced by the National Resistance Movement (NRM) administration after

---

[2] Resistance Councils (RCs) have been renamed Local Governing Councils (LCs). In addition, the new Local Government Act supersedes the 1987 Resistance Councils Statute.

it came to power in 1986. It was based on the NRM political ideology of popular participation. This system consists of a hierarchy of democratic units beginning with the cell from which the RCI committee is elected. The Village (RCI) which includes all residents over the age of 18 elects an executive committee, which goes on to form the RCII (parish) level council. This process is repeated through to the RCIII (Sub-county), RCIV (county) and RCV (District) levels.

According to the 1987 Resistance Councils and Committees statute, the objectives of this system are the following:

– to create democratic institutions to be used as a vehicle for participation of the grassroots in decision making;

– to mobilize the masses for economic development;

– to eliminate dual administration (field administration and local government) at the district level; and

– to promote accountability and good governance at the local level.

It is a structure of governance that has in the last ten years become strongly entrenched in the local politics of the country. The resistance council system through dispersion of powers in society has been instrumental in paving the way from one of extreme dictatorship to relative democracy. The resistance council system has now been incorporated into the national decentralization program, thereby making it more of a civic-oriented system of governance rather than a political one. And it is now known as local governing council. The council committees constitute the political organizations established at each level, while the chiefs are civil servants who advise the local governing counselors, and who implement their decisions. However, the RC system in Uganda still has some serious flaws because true democracy does not exist in all the RCs. Beyond that, part of the system is based on indirect rather than universal electorate. For political stability to be sustainable it is important that African leaders recognize and concede to the fact that there is a need to develop genuine decentralized structures of governance.

Economic integration

Whereas political union may not be feasible, Africa would definitely benefit from economic integration. And perhaps, in future, political integration can then build on economic integration.

Economic integration is no doubt one of the potential pillars of Africa's strategy for economic survival. Attempts at regional integration are manifested in all parts of the African continent through the various sub-regional groupings such as ECOWAS (West Africa), PTA (Eastern and Southern Africa), SADC (Southern Africa), and AMU (Maghreb countries), to mention but a few. South Africa is particularly looked to as a potential regional vehicle for growth. However, several factors have undermined African integration movements. These include the rigid structures of the African economies, lingering colonial ties, the few sub-regional complementarities, and poor economic infrastructure. In more recent times, the poor leadership, corruption and mistrust between African states have not been conducive to Integration. We should therefore take cognizance of past failures while at the same time forging a strategy for future cooperation.

In order to elevate our bargaining power in the face of strong regional blocks like the European Economic Union, the North America Free Trade Area (NAFTA), and Asian Pacific Economic Cooperation (APEC), Africa needs to rethink its economic integration strategy by consolidating its trade blocs as they stand, and in addition, having an umbrella integration forum.

Notwithstanding the fact that the importance of economic integration is high on the African development policy agenda and will carry on into the next century, the need for innovative development thinking and advocacy for change is real.

While the Afropessimists clutch on to the dependency theory framework as a tool of analysis of the political economy of Africa, the visionaries look to democratic innovation enabled through a better understanding of the African institutional set-up.

Institutional innovation

Institutional innovation that focuses on the structure of our societies seems to be the way forward. In this sense, institutions refer to the rules and conventions of society that facilitate coordination among people regarding their behavior. The institutionalist perspective can be of considerable analytical power in understanding the structural dynamics of the African nation states. Daniel Bromley says (1985:780–81):

> This matter of the structural dimensions of the emerging economy is critical for the simple reason that most tropical countries are still groping with overcoming a colonial past... Alien institutional arrangements were superimposed on top of traditional structures and these structures facilitated profitable trade for the colonial powers. At independence, new nation states... were faced with the imposition of yet another set of institutional arrangements. Tribes, clans, and other ethnic entities were consolidated under one European concept of statehood.... It is that process which is still going on.

It is futile for one to think that the process can be reversed, and preferable for us to work on how best we can, within our nation states, create workable indigenous structures that address our political, economic and social needs.

Institutional economics is emerging as a powerful analytical and conceptual framework for the understanding of the workings of the political economy of the developing world. Institutional economics does so by focusing on the structural aspect of the economy, unlike the orthodox economists who assume that Institutions are exogenous and go on to model economic development on the assumption of the existence of fully functioning markets. But how, then, do we explain the continuous grappling with market-driven policies in an attempt to create sustainable growth and development after over a decade of structural adjustment? Daniel Bromley sums it up best in the following words:

> ... the problem of development economics is not one of getting prices right. Rather, the problem is to get the rules right.[3]

It is through focusing on institutional arrangements in the context of Africa and by defining the role of institutions and institutional change in the process of economic development that Africa will be free of the bondage of underdevelopment.

The African development crisis can certainly be addressed through a more critical analysis of the set of fundamental political, social, legal ground rules that establish the basis of institutional arrangements. As Nissanke and Aryeetey (1997) argue:

> given that each country has its own specific circumstances, experiences, institutions and history, all of which should be taken into account in designing its own architecture of institutional arrangements and development policies.

The African continent has undergone numerous institutional experiments, whose failure can be attributed to a great extent to the lack of coherent integration with the African circumstances as set out by our diverse traditional heritage. Indeed, institutional economics has comparative advantages over time, as it places the nature of sources of dynamism at the center of analysis (Harris et. al. 1995 and Bardham 1988; cited in Nissanke and Aryeetey 1997). In this case, Africa is the center of analysis.

In many African countries, there is recognition of the need to study more deeply our institutions of governance and the overall institutional environment in a bid to create an African development paradigm. The future will see a stronger move towards adaptability rather than the replication of western models as a policy guide to achieving sustainable development.

Cultural preservation

Towards the end of the century, the flame for cultural preservation and harmonious coexistence seems to have been strongly rekindled. Take the instances of the newly restored tribal kings in the Republic of Uganda in 1993, the ex-

---

[3] Bromley, D., "Institutions and Institutional change" in *National Economic Development*. Internationale Agrapolitik und Entwicklung der Weltagrawirtschaft. Landwirtschaftsverlag GmbH, Münster-Hiltrup. p. 226.

tremely strong influence of the Ashanti in the Republic of Ghana, and the restlessness of the Zulu. The issue of traditional rulers remains to be resolved in many modern African societies. As Ken Saro-Wiwa (1995:191) so aptly puts it in his detention diary:

> Africa's tribes and ethnic groups are ancient and enduring social organizations complete with their own mores and visions, which no colonialism has been able to destroy over the centuries. The African nation-state as presently conceived has only succeeded in stultifying them...

Interestingly enough, as early as 1961 David Apter (1961:ix) in his study of Uganda was able to remark:

> By their special relationships with British authorities as well as their devotion to their institutions, these people have successfully prevented a wholesale assault on their ethnic autonomy. Neither colonial officials nor nationalists have been successful in whittling away the autonomous position of Buganda within Uganda or within a larger context of East African nationalism.

These remarks were made before Uganda attained Independence in October 1962 and more than thirty years later, the conflict between Buganda and the Government of Uganda is yet to be resolved. The new South Africa is no different. The Zulu leadership enjoyed a rather special relationship with the Apartheid government and is now battling with the ANC government to accommodate traditionalism within the mainstream political realm of the new South Africa.

Traditional knowledge can best be married with the modern ideals of democracy through creating viable local governance systems which enable the operationalization of the seemingly complex and sophisticated national political goals into simple rules of governing for the populace. Going back to the local governance system in Uganda as previously discussed; the blending of the old and new value systems of governance is possible and is perhaps the best way to ensure local participation, justice, community security, and a community sense of belonging. How else could the complex and highly westernized process of democratization be transformed into something simple and meaningful to the masses that hold on to their traditions?

The African visionaries should, therefore, appreciate the uniqueness of the cultural fabric of African society. The preservation and maintenance of cultural institutions is to be achieved by insulating them from politics. It is these very institutions that make us African and should be carried forward for generations to come.

Neo-Africanism

My vision of the future of African development is one in which the African scene is fully revitalized culturally. Perhaps more important is the strengthening of African nations by blending both the traditional and modern approaches in all spheres – political, economic and social. An African renaissance firmly holding its own against the increasing marginalization created by the fast-moving global tide. Neo-Africanism is merely the process by which Africans over time establish African rules of the game.

A few scenarios come to mind in regard to the process of Neo-Africanism. Politically, this chapter has elaborated the local governance structure in Uganda that draws on a strong system of traditional authority. This system of governance that has been adapted and made more flexible so as to accommodate the new values of modern progressive state can be deepened. Traditional chiefs that still play a vital advisory role in our communities can be formally drawn into the mainstream local governance structures of the African State.

The chapter has also highlighted the fundamental characteristics of the African dual economy. At the core of this economy is the familial entrepreneurial spirit, which is best depicted by the 'informal sector'. The future under the auspices of true African leaders that respond to the domestic needs of the African people will be one of indigenization of our economies. This will mean more policy support for small and micro enterprises. The fallacy of small African economies transforming into industrially-driven giants hopefully will have worn away. African leaders with political will and wisdom will reject economic experiments of the orthodox economic schools. Such experiments that have been carried out since independence have only served to create 'white elephant' economic projects. The bulk of the African population has not benefited from any 'trickle down' economic effects of such donor-driven experiments.

Another example is the dilemma of suitability of technology. African-tailored intermediate technology originating both from traditional practices and modern research and development by African scientists will occupy a central place in the development agenda of neo-African leaders. It will, however, be important to create partnerships with donors of the western world in facilitating such developments.

In the event that neo-Africanism does not gain full momentum thirty years from now, the continent will be as restless as it is today.

CONCLUSION

The stark reality about Africa is that government-led development continues to be crucial for any progress. The challenge that remains is how to define this role. The role of the state needs to be redefined in the African context by Africans rather than prescribed from out of Africa.

In the African context, the state has to find a mechanism by which it can juggle the dual role of pioneer of development and by the same token create an enabling framework for private sector exchanges. How "market- friendly" should the market approach become given the structural rigidities, and general lack of economic viability? How feasible is private sector development under the circumstances of low rates of capitalization of indigenous entrepreneurs against the backdrop of weak financial systems? These are some of the issues that must be addressed when redefining the role of the state in Africa.

In addition, indigenization is crucial to our future development. Rather than searching for answers in the 'orthodox' structural transformation of the agrarian economy into an industrialized one, it is more fruitful to encourage and innovate where necessary our home grown enterprises, modes of production, and intermediate technology that suit the conditions in Africa. Hence, developing local capacity.

Furthermore, as the world becomes more of a global village, Africa needs to create a niche for itself and carve out its future role. The most obvious step forward would be to enhance economic growth and strength through regional trade blocs which would then have a stronger bargaining position for Africa on the world market.

The African countries that are today referred to as success stories, Uganda for instance, have been able to achieve economic progress not only because of political stability, and exceptional donor support, but also due to their considerable latitude in tailoring their own political and social programs. Neo-Africanism is what the future holds!

REFERENCES

Adam, C.S. and S.A. O'Connell, "Aid, taxation and development: analytical perspectives on aid effectiveness in sub-Saharan Africa", World Bank Working Paper, February, 1998.

Akin Mabogunje, "Overview of Research Priorities in Africa," in Richard Stren (ed.). *Urban Research In The Developing World.* Centre for Urban and Community Studies, University of Toronto, Canada, 1994.

Allen, Chris. "Understanding African Politics," *Review of African Political Economy,* 22(65), 301–320 (1995).

Apter, David. *The Political Kingdom in Uganda:* A *study of Bureaucratic Nationalism.* Princeton University Press. Princeton, New Jersey, 1961.

Bromley, D., "Resources and Economic Development: An Institutionalist Perspective," *Journal of Economic Issues,* 19(3) 779–796 (1985).

Bromley, D., "Institutions and Institutional Change", *National Economic Development.* Internationale Agrapolitik und Entwicklung der Weltagrawirtschaft. Landwirtschaftsverlag GmbH, Münster-Hiltrup.

Collier, Paul. "Aid and Economic Development in Africa", paper presented at the AERC Conference on Comparative African and East Asian Development Experiences, 36 November 1997, Johannesburg, South Africa.

Nissanke, M. and Aryeetey, E. "Comparative Institutional Analysis: Sub-Saharan Africa – East Asia", paper presented at the AERC conference on Comparative African and East Asian Development Experiences, 3–6 November 1997, Johannesburg, South Africa.

Saro-Wiwa, K., *A Month and a Day: A Detention Diary.* Penguin Group, Penguin Books, London, 1995.

Stren, Richard, "Urban Research in the Developing World". in Richard Stren (ed.) *Urban Research in the Developing World, Vol.2: Africa.* Centre for Urban and community studies, University of Toronto, Toronto. 1994.

UNDP. *Human Development Report.* Oxford University Press, Oxford. 1995.

CHAPTER 9

A Vision for the Future of Zambia and Africa

Lawrence Mukuka

THE ZAMBIAN CONTEXT

A mere continuation of the present political and economic trends in Zambia foretells a very gloomy picture for the country in the next thirty years unless drastic changes guided by a common vision for national development takes place.

Looking at the future, it is urgently necessary that the country and the rest of the continent solve their political problems because these constitute the main obstacle to economic development. Once these problems are solved, then Zambia and the African continent will be half way to achieving their economic development. In Africa, there is overwhelming evidence of how political conflicts over tribalism and ethnicity, regionalism, religion, intolerance, gender, income and class, have ripped countries apart and reversed the pace of advancement. Needless to say, Zambia has had its own share of these problems.

The economic consequences of the political problems in Zambia and the rest of Africa have been severe. The prevalence of poverty, illiteracy, disease, hunger and ignorance have, in turn, increased the magnitude of the political crisis and created a vicious circle. Zambia is currently witnessing the beginning of democracy. The critical task at hand is to nurture and support the growth of the democratic process. The biggest fear, however, is that, if this opportunity to build democracy in Zambia is squandered, the country's political and economic development will experience a potentially devastating setback. Therefore, the ambition, hope and goal for the future of Zambia should be first to build a vibrant democratic, peaceful and secure Zambian society; and second, to build a strong and sustainable productive economy.

In order to realize this vision, the Zambian government must deliberately and carefully create a genuine and truly enabling environment that should provide opportunities for every Zambian, in rural and urban areas, to earn a decent and sustainable living. This implies a change in the attitudes, practices and legislation that in the past have not been beneficial nor favorable to Zambian citizens.

The Zambian government must also create a competitive and entrepreneurial economic environment. Such an environment must not only attract foreign business and investment into the country, it should also deliberately support local business through the provision of carefully directed innovative incentives, rebates and subsidies, and meaningful and limited protectionism. In addition, the environment must be stable, and cooperation between business and government must be nurtured.

Although the need for foreign investment is extremely important in order to bring the needed capital into the country, it cannot substitute fully for locally-generated resources. Therefore, it would be ludicrous, if not suicidal to ignore resources inside Zambia. The capacity of Zambians needs to be developed so that the country can have competent managers, a skilled labor force, and experienced business leaders and entrepreneurs who are capable of leading the country in different spheres and creating quality products.

Simply put, Zambia should build on its strengths by following the dictates of comparative advantage which stress reliance on factor endowments. For example, the Southeast Asian countries of Korea, Thailand, and the city-states of Hong Kong and Singapore, which were endowed with few natural resources and capital but abundant unskilled labor, based their early development strategies on labor-intensive manufactures. Their highly productive agricultural land and other natural resources built their export base during the early stages of rapid economic growth. In order to maintain their cost advantage, they also invested in traditional exports such as oil, natural gas, metals, timber, rice, palm oil and rubber, and diversified within primary products into exports of coffee, tea, cocoa and fruits (Lindauer et al., 1994). Once these countries moved into manufacturing for export and adopted an import substitution strategy, they did so from a solid base of primary export earnings. This strategy helped them to avoid the chronic shortage of foreign exchange that crippled the manufacturing sector in Africa in the 1980s. In addition, the governments of these countries invested in research, infrastructure, education and health in order to raise productivity in agriculture.

What is interesting about these Southeast Asian countries is that they appeared to be worse off than Africa in the late 1950s and 1960s. In many cases, they were characterized by a low-level equilibrium trap with large and growing populations, unstable governments, and a weak natural resource base.

Zambia and the rest of Africa must learn from the experiences of these Southeast Asian countries. It is necessary to build on Zambia's strengths, make the best use of what already exists in the country, and concentrate on what Zambia can do best. Unfortunately, the tragedy in Zambia and Sub-Saharan Africa at large is that because of high levels of illiteracy, lack of exposure and experience, many leaders fall victim to what can be called the ignorance trap.

As a result, many leaders make terrible and costly mistakes because they do not consult with those that might know.

A VISION FOR ZAMBIA

My vision for Zambia's economic development and prosperity can be summarized by the acronym "DREAM", in which the letters stand for *Development* and full mobilization of the available and potential internal and external human and natural *Resources* for the *Empowerment* and *Advancement* of every *Member* of the Zambian society. In the early stages of Zambia's economic development, this vision can be achieved by concentrating on the quadruple foundation of agriculture, mining, tourism and human resource development.

The three main aspirations of this Zambian Dream on the individual household level are:

- family household food security, i.e., availability of and accessibility to sufficient food for every Zambian family household at all times;

- home ownership, i.e., every Zambian family household to own at least a three-roomed fire-burned brick house with a good thatch or better; and

- freedom and opportunity to achieve and enjoy the basic human needs, i.e., every Zambian family household to be able to satisfy their needs. That is, all Zambians must have sufficient food, clean water and sanitation, clothing. shelter, health care, quality education, security, and have the freedom to exercise their fundamental human rights.

Agriculture

Agriculture is not only a necessary precondition for any successful national development strategy, it is also the basis and springboard upon and from which many other development processes are based and launched. In Europe, it was the agricultural revolution with such early revolutionary innovations as crop rotation, the introduction of new crops such as turnips, clover and potatoes, improvements in ploughing, the invention of the scythe, crop and animal breeding, and increased use of horses instead of oxen in the 18th century, that set in motion the process of development. Agriculture provided the capital needed to finance the industrial development. The production of iron and steel in the 18th and 19th centuries was driven by widespread demand for agricultural implements (Murdock, 1980).

After Europe, the same path of development with agriculture as the engine of economic growth was repeated in North America, Australia, Japan, Taiwan and China with tremendous success. In addition to agriculture, advances in mining, industry and the expansion of internal trade and new markets accelerated their economic progress. In recent years, the Southeast Asian countries of

Indonesia, Malaysia, and Thailand followed this path of development, and made significant progress compared to the majority of countries in Sub-Saharan Africa, including Zambia.

Agriculture is very important in the early stages of economic development because it also forms the foundation upon which the country's primary, secondary and tertiary industries are built. Agriculture contributes directly to the country's economic development in many important ways, including:

– providing food for workers in other sectors, national food security and improved nutritional standards;

– creating employment and surplus capital to finance industrial development;

– raising the purchasing power of the people through income generation;

– producing raw materials for use in industry and manufacturing; and

– earning of foreign exchange needed to finance industrial imports.

In spite of the critical role of agriculture in development, the agricultural sector in Zambia has never been the engine of economic growth, and this has subsequently been the main cause of poverty, food scarcity, and the inflationary increases in the price of food in the country. In order to make agriculture succeed in Zambia, we must have stronger political will, commitment and investment than the case in the past. Agriculture in Zambia is the largest sector of the economy, supports the bulk of the population, and has the largest potential internal market and the greatest growth prospects. Successful agriculture (i.e. one that creates food security, surplus capital, employment and income, raw materials and foreign exchange) does not result from the production of only one or two cash crops but from a carefully and painstakingly planned and executed package of necessary prerequisite components that includes:

– national 'agriculture-first' or 'perish' policy and its related poverty reduction objectives and strategies;

– unskewed patterns of land distribution and ownership;

– high governmental and private investment in agriculture and food production;

– improved access to credit, capital, modern technology, inputs, and processing facilities;

– even distribution of food within the country;

– reliance both on rain and irrigation for increased agricultural production;

– increased use of fertilizers, improved hybrid cultivars, inter-cropping and extension services in order to increase and maximize yield per area cultivated;

– improved feeder road system, storage, and marketing facilities;

- expanded internal markets for agricultural products and other biological resources;
- increased use of alternative energy sources and appropriate machinery and technology such as wind mills, water energy, thermal energy and biomass energy;
- increased knowledge about nitrogen-fixing strains of cereals and grasses;
- increased use of sustainable patterns of agricultural production to avoid environmental degradation:
- expansion of markets for agricultural produce and increased revenues from profitable crops;
- established industries to produce or service agricultural inputs (i.e., fertilizer, protection chemicals, machinery, seeds) or purchase agricultural outputs (i.e., textiles, paper, plastics, tobacco, food and drink industries);
- balanced production of cash crops and staple food crops; and
- well developed agricultural institutions with sufficient capacity to serve the agricultural sector.

Successful agriculture requires carefully targeted and limited government subsidies. In the short term, this may appear to be a financial burden on the government and the country but the long run benefits far exceed the costs by facilitating accelerated economic growth and increased food security.

Zambia can capitalize greatly on its large land mass. The country is bigger than the following countries: UK, Germany, France, Italy, Japan, and Spain. In addition, Zambia must begin to capitalize on its comparative advantage in agriculture and agro-industry. This can be enhanced by diversifying producers and products and adding value to products by encouraging and supporting further processing. The government should carefully target the small-scale producers, who form the majority of agricultural producers in the country, and provide them with special opportunities. An improved agricultural sector and household food security would help to expand economic opportunities and accelerate growth and development both in the rural and urban areas.

Mining

Zambia is located in the 'Gulf of minerals', as Southern Africa was often referred to during the cold war era, in comparison to the 'Gulf of Oil' of the Arab countries. The country is very rich in minerals, including cobalt, copper, zinc, gold, lead, vanadium, manganese, coal, emerald and many others that have not been fully explored and identified. Exploitation of mineral resources along with an improved agricultural sector should be the main source of foreign exchange earnings for the country. The country should focus on the highly productive sectors of mining, such as gemstone extraction.

Tourism

Zambia's moderate climate is one of the best in the world and it has earned the country the name of an 'air conditioned state'. Temperatures are mild and dry between May and August, hot and dry between September and November, and warm and wet between December and April. The country is ideal for outdoor activities such as camping, hunting and walking safaris, and it offers limitless opportunities for the use of alternative sources of energy.

A sizeable portion of the country is flat land, which should make it much easier for the construction of major agricultural irrigation canals, laying of water pipes to water-deficient areas, and transport roads and highways. Zambia is one of the few countries in Southern Africa with a large body of surface and underground water. This water area, which should be used for agricultural irrigation, fishing, recreation, tourism, transport and hydro-energy, includes the major lakes and rivers in the world. Examples are: lakes Tanganyika, Lusiwasi, Mweru, Mweru wantipa, and Kampolombo together with many other small lakes, lagoons and dams. There is also the Zambezi river. In addition, hundreds of smaller but perennial rivers and streams, are scattered all over the country.

There are already a good number of tourist attractions in unspoiled natural environment in the country, to which new ones could be added. Existing tourist attractions include water falls, leisure bays, cultural ceremonies like Kuomboka, N'chwala,, Likumbi lya mize, Umutomboko, and Shimunenga. Other attractions include a wide variety of plant, bird and animal species (700 bird species and 35 large mammals, some unique to Zambia), hot springs, and historical rock paintings and sites. In addition, there are over twenty national parks and game reserves occupying roughly 32 percent of Zambia's land mass. With a proper market-oriented management and marketing, these attractions could operate efficiently and productively to earn large amounts of local and foreign income for the country.

Therefore, in order to promote and invigorate the country's dormant tourist industry, there is a need to:

– maintain and preserve the tourist attractions located in the unspoiled, 'under-toured' and natural bush countryside, and capitalize on the Zambian wilderness experience;

– employ market-oriented management and marketing strategies aimed at achieving efficiency, productivity and attracting local and foreign holiday makers and tourists;

- reduce prohibitive hotel taxes and duties, cumbersome visa, customs and departure fee requirements and reduce fuel prices to entice holiday makers and tourists, and increase regional competitiveness;

- reduce crime, poverty (the biggest generator of crime in Zambia) and clean up cities to make Zambia safe and attractive for tourists;

- fight poachers who may endanger the lives of holiday makers and tourists while in the wilderness; and

- improve public transport, roads to major parks, and air links which have been a hindrance to tourism development in the country.

Other national assets of Zambia

Zambia is one of the most urbanized countries in Africa. It ranked as the fifth most urbanized country in Africa in 1988. Currently, the country's urbanization rate is over 42 percent. This implies that there is a large urban market to absorb agricultural products. The urban market can be further developed to absorb non-agricultural produce. Its potential for commerce is still untapped.

Zambia's peace and stability and its central location in the Southern, Eastern and Central African region gives the country an important political role in international and regional politics of Sub-Saharan Africa. Its access to all provincial capitals by trunk road, and three rail routes to the sea (when Bengwela route resumes) give Zambia, currently a sleeping giant, the competitive edge to participate fully and actively in the economic and political development of the sub-region, and Africa as a whole.

Zambia's demographic structure is another asset. Three quarters of the Zambian population is below 45 years of age. This indicates that Zambia is a very youthful nation and, generally, young people are known to be energetic, innovative, imaginative and forward looking. This is a valuable resource that can be used for national development.

Educationally, Zambia started from a very weak position, although this has changed over the years. However, there is still an abundance of unskilled labor, which could be employed in labour-intensive and capital-saving development projects, particularly agriculture and manufacturing.

Zambia's investment in its people (i.e. increasing people's access to quality education, health care, family planning, and good nutrition) will be more profitable than investing in machines, buildings and other material capital in the long-run. There are many multiplier effects and social spill-over benefits that could be gained from Zambia's investment in the improvement of human capital. For example, developed human capital increases the capacity of labor to contribute to gross national product and broadens people's capacities to think, act and participate in the economic development process. Education promotes better functioning of the democratic process as a result of voter literacy and more enlightened citizens. In addition, it helps to improve community sanitation, reduce the crime rate and improves government services for the community.

The need for Zambia to develop its human resources and make its people resourceful is paramount in order for the country to develop. The country should:

- reform its national philosophy and direction of education to include 10 years of compulsory free education for self-reliance, entrepreneurship, leadership and development;

- expand and improve education at all levels, and the learning-by-doing process (adult literacy) in order to upgrade work-force productivity both in agriculture and industry, and develop the required entrepreneurial, leadership and managerial skills in the country;

- expand and promote high quality health care (emphasizing preventive medicine, health education, mother and child-care, reproductive health and sexual health care);

- increase access to information by building infrastructure for radio, television, telephone and Internet;

- develop and expand countryside special education and rehabilitative programs for children and adults with hearing, physical, mental and visual disabilities and/or impairment; and

- promote and increase education enrollment, retention, and progression for girls in the country, and ensure the widest and earliest possible access by girls and women to secondary and higher levels of education, including vocational and technical training.

If we may summarize thus far, the main reason why Zambia, which is so generously endowed with human and natural resources, has sunk so much into poverty has been the failure to manage the country's enormous resources productively. This manmade or structural poverty in Zambia has been caused by the distortions and biases in the country's political, economic, educational and cultural institutions, as well as in its position in the world economic system over a period of time. Therefore, the fight against these distortions and biases requires a visionary leadership, comprehensive structural reforms, and a proactive, strong, purposeful and business-oriented national foreign policy. The nation's foreign policy should be based on poverty reduction and self-reliance at home, dismantling of international trade protectionism, securing fair terms of trade, attracting foreign investment, and solving Zambia's debt crisis.

POLITICS: THE ROOT OF THE AFRICAN CRISIS

It has been argued that the number one problem facing Africa is political. This argument is profound in the sense that without political stability, visionary, knowledgeable and hardworking political leadership, economic development will always be elusive. Many crises on the African continent are a result of the unsettled political question.

One of the causes of Africa's problems of political instability and economic fragility is the in-adaptability of the Western political and state-system into Africa's predominantly traditional way of life. Factors that favored state formation in Europe were and still are extremely and conspicuously absent in Africa. Historical research on state-formation in Europe emphasizes the importance of the feudal past and the following factors: socioeconomic changes; the contribution of the international economic system; the diffusion of Roman Law; the Renaissance; Christian religion; Greek philosophy; rise of the market economy; the works at the Henry the Navigator's School of Navigation at Sagres on Cape St. Vincent; intra-European trade; resource endowment and capital accumulation; cultural homogeneity of language and religion; openness of the European periphery to the outside; pressure exerted on European political life by the Byzantine and various Muslim empires; trade merchants; a continuous supply of political entrepreneurs; pre-existing decentralized political structures; and availability of extractable resources (Jones, 1981; Bertrand, 1983).

State-formation in Europe was not a mere result of economic modernization such as the rise of capitalism, the opening of trade routes or the growth of industry, but it was a political response to the crises that beset several feudal societies during the late Middle Ages. It was a political response that some European societies were forced to make to an increasing division of labor coupled with strong resistance to social change on the part of certain elements of feudal society. In addition, it was a way of reconciling the growing political incapacity of the great lords with the fact that they still maintained substantial control over economic and social life. In the European sense, the state implies a system of permanently institutionalized roles which has the exclusive right to the legitimate use of force, whereby it exerts sovereign power over a given territory, including its remote provinces, and defends the borders of that territory against foreign incursion. The system is also institutionalized in the form of a political and administrative machine run by civil servants recruited on an impersonal basis according to meritocratic criteria (Bertrand, 1983).

On the other hand, the exportation to and importation of the European state model to Africa was not meant to provide a remedy for African crises but was a deliberate colonial tool to facilitate the creation of markets for European goods and access to cheap raw materials. In addition, it was a means for political and economic subjugation, exploitation of cheap labor and extraction of raw materials to meet the needs and interests of western colonial powers. At that time, Africa had not experienced widespread significant economic, socio-political and international transformations. When European culture, which contained the basic ideas behind the rise of the state was brought to Africa, it was not only alien but also incompatible and irrelevant to the indigenous way of life.

Colonialism forcefully integrated the colonies into an international political economy about which they had very limited knowledge and understanding. State-building in these societies has largely been an exercise in imitating models developed in industrial societies and artificially superimposed, with or without local consent, on economic, social, and political structures shaped by other ways of thinking. Bertrand (1983) observes that to this day, the state is no more than an imported artifact in both Africa and Asia, a pale copy of utterly alien European social and political systems, a foreign body that is not only ineffi-cient and a burden on society but also a fomenter of violence.

GLOBAL TRENDS AND DRIVING FORCES

The trends that will shape the world, the Sub-Saharan African region, Zambia and our communities in the coming decades, have resulted from many factors including the end of the cold war and the collapse of the Soviet Union and the Eastern Bloc countries. These have significantly changed the old international economic and political environment and transformed the dynamics of interna-tional diplomacy and security. Some of the far-reaching consequences of these changes include the shifts from autocratic to democratic systems, military to civilian rule, and from centralized to decentralized governance.

We are now witnessing the beginning of a New World Order, in which new actors are coming on the scene, and where diverse nations are being drawn together for some common concerns and are also in an all-out global economic competition. The economically weak are likely to benefit the least while the strong will benefit the most. Countries with strong and productive domestic capacities have already started to take advantage of the opportunities, which the New World Order has brought about through global democratization, pri-vatization and liberalization.

This new environment has a number of consequences. Some of these are: the revival of old loyalties and rivalries, rising ethnic, tribal, regional and reli-gious tensions, structural economic changes, shifting the balance of economic power away from old centers towards new regions and countries, globalization of production and finance, and rising cultural hegemony through information and communications technologies.

The full consequences of this New World Order or globalization are only beginning to be understood. However, a number of consequences are already evident. For example, it is now obvious that there is a close relationship between the economic and social elements of development policy. The social sector is becoming both a link and intersection between political questions and economic ones, thereby imposing priorities on every one of us. It is now clear that a stable political environment is a precondition for harmonious social development; maintaining political calm and meeting social needs are the two sides of the same coin. A state with poor social integration, in which many find themselves excluded, must live in fear of the most unpredictable social turmoil.

Many of these trends, especially those that have positive effects, need to be encouraged. However, those that undermine development such as ethnic, tribal, regional and religious tensions and rivalries should be discouraged. Increased economic growth and distribution of economic benefits should be given top priority in order to build strong African nations.

THE AFRICA OF MY DREAM

I would like to live in an Africa where the individual's basic human rights and needs, and household food security are guaranteed and protected. The African continent has the potential to achieve these goals. Its human and natural resources are enormous and the size of the continent alone is formidable. Africa, with its 11,700,000 square miles, is bigger than China with 3,705,390 square miles, USA with 3,618,779 square miles, India with 1,266,595 square miles, Europe with 1,905,000 square miles, Argentina with 1,065,189 square miles, and New Zealand with 103,736 square miles combined. Africa is over three times larger than the USA and spans seven time zones. In addition, the African continent has the largest reserves of untapped natural resources such as minerals which are essential to the great powers in time of peace and war; empty farmlands which could feed the whole continent and all of Western Europe; and its fertile soil is capable of producing 130 times what it yields today even if no additional acreage is cleared.

However, in order for this development vision of the future to be attained, the African continent in general, and Zambia in particular, need, first of all, to have a new breed of leaders who can successfully manage the economic, educational, cultural and political institutions. Leaders who are goal-oriented, hard working, democratic, disciplined and committed to elevating public goals above private gain; leaders who are honest, forward-looking, inspiring, competent, fair-minded, intelligent, courageous, dependable, mature, imaginative, ambitious, self-controlled and independent.

The new leadership must have a vision and be able to share that vision with others and build consensus for action. In addition, they must know that leadership is a relationship with the constituents and that they should be part of and not apart from it; link leadership to service and quality; enrich performance through diversity; know what the constituents expect; make credibility the foundation of leadership; appreciate constituents and their diversity; show appreciation by listening, soliciting feedback, promoting constructive controversy, engendering trust, and taking risks; acquire competence, self-confidence and evaluate values; find common ground and use shared values to make a difference; inspire confidence and build competence; foster mutual responsibility and serve a purpose; sustain hope, take charge, demonstrate courage of conviction, and give love and encouragement and perceive and visualize success, arouse positive thoughts and images, and make hope a priority (Kouzes, 1993).

Secondly, after a correct leadership is put in place, then the political problems should be resolved and consensus developed. This is a precondition for the third component, which is economic growth through using each country's endowments and comparative advantage. Zambia and Africa should embrace the model that the New Industrializing Countries (NICs) have been following. This model of development consists of market-based and outward-oriented export development strategy which is supported by relatively low and uniform protection of imports; a stable real exchange rate; well functioning internal markets with factor prices reflecting real scarcities; and with private enterprise as the engine of growth. Economic development should be so highly valued that the Zambian and other African governments must be willing to risk political capital in order to achieve growth, and they should also insulate economic policy-making from politics.

The role of enlightened people, especially the young men and women who have a lot to gain from a politically stable and productive economy, should be to advise the economic and political leadership and encourage and support those structural reforms that are aimed at economic growth and national development. In addition, they should be willing to share their knowledge and vision about the future and development with as many people as possible inside and outside of their own countries; encourage and monitor improvements in their countries' policies and programs; undertake research studies and advisory activities which facilitate and empower different stakeholders to accomplish mutually beneficial goals and objectives, and enable policy makers and program implementers to set new priorities for state-formation, institution-building and national development.

CONCLUSION

Despite the many political, economic and social problems which Africa and Zambia are facing, the future and opportunities for an economic takeoff and actual development look bright, particularly with the current policies of free market economy and the emphasis on self-reliance rather than state dependency. The time has come for each African country to take stock of its factor endowments, follow the path of comparative advantage and make full use of all its resources. In addition, each country must set goals and build a shared vision for development, and find a niche in the new world order for active participation with the aim of improving the quality of life of their citizens, reducing poverty and developing their economies.

Since most Africans reside in the rural areas, the only viable strategy for economic takeoff and development must be based on agriculture and rural development. This is more apparent for a country like Zambia, whose comparative advantage lies in the abundance of arable land, irrigation water, unskilled labor, expanded urban markets for agricultural produce and a large urban population. The quadruple foundation of agriculture, mining, tourism and human resources development for Zambia, must be built in order to attain the Zambian dream and vision for accelerated economic growth and national development.

REFERENCES

Bennis, Warren. *On Becoming a Leader*, New York: Addison-Wesley Publishing Company, Inc., 1989.

Bertrand, Badie. *The Sociology of the State*, Chicago: The University of Chicago Press, 1983.

Elliot, Charles (ed.). *Constraints on the Economic Development of Zambia*, Nairobi: Oxford University Press, 1988.

FAO. *Food Security: A Domestic Approach*, November 1996.

ILO/JASPA. *Narrowing the Gaps, Planning for Basic Needs and Productive Employment in Zambia*, Addis Ababa: United Printers, 1977.

Institute for Scientific Cooperation. *Economics*, Volume 53.

Jackson, R.H., and Resberg, C.H. *Personal Rule in Black Africa*, Berkeley: University of California Press, 1982.

Jones, E.L. *The European Miracle*, London: Cambridge University Press, 1981.

Kouzes, J. M. et al. *Credibility: How Leaders Gain and Lose it, Why People demand it*, San Francisco: Jossey-Bass Publishers, 1993.

Lele, Uma (ed.). *Aid to African Agriculture: Lessons from Two Decades of Donors' Experience*, London: The John Hopkins University Press, 1991.

Lindauer, David L. et al. *Asia and Africa: Legacies and opportunities in Development*, Boston: International Center for Economic Growth, 1994.

Munoz, Heraldo (ed.). *From Dependency to Development: Strategies to overcome Underdevelopment and Inequality*, Boulder, Colorado: Westview Press, 1981.

Murdock, William W. *The Poverty of Nations: The Political Economy of Hunger and Population*, Baltimore: The John Hopkins University Press, 1980.

Mwanakatwe, J.M. *The Growth of Education in Zambia Since Independence*, Lusaka: Oxford University Press, 1974.

National Tourist Board. *Zambia the Real Africa*. 1995.

Poggi, Gianfranco. *The Development of the Modern State*, Stanford: Stanford University Press, 1978.

The World Almanac and Book of Facts, 1991.

Tordoff, William (ed.). *Politics in Zambia*, Manchester University Press, 1974.

UNICEF. *The Progress of Nations*, 1995.

UNDP. *Human Development Report*, 1996.

United Nations. *Social Development Newsletter*, 1996.

World Bank. *Poverty Reduction: Handbook*, 1993.

Zambia Poverty Assessment, 1994

Tomorrow is the Product of Our Actions Today

Chika Nwobi

Tomorrow is the product of my actions today – this is my mother's philosophy. As I grew up, she never ceased to drum it into my head. After every chiding for one of my transgressions, she would add, as if she were icing a cake, that as I made my bed as a youngster, so would I lie on it as an adult. I have grown to realize that she was right. In fact, I know now that this theory does not apply to me alone. The laws of destiny that dictate my future dictate Africa's also. As I sit here contemplating our precious continent's future, I can hear "Mama Africa" telling her children (all Africans) the same thing that my mother told me. I know that, like my mother, "Mama Africa" will be proven right. By observing how we Africans are laying our continental bed, we can predict what state the continent will be in when, in the year 2026, we want to lie down.

NEW TRENDS

As the whole world moves into the 21st century, the continents and their constituting countries are displaying significant differences in approach. The Americas (the United States especially), Europe, and Asia are moving with bold, calculated strides towards the new millennium while Africa is stumbling along behind. Two inextricably connected trends that will shape the world's future are the information revolution and the globalization of the economy. Briefly, I will explain the two concepts while observing Africa and her neighbors' reaction to these developments.

The information revolution

We find ourselves at the dawn of a new era – the Information Age. The term Information Age refers to the time (now and in the future) when, like bronze in the Bronze Age and stone in the Stone Age, information (its processing and handling to be more exact) will be central to most economic activity. In anticipation, the United States, the Far East Asian countries (Taiwan, Singapore, etc.), and the West European countries are leading the way by embracing the Information Revolution while preparing to take advantage of the changes it will bring.

The Information Revolution is the vehicle that is carrying and that will deliver the Information Age. The term refers to the series of technological break-throughs that began with the development of the personal computer in 1950 and that continually enable us to process and exchange information faster and cheaper. In the Information Age, businesses will be able to communicate with their branches or customers across the world at any time and for almost no cost. Their communication will not be just audio, as with the telephone, but also visual. A business executive in Tokyo will be able to attend and participate in a meeting in London without ever leaving his office; any student in Paris will be able to attend a lecture in Montreal.

It should be noted that though I have been writing in the future tense (that these things will happen in years to come), these innovations are already in use, albeit very sparsely. As a matter of fact, it is from hearing and seeing the yet unripe fruits of the Information Revolution that I know that in the future such technology will become commonplace. After all, no one who has enjoyed the luxury of a "water closet toilet" will elect to use the pit latrine in the future.

In the United States, the technology already exists but is at an early and concomitantly expensive stage of development. However, both the public and private sectors of most developed countries are investing extensively in the Information Revolution. The Information Age is only an infant now, but as it matures, it will change the way people learn, shop, trade and live.

The global economy

Global economy is defined as the "interconnected economic activity through-out the world that pays little regard to national borders". In an increasingly global economy, international trade, unhindered by closed markets, will enable countries to enjoy the fruits of economic comparative advantage. A sign of things to come is the vigor with which governments are dismantling existing trade barriers through multilateral trade agreements like the North American Free Trade Agreement (NAFTA) and the Asia-Pacific Economic Cooperation (APEC), and communities like the European Union. The Information Revolution and the globalization of trade have a special relationship. The Information Revolution will continue to facilitate global trade by providing easy and effective means for governments and businesses to communicate. As the benefits of global trade become ever more apparent, the Information Revolution will be fueled increasingly by investment and research.

In his book, *The Road Ahead,* Bill Gates writes,

> Citizens of the information society will enjoy new opportunities for productivity, learning, and entertainment. Countries that move boldly and in concert with each other will enjoy economic rewards. Whole new markets will emerge, and a myriad new opportunities for employment will be created. (p.257)

Bill Gates knows what he is talking about. He is the chairman of Microsoft Corporation, the biggest force in the computer software industry and one of the most significant proponents of the current Information Revolution. He envisions a future in which people from different countries, and on different continents, can benefit increasingly from a world made smaller by technology. He sees what I see, but the question is does Africa?

HOW SHE IS LAYING HER BED

In Igboland, we have a proverb, which says 'that one does not enter into private consultations with a deaf man'. As the information revolution and global trade carry other continents to unprecedented heights, Africa, if the current trends continue, will be the proverbial deaf man, left out due to his deficiency. Africa will have neither the technological prowess nor the economic clout to attract interest. I will not expound here on the innumerable ailments which plague Africa because I have never heard of the man who needs a flashlight to check whether the sun has risen. The symptoms of our cancer of corruption and tribalism should be obvious to all that care to look. What I will do, however, is address the ways we are investing in the future using Nigeria as an example.

In Nigeria, for example, our leaders constantly find themselves engaged in political battles for control of the government. Consequently, they see themselves as carrying elephants on their heads. You and I know that he who is carrying an elephant on his head and is yet trying to pick up worms with his feet is either very foolish or very strong. It is therefore not surprising to see that our leaders think it foolish to busy themselves with developing education and technological research which are mere worms in their eyes. This attitude causes them to spend available resources on winning support and loyalty through bribery and favoritism. Moreover, a large portion of the national revenue is stored in these leaders' private foreign accounts just in case any "Kabila" emerges to usurp power and our incumbent generals have to do a "Mobutu". Unfortunately, Nigerians pay for these practices with teachers' salaries and research grants.

Sadly, the youth too are quite disappointing. Those of us that live in modern cities have emulated American youths and adopted the worst of their habits. For example, in Nigeria we have emulated the American gangster culture in our university cults. What we have failed to realize is that the gang members in America are the underprivileged in that society, mostly from broken homes and with neither college education nor the motivation to pursue it. The young men in the Nigerian cults, on the other hand, are the hope for Nigeria's future. They are the fortunate few, lucky enough to get into universities. But sadly, they are not collecting the education that they are being offered, poor as it may be.

In rural areas, there is a different kind of misplacement of priorities. My fellow Igbos are a good example. Young men and little boys in the rural parts of Eastern Nigeria are caught up in the "get rich quick" syndrome. Impatient with seemingly unrewarding education, my brothers are dropping out of school en masse after their elementary school years to pursue commercial trade in the bigger commercial cities.

Not only are we neglecting education, but we are also abandoning agriculture. The way things are right now, one would hardly be surprised to hear that in a poll of all the Igbo villages, not a single nine year old boy declares his future ambition as wanting to become a successful farmer. Nigeria has become a nation so drunk with petroleum resources that we are ignoring every other potential source of revenue. We are currently complaining about hardship, but we will really see woe betide us in Nigeria if, in the not too distant future, Dr. Harold P. Furth at Princeton University completes his nuclear fusion experiments, or Dr. William Hoagland at Massachusetts Institute of Technology perfects his solar energy cells. Either of the two will provide a suitable and infinitely cheaper alternative to petroleum energy. To Nigerians, this should be a frightening possibility.

My sisters are not making much headway either. All over Africa, they are still bridled to matrimony by the society. In many cases, girls opt out of career and academic opportunities because they do not want to be so successful that they become unattractive to the proud African men who still admire inferiority in their search for subservient wives. In Nigeria, Ethiopia, Sudan, Ghana and many other parts of East and West Africa, very young girls are plucked, though yet unripe, from the trees of education and sold into marriage. Deprived of the chance to mature physically and intellectually, my sisters' immense potential is being wasted. Surely, this will yield a harvest of inauspicious mothers and parasitic citizens. Who, then, will take the blame?

In summation, I ask myself more questions: who will go into private consultations with a deaf man? Who will move "boldly and in concert with" an illiterate graduate? Who will conduct business with my monolingual illiterate brother? The answer is easy: no one will. And Africa will suffer. Without foreign investments and foreign markets for our exports, our economies will decay. Unless of course we listen to Mama Africa's cry and ask ourselves how we want our bed to be in 2026; then set out to lay it that way.

HOW SHE SHOULD LAY HER BED

President Bill Clinton's 1997 inaugural speech draws one's attention to the massive difference in stages of development between Africa and North America. Clinton states,

We began the nineteenth century with a choice to spread our nation from coast to coast. We began the twentieth century, with a choice to harness the Industrial Revolution to our values of free enterprise, conservation and human decency. Those choices made all the difference. At the dawn of the 21st century, a free people must now choose to shape the forces of the Information Age and the global society, to unleash the limitless potential of all our people....

In a sense, Africa is about two centuries behind the United States. The choices the Americans made about their borders and territories in the nineteenth century are still before us in Africa today, as we in Nigeria decide whether we want thirty-six or fifty-four states in our country. In a situation such as ours, it can safely be said that we are yet to fully tap into the benefits of the Industrial Revolution as the Americans have done in this twentieth century. Ask the Ogoni people of Nigeria about the conservation and human decency that Clinton speaks of and they will tell you that no such thing exists in the Africa they know. Their land has been poisoned from the operations petroleum companies. And to their cries for compensation and relief, the Ogonis have received brutal military abuse from the Nigerian Government. Nigeria and the rest of Africa seem too far behind. So where is the hope?

I believe that despite the great obstacles we have put in our way, Africa can break into the 21st century private consultations between the other continents. In as little as thirty years we can lay the kind of bed the Americans have taken twenty decades to lay. The first thing we need is leaders. We need leaders to inspire us and make us proud of our motherland. That is, admirable leaders who will give their fellow citizens reasons to be proud of their country and with that comes patriotism. We do not necessarily need professors or generals or political scientists to lead us, we need individuals of integrity, committed to serving their nations before themselves.

Indeed, if such admirable leaders emerge in Africa, the future will be very bright for the continent. Africans that have migrated in search of academic and career success in the Western World will likely return home to devote their physical, intellectual and financial resources to the betterment of the countries. As the people start to care about their countries, corruption and tribalism will begin to wane.

My vision may seem too fantastic to some, but I dream it only because I see it. I see that our present leaders have the potential to make the difference. Nelson Mandela has already made the difference in South Africa and now that the country is fairly secure with its new majority rule, he has begun to play a more active role in African politics. Ghana's Jerry Rawlings is another reason to be hopeful. He has successfully combined the military toughness needed to rule our tribally diverse countries with the democratic process needed to win Western support. Now Ghana is joining Nigeria as a West African regional big brother by extending a helping hand to the Liberians as they attempt to rebuild their country.

General Sani Abacha has shown himself capable of carrying the Nigerian elephant on his head quite comfortably, though the worms have been totally neglected. Now he can take any of two options to win himself a place in history as a national hero. The easier option is to conduct fair elections and hand over to whomsoever Nigerians elect. In addition to being the easier, this option is also the more uncertain and more unlikely one. It is uncertain because there is a strong likelihood that after a few years of civilian rule, a fresh set of hungry army majors will emerge to destroy the existing democracy through a coup. It is unlikely because Abacha is, by all indications, very comfortable where he is seated. If he does stay to rule Nigeria, say for six more years as a civilian, he will be choosing the more difficult, yet more likely option. It is quite apparent that he has the strength, resolve and military intelligence to keep the armed forces in check.

The real battle will be in fighting the culture of corruption and indiscipline and winning the people's admiration and respect. This is a battle that must be waged internally first. He must expel the demons of corruption within him and his inner clique just as the late Muritala Mohammed did when, upon assuming leadership of Nigeria, he repented of his past corrupt activities and returned to the state what originally belonged to it. After setting the example, Mohammed took the campaign to the people. Abacha should know that when the bath water is poured directly on the head, it will trickle or flow down and sanitize the rest of the body.

Healed of our disease of corruption, Nigeria can start to build itself up. But we must remember that one does not lick hot soup in a hurry. National development is a meticulous process that involves long term planning and investment. And for long term results, the place to invest is in the youth. This means making education a national priority. Once corruption is done away with, Nigeria will be able to afford to train and pay teachers. We will be able to afford textbooks in our schools and even computers in our colleges and universities. We will be able to start preparing our youngsters to live in a global society in the Information Age.

But even before we, the next generation, are ready to take the reins, there is much that can be done. The present rulers should try to win the favor of the already developed nations in the West, because it will probably be easier to attend the private meeting if we are invited, instead of trying to break in. Keeping the West happy is not such a difficult task. Our Generals do not have to assassinate or incarcerate their political opponents in order to maintain leadership. Instead, they can silence their opponents by implementing responsible policies.

African economies must be opened up to attract foreign investments. Our leaders must remember that open economy or not, no one will invest in Africa if the threat of losing everything in a coup or war still exists. Nigeria must help bring stability to politics in the continent through economic and military assistance. South Africa and Nigeria must stop bickering at each other and pool their resources to help their smaller neighbors. In addition, African countries must engage in strategic long-term planning such as the Vision 2010 program currently taking place in Nigeria. Moreover, governments must implement the recommendations.

And. And. And, I am tired. I think I have run out of ideas for ways to improve Africa. But I thank God that it is not yet my job to come up with the ideas. I thank God that there are thousands of intelligent economists, political scientists, army generals, engineers, farmers, and carpenters, in the African continent whose duty it is to come up with the ideas and implement them now. I pray that they will hear Mama Africa's cry and I pray that when it is my turn, I will not forget her words: "Africans, as you lay your bed...."

REFERENCES

Gates, Bill, *The Road Ahead*, Penguin Group, New York, 1995.
Macionis, John, *Sociology*, Prentice-Hall Inc, New Jersey, 1995.

CHAPTER 11

The Future of Africa
Lies in Home-grown Solutions

Levi M. Obijiofor

PREAMBLE

In his analysis of images of Pakistan's future, Sohail Inayatullah (1992) raised three fundamental questions which should guide such an exercise. The questions are: "Where are we going? What are the possibilities ahead? What strategies can we use to realize our goals?" In my view, these questions also apply to any attempt to chart the future visions of Africa. By raising the same questions with regard to Africa, we would be analyzing past and present Africa and, on the basis of this analysis, envision a future for Africa which should avoid repeating the errors of the past and present.

This essay incorporates my vision of the future of Africa, including some of the African qualities or characteristics that are important to a realization of this vision. Against this background, the essay also analyzes some of the problems and obstacles that lie in the way of Africa and at the same time draws Africa's attention to the experiences of the fast-developing Asian countries. Here, I argue that Africa has a lot to learn from South East Asia without necessarily copying the Asian examples. Finally, I outline the strategies that, hopefully, will lead to the desired African future.

VISION OF AFRICA

My vision of the future of Africa is anchored on unity, without which the foundation of the future transformation of Africa would be laid merely on soggy soil. A united Africa is envisioned on the basis that unity is strength. It is easier for Africa to tackle its socioeconomic and political problems as a united body rather than a loose entity. To achieve remarkable results in economic, political and social fronts, the disparate peoples of Africa must first identify themselves as people with common interests, agree to work together toward a common goal, adopt common approaches, and enact common laws and policies to achieve their objectives. In essence, my vision of the future of Africa calls for integration rather than division/disintegration, greater participation in decision making rather than paternalistic dependence. To facilitate this vision, age-old fears and suspicions, which have divided African people, must be expelled.

This is my preferred vision of a future Africa. It is very much like the European Union, with an African parliament enacting common laws and policies on trade, labor, business and economy, currency, human rights, immigration, crime, sports and so on. This vision is not unattainable. A union of African states is not an entirely new concept. The idea has been mooted and canvassed many times and has been dressed in various garbs such as Pan-Africanism, United States of Africa, and many more. The union of African states represents Africa's response to emerging global economic blocs and interest groups. It is also Africa's way of taking care of its destiny without relying on European, Western, or other developed economies. In essence, the union of African states underscores my vision of a great Africa where people of all ethnic groups can work, live and interact freely and peacefully without discrimination or harassment. In this dispensation, Africa should be able to muster a multilateral force capable of responding to emergency humanitarian situations caused by natural disasters, inter-ethnic quarrels, border disputes, or cross-border guerrilla warfare. Differences in culture, language, and religion should enrich, not divide, Africa. This is a vision for a truly independent Africa where political leaders are accountable to their people and not to neo-colonial foreign interests. It is also an Africa that can stand technologically on its own two feet without regularly kowtowing to the whims and idiosyncrasies of foreign powers, or struggling to import foreign technologies that are not appropriate to the African situation.

While it is in the interests of Africa to move forward rather than look backwards, it must be stated that looking backwards is not entirely problematic, as doing so would enable Africa to draw on the lessons of history. History itself is full of accounts of countries, societies and peoples that were virtually on the brink of collapse but were able to pick up the pieces and prosper. This is the reason why Africa's future should be seen in a positive light. Human and material resources are in abundance. These should be activated to lead Africa's emergence as a continental and global power.

Africa can also turn its present image of the "problem continent" into one of glory land. It has already been argued that communities need to feel "hurt" to be motivated to develop (Wildman, 1992). Africa has experienced enough pain and agony. Perhaps these numerous problems should act as a catalyst to transform Africa. As Paul Wildman (1992) stated, when communities are neglected and abandoned, the members realize that they have no choice but to do something for themselves. "When communities get so desperate they say 'we'll try anything,' ... this is why CED (community education development) works in third world nations ... where communities have nowhere else to turn" (p. 5). This philosophy can work well for Africa where group solidarity is known to be effective in community development.

AFRICAN CHARACTERISTICS

Group solidarity is an important African characteristic upon which Africa's future development can be built. For example, in African communities, collective decisions are cherished and valued because they promote popular participation, consensus and the feeling of camaraderie. This is why African societies are characterized as communal in nature, a point underscored by Jegede (1994) thus: "Group allegiance is valued over individual excellence. The community is almost personified, and takes precedence over every individual... Commitment to community loyalty is moral and spiritual" (p. 8). This is a quality that can be built on for the future development of Africa.

The essence of group solidarity in a multiethnic society such as Africa is that it effectively neutralizes feelings of marginalization and neglect among minority ethnic groups, as every group becomes the master of its own destiny. Group decision-making also has implications for the behavior and conduct of individual citizens and, most especially, for the way in which new ideas are assessed, endorsed or rejected.

Another African element that can be relied upon to make a union of African states attainable is respect for elders. This relates to the way Africans defer to elders based on the cultural assumption that old age is synonymous with wisdom. This perception of elders as repositories for knowledge runs counter to what obtains in many Western societies in which "old people are often perceived as individuals whose decline in physical and cognitive capabilities makes them burdens rather than assets" (Prior, 1994, p. 26). However, in Africa, respect for old age implies that elders also function as defenders of culture and tradition. Consequently, elders act as gatekeepers who determine whether new ideas threaten or uphold local cultural values.

Franz Shurmann (1996) has argued that, far from the view that Africa's problems are insurmountable, "Africans have three strong survival factors rooted in their history: family, villages and markets" (p. 6). All three factors are also instrumental in sustaining communal cohesion in African societies and could play major roles in Africa's transformation. To these three factors, I will also add a fourth factor: the role of "age grades" (an "age grade" is a formal organization in which membership is based on a predetermined age range; an age grade must not be confused with social clubs or groups) in the development of rural communities in Africa. But first, let us briefly examine the role of the family in the life of an African. The family as a social unit is highly valued in Africa. Hence, there is a strong sense of obligation to one's family and this entails providing for the upkeep of members of a family. The family in Africa is highly valued because it provides the platform on which members receive or offer assistance, encouragement and advice (see Uchendu, 1965). The African family unit thus functions as a cushion that helps to shield members from the shocks and uncertainties of life.

Back to the function of "age grades" in local communities. Age grades are useful not only at the local level of development but also at the national level. At the local level, age grade members tackle problems affecting their members and their communities. The phenomenon of age grade is prominent in rural communities of Nigeria, especially the eastern part of the country. Age grades liaise with village leaders to identify areas where they could assist in the development of the village. As there are different age grades based on different age ranges, age grades thus compete among themselves to provide financial assistance and infrastructural facilities to the villages. In my view, there is no reason why the activities of these age groups cannot be lifted to the national or continental level. Writing about the activities of age groups in Igbo-speaking communities of Nigeria, Victor Uchendu (1965) noted:

> The executive function of the village is vested in the youth through their age grade organization. Besides serving as a social indicator which separates the seniors from the juniors, the age-grade association is a means of allocating public duties, guarding public morality through the censorship of members' behavior, and providing companionship and mutual insurance for members (p. 43).

One observes from the preceding passage that age grades contribute to the daily functioning of the village and, above all, also moderate the behavior and conduct of their members. These are some of the unique qualities that can be utilized to the benefit of Africa.

Africans are also known to be inventive and can adapt to situations which people from other cultures find difficult. In this regard, Africans will find no problems relying on local and unique talents. These are crucial elements in the design and production of local technology, arts and craft. Indeed, indigenous solutions to Africa's problems are the only reliable and realistic way forward. In the Western world, relying on indigenous solutions (self-reliance) is widely referred to as do-it-yourself (DIY).

The concept of do-it-yourself does not only apply to minor tasks performed by individuals at home, it also applies to national, regional, sub-regional and continental issues. Therefore, it is imperative that Africa should not wait for an economic lifejacket from the developed West. It will never come. The West is more concerned now with the economic plight of its citizens than attending to the problems of Africa. Indeed the world is becoming weary of attending to Africa's problems. Decades of foreign aid and assistance suggest that they only offer temporary relief but not an effective shield against further dependence. Experience indicates that poor African nations may attract occasional crumbs and sympathetic arguments but no respect from the international community. In the final analysis, the solution to Africa's socioeconomic woes lies in harnessing the abundant local resources and talents as well as unique characteristics of the African people.

The concept of do-it-yourself or self-empowerment recognizes the need to tap local resources, generate initiatives and involve local people as the principal drivers of the development train. In other words, self-reliance encourages local participation and involvement of people in decision-making and project implementation. In this regard, Wimal Dissanayake (1981) observed that, in most developing countries, "the greatest resource for development is the people themselves" (p. 225).

CHALLENGES AND PROBLEMS

The vision of Africa's future outlined above is indeed a feel-good vision for a troubled continent. But it is not utopian. As pointed out earlier, it is practical, realistic and achievable because it is a vision based on indigenous knowledge and ideas. It is also a vision drawn from Africa's experiences. However, huge problems abound which could constitute obstacles to the attainment of this dream. Again, we pause to ponder over Inayatullah's second question – "What are the possibilities ahead?" To understand where we are going, we must take stock of the past and present.

For decades, development scholars and researchers have tried to explain why relatively few countries have attained socioeconomic, scientific and technological advancement while many others are overwhelmed by problems of underdevelopment. Theories have been formulated, as have hypotheses, but they remain unsatisfactory.

In the opening sentence of his essay, "The Impulse to Modernization," McClelland (1961) raised an important question which, for years, posed a problem – and still does – to development scholars. McClelland's question: "Why do some nations 'take off into rapid economic and social growth, while others stand still or decline?" (p. 26) has been replicated in another form by Portes (1976): "What forces, present in some societies, have been absent in others and hence prevented their rapid advance toward industrialism?" (p. 56).

The answers to these questions have generally been linked to historical, geographical, economic, structural, philosophical, religious, socio-cultural, political, and behavioral factors. It is necessary to examine briefly a number of perspectives so as to gain an insight into how they explain or ignore the African situation.

Before World War II, many African countries were colonial outposts of the major industrial powers. As Ihonvbere (1996) noted: "Africa's historical experience of slavery and colonialism severely deformed, distorted, disarticulated and underdeveloped the entire region. It culminated in the marginalization of Africa in the global capitalist system and its domination by profit and hegemony-seeking transnational corporations" (p. 17). The end of World War II and its social and economic consequences for the colonial powers, as well as the emergence of the United States as a major world power with an anticolonial foreign policy combined, among other factors, to weaken the political and economic base of some of the colonialists (see, for example, Diwan and Livingston, 1979).

In the post-war clamor for freedom and independence fuelled by the notion that colonialism was responsible for the impoverishment of many countries, some of the colonial powers were forced to leave quietly while others fought bloody battles with nationalists before relinquishing political authority. But even as they departed, the colonial forces managed to fasten the economic lifejacket ever more tightly around their waists, making it imperative that political independence without economic emancipation is nothing short of half-baked freedom. Within a short time, the bogey of political independence was unmasked. The developing countries found themselves manacled by new forms of colonialism (see Lerner, 1980; Diwan and Livingston, 1979). In short, things did not work out the way they were envisioned by the freedom fighters.

In Africa, Ali Mazrui illustrated how the balkanization of the continent by European colonial administrations sowed the seeds of internal political unrest in many countries, decades after the attainment of independence.

> It was... in Africa that Europe practiced the art of partition at its most elaborate. Where Europe attempted to unify those who were different, it sowed the seeds of future separatism... Where Europe divided, it sometimes left behind latent passions for reunification – and political killings at the grassroots level have resulted from such division. In short, balkanization is a breeding-ground for political violence, including the phenomenon of assassination. And balkanization is what Africa is burdened with for the time being (Mazrui, 1973, p. 183).

To add to this view, Africa is also burdened with urgent problems of poverty, famine and drought, over-population, desertification, and poor health care. And that is not all. There are a host of problems – internal as well as externally contrived – such as obstacles to free trade in the form of regional economic blocs, leadership problems in Africa, the subjugation of women, and illiteracy.

For Africa to make an impact in the world and earn much-needed foreign exchange, it needs to overcome the structural obstacles created by the international economic and political systems, whereby Africa is dependent on the Western industrialized countries for virtually everything. Ashby et al. (1980) explained this skewed relationship thus:

> The limited industrial expansion and relative agricultural stagnation in poor countries is seen to have evolved historically from international relations of colonialism and unequal power, and hence exchange, between producers of raw materials and industrial capital goods. These relations have sustained a distribution of wealth and power within poorer nations... (p. 159).

This international economic structure also explains why raw materials produced in Africa are taken to the West, processed and re-imported into Africa in the form of finished goods sold at exorbitant prices. Mention must be made of the activities of multinational companies that promote the official and unofficial transfer of funds generated in developing countries to their parent companies in Europe and North America. These and other factors have combined to make Africa a consumer of goods and services produced in the West. The imposition by the West of discriminatory production standards on African products denies Africa the opportunity to export its own finished products. Another problem is the emergence of regional economic blocs such as the European Union (EU), Asia-Pacific Economic Cooperation forum (APEC), and the North American Free Trade Agreement (NAFTA). These trading blocs promote free trade among member countries while making entry by non-members into their markets difficult.

Apart from foreign-induced obstacles to Africa's development, one must also identify internal problems such as the continent's history of incompetent leaders. Incompetent leaders in Africa have shown themselves to be visionless, vicious, dictatorial and unaccountable. Thus, one must hold them responsible for dragging Africa backwards while the rest of the world was moving forward. Lack of accountability and responsibility leads to gross corruption and acts of economic misdemeanor. In this regard, unbridled corruption becomes an endemic feature of Africa's socioeconomic and political leadership. This partly explains why many non-Africans tend to perceive Africa as a rudderless ship. The problem of leadership can only be solved by Africans themselves, and underpins Africa's ability to undergo any form of socioeconomic transformation. To experience social change, Africa needs a crop of dedicated and selfless leaders who possess the vision and drive to steer the continent's socioeconomic development. Without this, there will be no progress. It takes such leadership to transform a country, as South East Asian countries illustrate. Here are a few examples. Lee Kuan Yew is widely regarded as the father of modern Singapore. He was instrumental in the economic and technological transformation of Singapore. In the same region, Mahathir Mohammed is credited with the economic development of Malaysia. In Indonesia, reference is made to the vision and foresight of Suharto and Sukarno. Africa seems to suffer from a dearth of such leaders. Why? To attempt an answer, we need to revisit the impact of colonialism on the attitudes of the colonized people. It has been suggested (Inayatullah, 1996) that lack of genuine leaders in Africa could be attributed to Africa's colonial experience. Specifically, the argument goes that in fighting to overturn colonialism, post-independent African leaders ended up adopting the values of their enemies – tyranny – as a way to hold on to power. Regardless of whether this thesis is a correct or incorrect interpretation of history, it raises the question about the dominance (until recently) of military dictators or one-party political systems in Africa.

Another challenge facing Africa concerns the subjugation of women in all spheres of life. The question that must be tackled is how to integrate women into society in such a way that their potential can be fully utilized. To achieve the vision of Africa canvassed in this essay, it is necessary to try groundbreaking or outrageous ideas. One of these ideas is leadership by women in Africa. The idea of elevating women to leadership positions may sound unacceptable to many African men given their patriarchal background. However, it is my considered opinion that African male leaders have failed Africa and that women should be given the opportunity to lead the continent out of its predicament.

Owing to some inexplicable traditional reasons, African women have been suppressed for so long that their leadership qualities and all other qualities remain unknown and untapped because they were untested. Why impose women leaders on Africa? My response here is simple. Equity, justice and fairness demand that we try women in all areas where men have failed Africa. If gender is not at the root of Africa's problems, no one should criticize women's leadership potential until they have been given the opportunity to lead. The experiment in war-torn Liberia in West Africa is a clear but limited example that women may carve out a path where men encounter obstacles. For many years, Liberia was engulfed in a brutal civil war in which no fewer than four factions were struggling for power. Many peace accords were signed but they were also broken with the same frequency. The last peace accord signed in the Nigerian capital city of Abuja, led to disarmament and a successful election. The successful resolution of the Liberian crisis is due, in part, to the appointment of a woman to head the interim government during the Abuja meeting. This example underscores my view that African women should take over leadership positions where men have failed. Elsewhere in the world, there are instances where women have held or are still holding the mantle of leadership. Examples include Bangladesh, Britain, India, Israel, Norway, Pakistan, and Sri Lanka, among others.

The widening gender gap in Africa must be halted. And so too must those norms of communication which limit areas of discourse open to women. It is no secret that African women and girls are discriminated against merely on ill-founded cultural grounds. Many people believe, for example, that the exclusion of African women from educational institutions denies the continent an opportunity to tap the vast amount of human resources possessed by women. In many rural communities, women are active in the local economy. Discrimination against women in any form must be abolished to fully integrate African women into the future African society. African women need to be free to work in any profession, they also need to be free to communicate and explore subject areas hitherto regarded as taboo. This will not only change the way women are perceived but will also lead to growing acceptance of the important role of women in Africa. In this way, Africa would be laying the foundation for a future that is not gender based. As African women have been active and successful in sustaining the rural economy, the increasing realization of the usefulness to Africa of the world-view and contribution of women will lead to their greater participation and equal acceptance of their role in society.

An apparent threat to the vision of a union of African states is lack of unity and the increasing polarization of the continent. Polarization implies disunity and less loyalty to the African cause. This is contrary to the prescribed vision of Africa. On the international front, for example, African interests are now polarized into Francophone and Anglophone Africa (reflecting allegiance to two of the major colonial players in the continent) as well as Arab-Africa interests and Sub-Saharan African interests. This development continues to test African loyalty to Africa. These allegiances take precedence over the wholesome interests of Africa. Unity is compromised and with it goes African solidarity and most especially Africa's ability to secure its interests in the comity of nations. The bedrock of a union of African states is unity, solidarity, and stability. Without this support base, the vision of a desirable future for Africa remains a dream.

The alternative to a united Africa is further ethnicization and balkanization of the continent. Surely, the easiest way to scupper the idea of a united Africa is to give voice to the myriad ethnic groups. It is fine to campaign for the rights of all ethnic groups to exist and perhaps metamorphose into independent autonomous states, but one must ask whether those ethnic groups would be viable as independent states, or whether their interests and concerns can be accommodated within the existing nation states. There is a major problem with granting autonomy and independence to ethnic groups: one is never enough, once it starts, there is never an end to the clamor. In other words, every new state based on ethnic affiliation implies the emergence of a new breed of disaffected minorities. The proliferation of unviable states is what Africa must avoid.

THE ASIAN EXPERIENCE: LESSONS FOR AFRICA

Long before now, human understanding of the universe was strongly influenced by arguments of Western philosophers and scientists in which truth was presented as absolute, reality viewed through only one prism, and science and reason held as the solution to every problem. In that era of modernism, progress was conceived as modernization and consequently as the ultimate goal of society. The dominant belief was that there was only one path through which modernization or development could be achieved – industrialization, urbanization and capital intensive technology – the central pillars of Western socioeconomic values. For example, dominant theories of socioeconomic development projected underdeveloped societies as backward, traditional, disadvantaged and impoverished. However, a clear indication that Western models of development do not apply globally can be gleaned from the forces driving socioeconomic development in South East Asia.

Whereas dominant theories of development perceived traditional and socio-cultural values as impediments to development, more recent Western authors (Servaes, 1986; Walsh, 1993); Levy Jr., 1992; Little and Reed, 1989) now highlight the importance of these factors. Adherence to these values is now identified as one of the major factors influencing the development of certain Asian countries such as Singapore, China, South Korea, Taiwan, Malaysia and Japan. The values associated with the development of these countries include: respect for elders; high regard for family values; competitive education; high value on communal association, and respect for traditional institutions. These socio-cultural values, among others, constitute the chief elements of the Confucian philosophy, a philosophy that has now been identified as the cornerstone of Asian development. For example, Levy Jr. has observed that:

> Some of the most successful cases of modernization have been in societies, or countries, in which the Confucian ethic has, for many centuries, loomed large in the religious aspects of life. Among the most spectacular examples in the twentieth century are the Republic of China, Singapore-Malaysia, Hong Kong, and South Korea, Japan, and more recently the People's Republic of China (p. 15).

This view, if upheld, invalidates or challenges the Western concept of development widely regarded as universally applicable. Servaes (1986) has articulated the point thus:

> In contrast with the more economically and politically oriented approach in modernization and dependency paradigms, the central idea here is that there is no universal development model; development is an integral, multidimensional and dialectic process that can differ from society to society. In other words, each society must delineate its own path to development (p. 211).

Little and Reed also underscored this point. The Western philosophy of development could not be applied in Asia because it:

> was too culturally specific to be readily utilized by some other cultural traditions. Its emphasis on individualism, consumption, the notion of the perfect market, and an open global trading system could cause economic decline, social decay, and political disruption in communities whose indigenous values and institutions did not enable them to handle robustly negative external influences (p. 41).

As a counterpoint to the dominant models of development, Asian societies have placed emphasis on the community rather than the individual, on production rather than consumption, on managing the imperfections of the market rather than paying homage to the perfect market ... (Little and Reed, 1989, p.41). Indeed, events in Asian societies have shown that, with regard to socioeconomic development, what is good for the goose cannot always be assumed to be good for the gander as well.

The lesson for Africa is that Western prescriptions for development may not also be suitable to African conditions. Adherence to and recognition of African values could well prove to be the main drivers of African transformation. The experience from Asia points not only to the multidimensional nature of development but also underscores the need for each country, region, or continent to recognize its peculiar circumstances and situation, determine the needs of its people, and set its own development objectives and agenda.

AFRICA'S FUTURE

Herein lies the key to Africa's development. But how and from where does one begin to tackle Africa's huge problems such as lack of basic social services; crippling poverty; high mortality rates; mounting foreign debt; social unrest and political instability; as well as corruption? In other words, what should be done? At first mention, these problems and many others appear insurmountable; however, it should be pointed out that no developed country achieved its present status without experiencing some socio-political and economic hiccups. As various regions forge economic unions to bolster their socioeconomic status, Africa needs to understand the key phrase in modern economic development – self-reliance. This is the key to Africa's future development. Aside from focusing on local human and material resources, there are other issues that must be examined.

Africa is now devastated by age-old ethnic conflicts which have displaced hundreds of thousands of people and pitched brothers against sisters, husbands against wives, and cousins against uncles. Ethnic conflicts represent the most severe threat to the realization of a union of African states because ethnic loyalty is often (if not always) stronger than regional, continental or national loyalty. If this is the situation, should the African continent be further carved up to accommodate every ethnic group? Based on experience, balkanization will not solve the ethnic question. As stated earlier, every new state implies the emergence of new interest groups and a new breed of disaffected minorities. There must be an end to the myriads of ethnic conflicts and mass genocide taking place in various parts of Africa.

It is a well-acknowledged fact that there is a relationship between internecine conflicts/wars and the issue of poverty in Africa because human and material resources are directed into the wars. Closely tied to this is the struggle in Africa for a sphere of influence among foreign powers. These factors in no small way engender and sustain poverty in Africa. As ethnic wars are manifestations of long-held feelings of bitterness resulting from marginalization, insecurity, neglect and subjugation, the solution to the problem must be a political dispensation that guarantees all groups equal access to economic and political power. That political setup can be achieved in a union of African states.

Furthermore, African leaders and people must first be rid of all traces of colonial mentality whereby "nearly all African ideas and social institutions were categorized as backward, and their European counterparts as progressive" (Sogolo, 1994). This is another key to Africa's future development. It is true that the colonial dominance of Africa ended several decades ago, yet its impact is still manifest in various forms on the continent. The colonial mentality explains why many Africans first think and then act in terms of the mental constructs provided by their former colonizers. Africans, in particular African leaders, tend to judge their performance or policies on the basis of concepts developed by the industrial powers. Sometimes, decisions are held back until formal consultations have taken place with neo-colonial powers. It is the colonial mentality that makes one feel 'inferior' and unimpressive even when one has adopted the right approach to a particular continental problem. Africans must begin to tackle their problems based on local knowledge, experience and the unique African ways of problem solving.

But the elimination of the colonial mentality will not be easy given that most of the continent still conducts official and unofficial business in the foreign languages imposed by the colonialists. To a large extent, language shapes the way people think and reason. When people are born in an environment in which events and objects have been labeled and given meaning, they grow up to accept most of the things the way they are described not in their local languages but in the official language(s) of the colonizers. It is in this way, too, that language helps to create and sustain social reality for people. This is how Africa's indigenous languages and modes of thinking have been subordinated to foreign languages. The local languages are perceived as inferior and subordinated to foreign languages. This point is well illustrated by Berger and Luckmann (1966). However, one must not tie Africa's socioeconomic and political problems solely on the tenterhooks of colonial experience. Africans themselves must take some of the blame for these problems.

Beyond the issue of language, there is also the question of dependence on foreign imported food and luxury products. A nation or continent that cannot feed its population is dependent on foreign imports and is forever condemned to massive loss of scarce foreign exchange through importation. Consequently, such a nation becomes perpetually tied to the underbelly of its benefactors. To get out of this stranglehold, Africans must return to the land, to agriculture, previously the mainstay of the African economy. Adebayo Adedeji, former

Executive Secretary of the United Nations Economic Commission for Africa (ECA), has painted a clear picture of what happens when a continent finds itself in such a scenario. According to Adedeji (1990), although agricultural production in Africa rose marginally between 1970 and 1980, food output fell below the rate of population growth. And as the demand for consumer goods rose, so also were resources channeled to importation of goods. Thus, Africa had to rely on "external sources to finance its development". For how long shall this trend continue? Certainly not for long as Africa continues to attract less and less sympathy from aid donors and Western governments. In the coming millennium, Africa must be able to feed its population through vast improvements in agricultural production before it can address any other problem. The gory images on television of Africans buffeted by hunger and malnutrition and clinging desperately to bowls of cereals supplied by foreign governments and aid agencies in war-torn countries in East and West Africa must not be allowed to recur. Africa is blessed with arable land for agricultural cultivation.

There is also the need for Africans to engage in genuine brainstorming sessions to identify and outline those qualities that are unique to Africa and also map out strategies that would assist in the march towards socioeconomic development. Worthy of consideration, perhaps, although difficult to achieve is how to halt the brain drain in the continent and consequently depend less on foreign experts.

According to a 1994 World Bank report (see Blair and Jordan, 1994), "some 23,000 qualified academic staff are emigrating from Africa each year in search of better working conditions". This is a worrying figure because of the realization that Africa's best brains are engaged in the socioeconomic development of other parts of the world. To halt the flood of African experts to overseas countries, African leaders need to create the right and conducive work atmosphere, not necessarily huge salary structures. This is one of the lollipops that could be used to lure back African experts living overseas. Not huge salaries. Not expensive cars. Not unattainable conditions. Relying on Africans to solve Africa's problems is simply another way of practising self-reliance. In the absence of African experts, the task of transforming Africa would be more difficult, consume more time, and probably would not be well executed.

Closely associated with the engagement of African intellectuals and experts must be an aggressive policy on the development of science and technology, culture and infrastructure. If Africa is to emulate the emerging "Tigers" of South East Asia, it must be prepared to examine the position of science and technology, because this is one of the factors that has aided the development of South East Asia. Africa must identify and recognize this factor of development and be willing to invest in science and technology. However, as I have argued elsewhere with regard to the new communication technologies (Obijiofor, 1996), investing in the new information and communication technologies (ICTs) in Africa in the face of other competing basic needs presents Africa with a dilemma. The major issues revolve around the question of priorities. The principal question, in my view, is this: How appropriate is it for Africa to overlook the basic needs of its population and invest massively in the new communication technologies? In other words, will science and technology transform African economies, overcome problems of poverty and illiteracy, and end internecine civil wars?

There are divergent views among African scholars. Taking the Internet, for example, Jegede (1995) argues that 'If we had everyone in Africa electronically networked today, it would not necessarily develop Africa". However, relying on the same premise, Djamen et al. (1995) contend that "Electronic networking will not only enable Africans access global data but will also help the entire world to access information on Africa in Africa". As each side of the debate has its strong points, the overarching question remains: which way should Africa go?

Specifically with regard to the new information and communication technologies (most often referred to as the information superhighway), it is my view that Africa should start from the basics and opt for that technology which promotes greater interaction and sustains kinship relationships. In other words, the communication technology to be adopted by Africans must be one that is easily accessible, and which poses no challenge to socio-cultural practices. This is the key to understanding how Africans will adapt to the communication technologies of the future. A technology that meshes well with local cultural practices has a greater probability of being accepted. As Jegede stated: "Communication in traditional Africa takes place between human beings rather than the technical components of communication technology".

CONCLUSION

The task confronting Africa is enormous and urgent. And it is on the shoulders of Africans themselves that the ideas and strategies needed to tackle the continent's problems and work toward our visions for the continent must emerge. As President Jacques Chirac of France said during his visit to Africa in 1996, the future of Africa lies ultimately in Africa's ability to utilize its wisdom, experiences, history and traditional values to transform its peoples and societies. Our historical experiences may seem uninspiring and terrible, but there is still hope on the horizon. After all, according to a Somali proverb: "What you lose in the fire you must seek in the ashes". At this point in Africa's history, an introspective reflection is a much-needed tonic.

REFERENCES

Adedeji, Adebayo (1990) "The African Economy: Prospects for Recovery and Sustained Development," in Obasanjo, Olusegun and d'Orville, Hans (eds) *Challenges of Leadership in African Development.* New York: Taylor and Francis, Inc.

Ashby Jacqueline; Klees, Steven; Pachico, Douglas; and Wells, Stuart (1980) "Alternative Strategies in the Economic Analysis of Information/Education Projects," in McAnany, Emile G. (ed.) *Communications in the Rural Third World: The Role of Information in Development.* New York: Praeger Publishers.

Berger, Peter L. and Luckmann, Thomas (1966) *The Social Construction of Reality: A Treatise on the Sociology of Knowledge,* London: Allen Lane.

Blair, Robert and Jordan, Josephine (1994) "Staff Loss and Retention at Selected African Universities: A Synthesis Report," *AFTHR Technical Note No. 18.* Human Resources and Poverty Division, Technical Department, Africa Region. Washington, D.C.: World Bank.

Dissanayake, Wimal (1981) "Development and Communication: Four Approaches," *Media Asia,* Vol. 8.

Diwan, Romesh K. and Livingston, Dennis (1979) *Alternative Development Strategies and Appropriate Technology: Science Policy for an Equitable World Order.* New York: Oxford University Press, Inc.

Djarnen, Jean-Yves; Ramazani, Dunia; and Somé, Stéphane Soteg (1995) "Electronic networking in Africa: Emergence towards the Internet," *FID News Bulletin,* Vol. 45, Nos. 7/8, pp. 228–233.

Ihonvbere, Julius O. (1996) "Africa in the 1990s and beyond. Alternative prescriptions and projections". *Futures,* Volume 28, Number 1, pp. 15–35.

Inayatullah, Sohail (1992) "Images of Pakistan's future," *Futures,* Vol. 24, No. 9, November, pp. 867–878.

Inayatullah, Sohail (1996) *Personal Conversation,* The Communication Centre, Queensland University of Technology, Brisbane, Australia, Tuesday, 17 December.

Jegede, Olugbemiro J. (1994) "Indigenous African Mode of Thought and its Implications for Educating Future World Citizens". Paper submitted to *The Journal of Afro-Latin American Studies and Literature.*

Jegede, Olugbemiro J. (1995) "From talking drums to electronic networking: Africa's snailmobile through the cyberspace," FID *News Bulletin,* Vol. 45, Nos. 7/8, July/August, pp. 218–224.

Lerner, Daniel (1980) "The Revolutionary Elites and World Symbolism". in Lasswell, Harold; Lerner, Daniel; and Speier, Hans (eds) *Propaganda and Communication in World History,* Vol. 11. Honolulu: The University Press of Hawaii.

Levy Jr., Marion J. (1992) "Confucianism and Modernization," *Society, Vol.* 29, No. 4, May/June.

Little, Reg and Reed, Warren (1989) *The Confucian Renaissance.* Sydney: The Federation Press.

Mazrui, Ali A. (1973) "Thoughts on Assassination in Africa," in Prosser, Michael H. (ed.) *Intercommunication Among Nations and Peoples.* New York: Harper and Row, Publishers, Inc.

McClelland, David C. (1961) *The Achieving Society.* Princeton, New Jersey: D. Van Nostrand Co., Inc.

Obijiofor, Levi (1996) "Future Impact of New Communication Technologies: Beyond the Debate," *FUTURESCO,* No. 6, UNESCO, Paris.

Portes, Alejandro (1976) "On the Sociology of National Development: Theories and Issues," *American Journal of Sociology,* Vol. 82, No. 1, July.

Prior, Margot (1994) "The Folly of a Society that Pensions off Wisdom," *The Australian,* March 16, p. 26.

Schurmann, Franz (1996) "Africa is Saving Itself," *Choices (The Human Development Magazine, UNDP),* Volume 5, No. 1, pp. 4–9.

Servaes, Jan (1986) "Development Theory and Communication Policy: Power to the People!" *European Journal of Communication,* Vol. 1, No. 2, June.

Sogolo, Godwin (1994) "Prescriptions from a Lost Generation," in Kim, Tae-Chang and Dator, James A. (eds) *Creating a New History for Future Generations.* Kyoto, Japan: Institute for the Integrated Study of Future Generations.

Uchendu, Victor C. (1965) *The Igbo of Southeast Nigeria.* New York: Holt, Rinehart and Winston.

Walsh, James (1993) "Asia's Different Drum," *Time Magazine,* June 14.

Wildman, Paul (1992) *Development as if communities mattered. It's your community, it's your economy: Understanding the nuts and bolts of your community economy.* Community Education Development Series No. 4. Nundah, Brisbane: Prosperity Press.

CHAPTER 12

Africa in the 21st Century: A Case for Innovative Use of Technology

Bolanle A. Olaniran

"A dramatic 'powershift' is coming,
and all nations face one inescapable rule
*– Survival of the fastest". (*Alvin Toffler)

It is ironic that the words above used to read survival of the fittest. However, these words from Alvin Toffler can describe economic development and general standard of living around the globe today. The buzzword today is globalization. When we talk of globalization, we are not just talking about multinational corporations (MNCs); we are talking about the progressive interconnectedness of nations and people across geographic boundaries for economic, social, political and general well being. The vision of African communities in the 21st century would not be complete without drawing on globalization and technological perspectives. Thus, this chapter hopes to present a glimpse of Africa in the next century relative to other parts of the world. The focus is given primarily to technology, standards of living and general economic development and expectations. Analogies are specifically drawn in a view from the country of Nigeria. The next section presents a general glimpse of what one can expect from life in the year 2026.

A FUTURE FOR AFRICA?

You log on to your computer in Ibadan right from home, office, or perhaps through a laptop computer from a remote village on the beach. At the other end is a client at Iwo or Lokoja and maybe even in Addis Ababa, discussing the latest marketing strategy or ordering shipments. Pictures, images and voices are being relayed to clients in a similar manner. Both picture and voice are transmitted in real time. If that is hard to imagine, how about using a voice interactive computer without having to touch a single key on your computer keyboard. Thus, one's computer becomes a personal secretary, companion, and servant. You can ask your computer any question and have the computer help you solve problems. Telecommunication lines and desktop computers that permit transmission of data, audio, and video also allow people to work on budgets and proposals together. One does not have to travel down or send a representative for a meeting; the video-conferencing capabilities offered through one's computer would suffice. Better yet, one does not have to abandon one's work and responsibilities or spend many days addressing only one single task because of a travelling schedule. In essence, out of reach does not necessarily mean lack of access.

These are samples of what an office and interactions could be like in the envisioned Africa of the twenty-first century. Is this really possible? Sure! The picture is captured by a micro camera attached to a computer with a microphone to capture both picture and voice such that interactions can occur in real time.

Nevertheless, for Africa to move from where it is today to realize that possibility, certain things must happen. Different pieces of the puzzle must be put together for the technological possibilities to become reality. Namely, social, political, economic, and cultural problems in the African continent must be addressed.

Where do we go from here? While I am neither a soothsayer nor an astrologer for that matter, I see an African community (note: I use community rather than a specific nation) that offers great potential and hopes for a brighter future. However, the realization of this potential economically, socially, and politically depends on its technological infrastructure and capacity. In a nutshell, Africa must move away from being technology-dependent and must become society of innovators and technological pioneers.

It is crucial to note that without technology, global issues will lack their current vitality. Worthington (1993) echoes this sentiment when he claims that the power to organize human systems and control nature on such a grand scale will be impossible in the absence of technology. Thus, the crux of this paper focuses on examining this question and presents other variables that would facilitate realization of these benefits and technological developments. The key to this development lies in Africa's performance in the globalization process.

GLOBALIZATION

The need for transcendence of economic activities beyond national, geographic, and cultural boundaries characterizes the globalization process in which the world community has become, in Marshall McLuhan's terminology, a "global village". In essence, this tendency has resulted in a "hyper-competitive" global marketplace where comparative advantage does not derive merely from low labor costs and natural resources, or close access to markets. Instead, comparative advantage evolves from "knowledge-intensive", value-added technology that creates new products, processes and services (e.g., Brown, 1993; Merrifield, 1991; Simon, 1993; Yoda, 1990).

A potent force in this change or shift from the traditional form of economic competition is the increasing trend in technology competence and capability. The point that must be stressed in this development is knowledge. It is generally accepted that knowledge is power. Toffler (1990) argues that one must take the new role of knowledge in wealth creation into account. Thus, knowledge as presented here consists of imagination, values, images, motivation, education and technical skills. Nigeria and other African countries must find ways to not only acquire knowledge, but also learn to create and disseminate this critical resource.

In this realm, it is essential that Africa find ways to acquire knowledge. This process includes taking whatever steps necessary. It involves employing unconventional means of acquiring the knowledge, which comprises acquisition of technological secrets from those that have it by any means. Stealing technological secrets is nothing new. It is a booming business that provides a way to equalize the gaps between the haves and the have-nots (Toffler, 1993). The Pacific Rim countries have been able to perfect this process to an art form. Therefore, it is Africa's time to join in the hunt. While I am not encouraging industrial espionage or other non-ethical and immoral behavior, I am indicating that gaining knowledge via joint effort and first hand information is perhaps the fastest way for technological transfer. At the same time, globalization demands "strategic alliances" between nations and firms for joint development of technology (Hagedoorn & Shackenraad, 1992).

Succeeding in this process will involve taking responsibility and avoiding blame shifting so that "the old and former colonial bosses are responsible for all the ills and woes that plague the entire continent". I envision an Africa that needs and wants a share of the global economy and is a force to be reckoned with, if it decides to make the 21st century the African Era as its Asian counterparts have made the latter portion of the 20th century. At present, however, according to Dr Amoako (the executive secretary of the UN Economic Commission for Africa, ECA), "Africa represents the world's most serious economic challenge". I am sure we do not have to look far to see the truth in this statement. For the most part, food production in the region is based on self-subsistence. The technological know-how for mass production is below par. Those able to afford tractors and other agricultural production tools are often challenged by lack of spare parts when equipment breaks down. Clearly, there is a demarcation in the world hegemony of haves and have-nots. The haves are constantly in the midst of far-reaching technological frontiers while the have-nots continue to wallow in self-pity and outdated methods. Therefore, in breaking out of the doldrums of the old economic policies that have not worked, certain issues must be addressed: an emphasis on excellence at all levels; a focus on cost effectiveness and value creation; and effective partnering. All these must be incorporated if one is to participate in the latest global technological frontier.

EXCELLENCE

In globalization processes, it is evident that corporations that aim to wield power or survive must do so by developing strategic advantages in access to sophisticated technological resources, along with a strong regional market position (Simon, 1993). The same is true for nations or regional sectors. However, such market presence and advantages will come from excellence in technology and other supporting infrastructure such as a skilled labor force, communication systems and transportation, research and development, and manufacturing capabilities.

A starting point for a move towards development is communication and information technology. Currently, most people do not have access to even the most basic telephone service in Africa. Telephone systems, along with personal computers and the Internet, have brought a new meaning to the theme "reach out and touch someone". In the developed countries, telephone is not a luxury; it is a necessity for survival. In the new global economy, the ability to instantly communicate with others has become critical. Therefore, it would seem difficult for Africa to compete effectively when it may not be on the same level playing field. Hence, the first task is to invest in the telecommunication systems that will facilitate quicker and easier access to the information superhighway that propels the global economy today.

Currently in Africa, it is common knowledge that demand for telephones is greater than supply. The exorbitant initial application fee for a telephone hook-up is so outrageous that an average individual cannot afford it. Those who can afford a phone must deal with the inconvenience of not having direct access to international lines. More outrageous is that there are so few phone gateways that one often has to spend several hours to get through to one's destination. In the global economy, speed is everything. Any nation that chooses to do business the old fashioned way of relying on traditional travel and face-to-face interaction may be left behind. In other words, ensuring meaningful growth in the global economy demands a dramatic increase in the provision of basic infrastructure such as telephones, water, electricity, and transportation (Olowo, 1996). Thus, erratic supply of these basic needs by the government results not only in slowing economic and national growth but also contributes to increasing the cost of doing business in Africa. Therefore, easy access, knowledge, and use of telecommunication facilities are crucial in the struggle to improve profitability and competitiveness. The sophistication of telecommunication technology elsewhere, along the lines of email, video-conferencing, and picturephone, have changed the tide in market behavior competition-wise, as there is ever-increasing demand for faster processing of customer orders. (Colombo, 1992).

There is a greater need to put information in the hands of users. The Internet is one such place. However, Internet is still out of reach for most Africans. Very recently, a report indicated that only 20 African nations have internet access and access is limited to the capital cities, while 12 other countries are still at the planning stage (Jensen, 1996). This illustrates the slow rate at which technology transfer occurs in the region.

While it will be hard to compete with the larger economies of scale that PTTs enjoy in providing telecommunication services, this should not be viewed as an impossible task. For instance, the private sectors can form cooperatives to fund projects that will bring about the necessary telecommunication facilities. After all, the globalization process is all about greater interdependency and strong collaboration (Hagedoorn & Schakenraad, 1992; Schott, 1994) as a result of having to do more with less. Working together to provide telecommunication access that will benefit each of the cooperative's members would fall under this category and would speedup the growth-rate. In other words, the policy of businesses and the communities depending on state-run PTTs to provide all their telecommunication needs is no longer a wise choice.

There are several ways of doing this. One is to create new telecommunication service companies. The second option is to work with the existing PTTs through strategic partnerships. The third is to attract international service providers such as AT&T, MCI, Sprint, WorldComm and a host of others with specific expertise that can improve quality and access. Fourth, and the option that holds perhaps the most promise for Nigeria and other African countries, is to seek alternative telecommunication technology that does not carry the constraints and the financial burdens associated with older techniques and technologies, such as wireless and satellite-based telecommunication technologies. Among the service providers are Teledesic, who promise a space-based satellite system for broad-band multimedia communication, and Motorola's iridium for wireless communication. These companies provide an alternative for Africa to enter and participate in the new global economy. More importantly, this technology is currently available for use at a reasonable price. Developing countries might use it in areas not served by a regular telephone network or even by electricity. Craig McCaw the CEO of Teledesic says the services could be used in the center of remote villages where telephone services are currently not available (Kupfer & Davies, 1996).

At the center of this lies consumer choice and needs. After all, it is consumer choice that is responsible for a company's market shares, revenues, profits, and competitive opportunities. Thus, the question before all African nations involves determining how information technology can be adapted to help consumers select or prefer their locally-manufactured products. Engineers and manufacturers would have to play a significant role in this process by helping their respective companies to create and add value along with a focus on cost reduction techniques. With the shift away from a production-oriented to a consumer-driven economy, where demand lags behind supplies, strategies that delay incorporating consumer inputs will falter while those that take the time to figure-out consumer needs and speed the process of developing products that meet those needs will triumph. This represents another area where a good communication technology is required to provide links between consumers and manufacturers in order to allow customers to express their desires directly to the manufacturers for product customization rather than the standardization that characterizes mass production. A good place to start for those with Internet capability is to take advantage of the new World African Internet Society (WAIS) that was recently launched. The society aims to provide a link for collaborative effort between African businesses and the rest of the world (Nicholson, 1996). This could help entrepreneurs in scanning for ideas and also in determining ways to turn those ideas into final products and services.

FOOD PRODUCTION AND SELF SUFFICIENCY

The Nigerian economy, like most of the other African countries, is primarily agrarian. Yet Nigeria spends tremendous amount of money on importing food. The main reason is that the country's past and present approach to food production is based on subsistence farming due to lack of technological know-how. Thus, food production represents an area where Nigeria and many other African nations can dramatically reduce their dependency. Nigeria needs to aggressively pursue policies that focus on acquiring and domesticating technology. The nation is blessed with a significant amount of natural resources, perhaps more so than some developed countries. However, it lacks appropriate policies and the technical skills required to transform these resources into final products and services.

The essence of this argument is the idea that the new global economic order requires that overseas suppliers from developing countries advance their own technologies to meet the world's speed and standards. Otherwise they will be eliminated and become casualties of the information speed effect (Toffler, 1990). Given the importance of "value added", it is imperative for Nigeria to harness its human resources and utilize its raw materials and capital equipment base. This can be realized by developing a process in which technology is designed to utilize locally available resources. Consequently, these should be turned into final products that are produced not only cheaply but also with higher value.

In this case, domestic corporations will not have to depend on the government for protective policy to fight off cheap imports. For example, remnants of palm kernel, after palm oil has been extracted, can be a valuable component of poultry feeds. Poultry feeds could even become a valuable export and foreign exchange earner. Similarly, agricultural by-products and crude oil can also be put to good use.

Currently, the main focus of Nigeria is exports of crude oil. Nonetheless, it is absurd to see Nigeria, one of the giant oil producers suffering from petroleum scarcity. Apart from petroleum, Emmanuel Onuegbe (1996) proposes that Nigeria should get involved in the production of jet fuel as it is derived from crude oil. After all, it is a commodity that all nations need and use, as billions of people travel by air every year. It does not take much to become a dominant player in the global economy; all it takes is creativity to find a niche and apply appropriate technology, and effective marketing.

The Asia Pacific Rim LDCs have managed to realign the global economy and production. For instance, the USA is the largest producer of microprocessors but the main DRAM (Dynamic Random Access Memory) which the microprocessors depend on for storage are manufactured in Korea (Onuegbe, 1996). The same goes for laptops, which are predominantly manufactured in the USA. The screens for these laptops are manufactured in Japan. The "recursive interdependency" illustrated in the example demonstrates how a nation or region can contribute to capital production while at the same time adding value to the global economic process.

Furthermore, proper application of appropriate technology to create added value would help the cottage industries and other small-scale domestic firms to become large-scale operations. The 1995 Central Bank of Nigeria Report was right in suggesting that enhancing the value of domestically produced products will facilitate independence that will prepare the economy with the flexibility to withstand external shocks (Olowo, 1996). Local resources must be developed to have a significant impact on national development problems. Internal talent, and processes must be adapted towards a structure that focuses on stimulating creativity and productivity. Then, African nations can demonstrate to the outside world that they have the capacity to produce cost-effective products and they can enact incentives to encourage foreign investment. This would speed the move toward bridging the technology gap between Africa and the developed countries.

TRANSPORTATION

Transportation continues to be a priority for economic development. No distribution of products and services can exist without an adequate transportation system. At the same time, the need to get products to market at the right time has never been more pressing. Thus, it is crucial that shipment of products and delivery of services occur just on time.

In a sense, the globalization process has given new meaning to the notion of the "Just in time inventory". Africa is still at a disadvantage when compared to developed nations. There is a significant disparity in the numbers of good roads available for land transportation. At the same time, air transportation is almost out of reach for small businesses.

There is a need for safer vehicles and trailers that utilize communication and tracking technological devices to keep track of cargo movement and maintain contact with operational headquarters and provide drivers with necessary road assistance to fulfil timely delivery objectives. Maintaining constant information transmission between cargo vehicles, operational headquarters and destination points can result in an enhanced distribution process. This would also increase the likelihood of achieving the just-in-time inventory objective by firms. Furthermore, considerable improvements in the current rail, sea, and air transportation systems at an affordable price are necessary. Competent governments and merchants realize that a delivery delayed is equivalent to a delivery denied. While many multinational firms expand to less developed countries (LDCs) to explore cost benefits, the ability of LDCs to deliver products and services in a timely fashion will assume greater priority in that decision. Thus, less developed countries must prove that they are up to the task of swift and quick delivery.

EDUCATION

While it is clear that there is a need for Nigeria to join the technological revolution in order to move ahead in the global economy, one must not forget the role of knowledge in the process. The sophistication of technology and the need to apply it in the workplace will require a better trained work-force. Therefore, educational systems hold the key to the dissemination of the knowledge needed to facilitate technological acquisition and economic development.

The school system in Nigeria is in a gross state of disrepair. Teachers have no tools to teach and students cannot afford to buy books and materials. Despite the increasing importance of information technologies, most schools do not have access to computers. Can you imagine learning computer science without a personal computer? The same goes for other natural sciences. The effect of the school system is felt not only at the school level but also in other areas. For instance, poorly trained medical doctors are nothing short of quacks without the knowledge of simple, life saving-medical procedures. Furthermore, instructors frequently strike due to poor pay and inadequate resources. These conditions are a handicap to growth and development.

The rise of the Asian economies in the 20th century has shown that success or failure in the global economy does not depend on natural resources alone. Despite not having vast amounts of natural resources, they have managed to exert their dominance in major industrial sectors (Hax, 1989). In essence, the basic ingredient for developing competitive supremacy now lies in knowledge embodied in managerial, leadership, and technological competence.

The government, the community and old alumni of schools must come together and place a high priority on providing the present and future generations of students with modern equipment, the latest research journals and books to train the minds of the future. Japan has demonstrated a strong correlation between training and human productivity. With twice the engineering capacity per capita as compared to the USA, Japan has acquired the reputation for quality manufactured products (Hax, 1989).

The exact nature of education that will prepare future workers in a fast-changing job market is debatable. However, the education process would benefit tremendously by taking advantage of the present information superhighway made possible through the Internet and the World Wide Web that allows for easy access and exchange of ideas. Similarly, the dichotomy between the liberal arts – learning art, literature, music, science, math – and vocational specific job skills may have to be revamped for an approach that leans towards modified liberal arts with an emphasis on coordination and leadership skills.

One thing is certain, however, a significant portion of future job skills will have to be acquired on the job. Also, it will no longer pay to train a worker to work at a particular job or a single machine, as jobs and machines will change rapidly (Bailey, 1990). It is believed that workers who continuously acquire knowledge will have the edge (see Knestout & Siskos, 1996). Therefore, constant learning and skills upgrading will be advantageous for individuals and societies. Most importantly, individuals must be equipped with the knowledge to transform their ideas and skills into enterprising ventures.

Hence, Nigeria and other African countries must come to the realization that there is no substitute for good quality education. Otherwise, progress will continue to wane. China, Thailand, Korea, Indonesia and others have invested heavily in technical education, and they are reaping the results by moving up from the class of economically impoverished states. There is no reason why Nigeria and other African countries cannot do the same.

SOCIO-POLITICAL CLIMATE

Ever since its independence from England some 37 years ago, Nigeria has continuously seen its political structure bewildered by coup after coup, and ethnic and socio-political upheavals. Political uncertainties have cost Nigeria and many other African countries by clearly driving away investors and indirectly resulting in a brain drain. Foreign investment is a high-risk exercise as it is, without the pressure of political instability. Potential investors' greatest fears are uncertainty and instability. Given the opportunities available today, a large population and low labor costs are insufficient to encourage foreign investors. A stable political and policy environment is a basic minimum requirement.

Currently, Nigeria is making rather slow progress in returning to political stability. As one may note, the annulment of the June 12, 1993 elections is adversely affecting the current military regime and the nation. Some view the annulment as responsible for the trouble facing the current transition program. The government is focusing more on propaganda to mask the problems facing the nation. I believe that diverting money earmarked for propaganda into research and development activities can make a significant difference in the lives of the citizens. All eyes are on Nigeria, as to which direction it is going to take, whether it opts to go forward or backward. Furthermore, it is hard for economic policy to make significant progress when there is lack of continuity and a stable policy environment

Further contributing to the political dilemma in Nigeria is the inter-ethnic rivalry which always surrounds the debate around where the leaders ought to come from. The inter-ethnic rivalry is certainly not going to completely disappear, and a breakaway of the three dominant regions is hardly a solution. Therefore, the people must find a way to live together cooperatively and manage their differences like most developed nations. The USA, for instance, is made up of different ethnic groups. Despite their differences, the democratic political structure allows all groups the opportunity to make their point and to accept the consequences of the outcomes of elections. This not only creates a stable policy environment but also civility.

ALLIANCES AND PARTNERING

Taken as a whole, it seems impossible for any single African nation to implement these ideas. However, the interdependency among nations as globalization advances offers a way to make the process more economically feasible. The operative words in the globalization age are cooperation and collaboration. No nation or company can afford to stand like an island. Therefore, joint ventures and resource pooling are necessary for Nigeria and other African states to share the financial burden that comes with research and development of technology. Activities including development of cross-border trade, transport and communications, energy and minerals, harmonizing economic and monetary policies and promotion of regional convergence are a must. In addition, African countries should give priority to opportunities to share ideas, knowledge and expertise.

These tasks would have to go beyond mere regional alliances. Efforts should be made to cooperate with other LDCs who are currently enjoying access to modern technology (e.g. Koreans, Indians, Chinese, and others). This strategy may be more promising than dealing with the developed countries. It is important to note that as developed countries develop, they become less dependent on imports of raw materials from developing countries (Toffler, 1990). Therefore, it is necessary for Africa to engage in the "brain drain" by enticing teams of researchers and scientists to come and work in Africa. African countries should target minorities and persecuted groups from different countries rather than attempting to compete by offering large salaries. According to Toffler (1990), these groups of individuals offers "economic hybrid vigor" because: "They work hard, they innovate, they educate their children, and, even if they get rich in the process, they stimulate and accelerate the reflexes of the host economy" (p. 44).

TECHNOLOGY RESISTANCE AND LOCAL ISSUES

The solutions provided above focused on technology. It is also necessary to discuss the role of local culture and its effect on the adoption of technologies. New technologies, like other innovations, face resistance prior to their adoption. Resistance can be individual, institutional, or cultural in nature. Individual and institutional resistance emanates from various reasons, among which are fear, lack of capacity and cost. Technologies do not come cheap, and many individuals and institutions do not have the resources to acquire and maintain them. For instance, the basic cost of personal computers is more than double the per-capita income in Nigeria.

Similarly, there is lack of basic training to acquire the skills to use a computer or maintain one. Computer maintenance services are uncommon. In addition, the infrastructure in Nigeria is hardly conducive. For example, most technological products sold in Nigerian markets are not tropicalized to withstand the rigors of the climate and environment. For computers, erratic power supply plus hot and humid weather are key factors making their use very difficult.

On culture, one must examine existing processes. The Nigerian system is beset with bulging files that are ill maintained and ripe for computerization. Unfortunately, the fear of job loss is a real barrier. Resistance against streamlining paper work should be expected from clerical staff. They are likely to see computerization as a way of depriving them of a lucrative avenue for extra income that normally results from processing files for clients.

Overcoming resistance to technologies calls for good training. Individuals and institutions must be exposed to the benefits of computer technology. Potential users must be aware that technology is not here to replace humans but to ease the drudgery of work. They must also be alerted to the fact that information technology is a net job creator.

The relevance of technology in Africa is questionable as well. Technology has to be relevant. Arguably, most technologies brought to Nigeria in the past were not necessarily relevant. Thus, if a technology does not fit the task it is intended for or the environment in which it is to be used, obviously problems will arise. In this regard, Nigeria has done poorly when it comes to refining technologies to ensure that they are suitable for its environment and needs.

A GLIMPSE OF FUTURE POSSIBILITIES

If Africa decides to take an active role in the global economy by riding the technology wave, there are endless possibilities. Below is a brief glimpse of what can be expected.

Technology, as we know it, will be different. For instance, it is projected that improvement in computing power doubles every 18 months; in the next 15 years, standard desktop computers will be 1000 percent more powerful (Knestout & Siskos, 1997). Therefore, one could expect to see compact pocket-sized computers. Road congestion could be expected to reduce drastically as the need for travelling would be reduced considerably, as many workers become telecommuters – working from home.

Service providers will also find ways to jump on the technology bandwagon. For instance, one could expect telephones to be more friendly, so that one could tell bed-time stories and fables to children regardless of one's location. Individuals should be able to access and invest in any financial market in the world with a click on their computers. At the same time, medical services can tap into technology as different doctors and medical teams will be able to exchange ideas about treating patients. There would be opportunities to engage in collaborative surgical procedures where teams of medical experts from different locations coach one another through delicate and emergency procedures. More important, however, is that technology holds a long-anticipated hope for people living in rural areas where access to medical facilities is difficult. These individuals will be able to dial into a medical facility and obtain the necessary treatment and medical advice without having to leave the confines of their villages. Similarly, it would be conceivable to speak with people in foreign languages because these languages will be instantaneously translated.

The move toward electronic cash or e-cash as it is commonly referred to is expected. This trend will drastically reduce robberies as business and individuals have very little need to carry large sums of money around.

Efforts will be made towards alternative sources of energy whereby a house could be designed to switch from conventional electricity to solar energy through the use of photovoltaic panels in the building structure. These technologies will definitely become attractive in those regions where there are frequent interruptions in electricity supply.

Employment interviews and contract negotiations will be conducted electronically via video-conferencing. The filing or transfer of paper applications from one workstation to another, or office to office, will be transmitted electronically. There is no choice for service providers as strong competition force them to respond to consumer demands: hence, the decision to go technocratic.

At the same time, one can expect the industries of the future to focus more on environmental issues. Industrial waste disposal and recycling activities will be on the increase, as the increase in technology capabilities forces companies to be held more accountable for high standards by consumers and society at large. These standards and people's interest in preserving the environment will force companies to pay more attention to pollution control and hazardous waste disposal technologies. For instance, there is ongoing research into the process of converting waste oil into useable quality grade diesel fuel by an American firm, Green Oasis. Also, conversion of metal scraps, the kind that are currently found along the roadside with no proper disposal can be ground and reused. Furthermore, these tasks will provide entrepreneurs with a way to demonstrate their concerns for environmental preservation and also to make money from the "enviro-economic" process.

CONCLUSION

Realizing these benefits is a challenge that everyone (individuals, organizations, and government) must commit themselves to doing their very best to make sure their acts benefit others, their country, and finally themselves. It is time to put the blame game aside and assume responsibility for our future. Individual Africans must take initiatives and commit ourselves to engaging in activities that will change us and our continent, Africa, for the better. More important is the need for Africa to use its resources carefully and to focus on activities that have a measurable impact on Africa's development problems. Africa must adopt a structure and internal process that stimulates the creativity and productivity of its people. All its institutions must demonstrate self-accountability and accountability to stakeholders and the community that they serve. We may be able to run but we cannot hide. In the final analysis no one will do it for us, so what are we waiting for? The earlier we get on with the tasks before us, the better. All we have to do is get serious, get committed, and start somewhere. The end is closer than it seems and one should always remember that the journey of a thousand miles begins with the first step. Let us make Africa the most admired continent in the 21st century.

REFERENCES

Bailey, T. (1990). "Jobs of the future and skills they will require". *America Educator,* 14, pp. 10–44.

Brown, R. H. (1993, May 31). "The underlying principle of the economic system has changed profoundly says Secretary Brown". *Business America,* 114(11),pp. 6–7.

Colombo, Victor (1992). "Switzerland's communications model communities (CMC) project: Development of solutions for increasingly complex communication needs". *Telecommunication Journal,* 59, pp. 355–366.

Hagedoorn, L, & Schakenraad, J. (1992). "Leading companies and networks of strategic alliances in information technologies" *Research Policy,* 21, pp. 163–190.

Hax, A. (1989). "Building the firm of the future". *Sloan Management Review,* 30, pp. 75–82.

Jensen, M. (1996). "Internet update for ISOC" *Geneva's DEVSIG Meeting.* MikeJ@Wn.apc.org.

Knestout, 13., & Siskos, C. (1997, January). "Fifty years from now". *Kiplinger's Personal Finance Magazine.* pp. 98–104.

Kupfer, A., & Davies, E. (1996, May 27). "Craig McCaw sees an Internet in the sky". *Fortune,* 133(10), pp. 62–72.

Merrifield, D. B. (1991). "Value-added: The dominant factor in industrial competitiveness". *International Journal of Technology Management,* p. 226.

Nicholson, W. G. (1996, September 18). "World African Internet Society". Naijanet@mitvma.mit.edu.

Olaniran, B. A., & Williams, D. E. (1996). *Anticipatory model of crisis management in technology.* Working Paper.

Olowo, Bola, "Ensuring meaningful growth". *West Africa* p. 1154, (1996, July 22–28).

Onuegbe, E. (1996, December 23). "The dawning". *Naijanet Newsgroup.*

Schott, Thomas, "Collaboration in the invention of technology". *Social Science Research,* 23, pp. 23–56, (1994).

Simon, D. F. (1993). "The international technology market: Globalization, Regionalization and the Pacific Rim". *Business & the Contemporary World,* 5(2), pp. 50–66.

Toffler, A. (1990, November). "Toffler's next shock". *World Monitor,* 3(11), pp. 34–44.

Waddock, S. A., & Boyle, M. (1995). "The Dynamics of change in corporate community relations". *California Management Review,* 37, pp. 125–140.

Worthington, R. (1993). "Science and technology as a global system". *Technology, & Human Values,* 18, pp. 176–185.

Yoda, N. (1990). *Japan intelligence overcomes natural resources: Do not be arrogant.* Tokyo: Keizaikai Publishing Co.

CHAPTER 13

The Future of Africa:
A Crime and Justice Perspective

Paul O. Omaji

INTRODUCTION

As I reflect on Africa, the crime and justice situation leaves me with a troubling feeling about the continent's future.[1] The emerging culture of fear of criminal victimization or the collapse of justice in general threatens to portray Africa as a 'dark' continent once again. In Asia, Europe and the Western hemisphere, even among people who have never set foot on African soil, there is now a widespread impression that Africa is the crime continent of the World; that most systems of justice are little more than a sham; and that African leaders are not only losing the fight against crime but are in many cases guilty of complicity in the prevalence of crime and injustice.

Impressions may be wrong but their consequences are real. The veritable hesitation of people in these regions to deal with Africa in trade, tourism, industrial investment, education, or social interaction means that the crime and justice situation has a high potential to compromise Africa's future. In the growing globalized political economy, the prospect of this situation to not only turn Africa into a pariah continent but also damage its present and future generations, is frightening to contemplate. Against this backdrop, l believe that no functional vision for the future of Africa would be complete without strong research and policy-oriented attention to the area of crime and justice. Far more compelling, though, is the urgency with which such attention is now required, if irreparable damage is to be forestalled.

In this chapter, I present a panoramic view of the crime and justice situation in our continent, articulate a vision of a safe and secure continent, and outline 'what is to be done' in order to translate the vision into reality. My contribution aims largely to sensitize and mobilize the African person (spirit, mind, and body) to appreciate the current state of affairs and what needs to be done to ensure that the future of Africa is 'the Africa of the future' which nationals of all regions of the world can admire.

[1] I thank Professor Olu Jedege of the University of Southern Queensland, Australia, who has in many ways sharpened my thoughts about Africa. I am also thankful that he alerted me to this project on the Future of Africa.

IMAGES OF CRIME IN AFRICA TODAY

Criminality is one of the social ills that now define Africa as "the continent that has lost its way".[2] Many African countries are said to have witnessed in the 1990s a surge not only in the conventional crimes index such as violent, white collar, and political crimes but also in what I call 'modernist crimes', including drug trafficking and money laundering.[3] The incidence of the latter form of criminality means that Africa has now become very much drawn into the internationalized criminal networks in Asia and the Western hemisphere.

Clearly, as these networks become powerful enough to use their dirty money to undermine prudent banking practices and to exert political influence, Africa would be most vulnerable to blackmail and sabotage. Together with the corrosive impact that conventional and political crimes have on the feeling of safety, morale, and productivity, the whole situation carries a deadly prospect for the social stability and economic advancement of Africa.

From north to south and east to west, hardly any African country is perceived by the international community to be free, or at least safe, from crime and justice problems. All countries experience, albeit in varying degrees, the scourging menace of street, corporate, white collar, political, and organized crimes.

The northern region of Sub-Saharan Africa has been afflicted by petty crimes and, in some countries, violent crimes. Nationals and visitors in Chad, Mali, Mauritania, and Niger, for instance, have been warned about pick-pocketing, purse snatching, incidents of banditry and vehicle theft which have assumed endemic proportions in the nineties. Somalia has experienced a non-existent or dysfunctional government for some time and has continued to witness looting, banditry, and other forms of violent crime, particularly in the capital city of Mogadishu.

The southern region countries, including Angola, Botswana, Lesotho, Malawi, Mozambique, and South Africa, have witnessed increased incidents of break-ins, auto theft, armed robberies, car-jackings and other forms of violent crime. In those countries that have suffered armed conflict in recent times, the crime problem is compounded by the marauding bands of former soldiers and rebels who are well armed and out of work.

Among the countries in this region, South Africa's crime problem has been the subject of the most widespread discussion. One of the reasons for this disproportionate attention is the country's recent but long awaited transition to a

---

[2] Victoria Brittain uses this phrase to capture her argument that African nations are continuing in a downward spiral of development, disintegrating under the pressure of failing economies, environmental degradation, social stress, and political collapse. See *World Press Review* (July 1994).

[3] A recent forum where Africa's rising crime was demonstrated was the international conference on "crime and justice in the nineties", held in July 1996 at the University of South Africa, Pretoria. My experience at that conference confirmed the disquiet I have had for some time about the rhetoric and reality of crime and justice in Africa.

non-racial democracy. Besides placing the country in a renewed international spotlight, the transition has attracted the curiosity of criminologists who are interested in the nexus between social change and crime. Both popular and systematic works show that there is significant random street violence (e.g. car-jacking), which affects foreigners as well as local residents, especially in major cities such as Johannesburg.

Privileged groups in South Africa "live in jail-like homes guarded by vicious dogs, razor wire, and armed security guards summoned by panic buttons".[4] In the less privileged sections, mainly the black communities, the murder rate has escalated and vigilante justice is common.[5] Several studies reveal a sinister picture of South Africa as the world's crime capital. A report from South Africa's own government dubbed it "the most violent country outside a war-zone".[6]

Petty crimes and violent crimes are also features of the western region of Africa. In countries such as Benin, Burkina Faso, Cape Verde, Côte d'Ivoire, Gambia, Guinea, Liberia and Togo, crimes including pick-pocketing, purse snatching or 'grab and run' offences, and mugging are said to be widespread. Ghana and Nigeria are two countries in this region where violent crimes such as armed robbery, assault, burglary, car-jackings and extortion have become endemic. Both countries have also acquired some notoriety for official corruption, business scams and swindles.

In Nigeria, in particular, the criminal threat to life and property is such that some groups constantly ask: if the military government with its paraphernalia of arms and ammunition cannot make the lives of ordinary citizens secure, what hope do we have for security of human life and property when a civilian government assumes the reigns of power?[7] The rate at which human lives are being destroyed in Nigeria, especially by armed robbers and hired assassins has reached a most alarming stage.

Countries in the eastern region, including Burundi, Ethiopia, Kenya, Rwanda, Tanzania, and Uganda have all had their own share of crimes, petty and violent, at a level capable of compromising safety and hindering development. Banditry, looting, mugging, and armed robbery are among the significant unlawful antisocial conducts. At the time of writing this chapter, Burundi and Rwanda were still reeling from a rather insidious and politically motivated crime against society and humanity. In the central region of the continent, the Central African Republic, Congo, and Zaire have witnessed most forms of the

---

[4] Matloff, Judith, *The Christian Science Monitor*. November 13, 1995, 7.

[5] Contreras, Joseph, "Fortress Mentality: South Africa Crime Wave Scares Off Foreigners and Rattles the Citizenry", *Newsweek*. October 2, 1995, 23.

[6] Roddy, Michael, "Can Election Help Crime-Plagued South Africa?" *Reuters*. October 22, 1995.

[7] Comment by the Secretary General of the Christian Association of Nigeria, Charles Williams, published in *Nigeria Today*, Tuesday 19, November 1996.

major crimes, ranging from pick-pocketing, through assault on the streets and endemic banditry, to murder.

With regard to organized crime, evidence suggests that notorious criminal groups from around the world have, in recent times, conducted financial operations in a number of African countries. The International Narcotics Control Strategy Report (1993) provides an overview of the state of law and justice regarding narcotics crime in the world, among which Côte d'Ivoire, Nigeria and South Africa feature very prominently.

Côte d'Ivoire is most probably a transit and conversion point for money laundering. Jonathan Winner, the US Assistant Secretary of State for International Narcotics and Law Enforcement, while on a visit to Nigeria, stated that Nigeria has been ranked the third largest narcotics route in the world.[8] South African police have, in recent times, uncovered over 100 different criminal organizations and syndicates operating internally.[9] Further, there is the view that drug cartels and money launderers in Africa are aided and abetted by top serving and retired political or military officers. All of this represents an ominous influence on the future of Africa.

IMAGES OF JUSTICE IN AFRICA TODAY

Criminality is one definer of the character of a continent, as I have tried to show above. The legal response to this phenomenon, particularly the way justice agencies address crime in their respective communities is another, perhaps more potent, marker. In this regard, the justice systems in Africa have given the continent everything except a good name, a good life, and a peaceful conscience. There are widespread impressions that the policing, judging and correcting or punishing of crime in Africa not only fall far short of civilized standards but also fundamentally destroy the basis for individual reform and nation-building.

The police who are charged with the responsibility for general law enforcement or maintenance of public order and territorial security have been found to commit numerous and, on occasion, shocking abuses against the same people and communities they had vowed to protect. Evidence suggests that not all of such heavy-handedness by the law enforcement agencies can be justified by the nature of crimes involved. In some cases, no crime is involved.

In many African jurisdictions, the police have:

– abused their power to conduct searches with or without a judicial warrant, apprehended and taken people to local police stations to extort varying amounts of money for alleged crimes, a great number of which would be minor offences,

---

[8] *Nigeria Today*, Friday 13, December 1996.

[9] Grove, Major General W., "South Africa: The Drug Trade as a National and International Security Threat". *CJ International*. May–June 1995, 8.

– carried out extra-judicial killings of criminal suspects or political opponents,[10] and

– failed or delayed to take detainees to court to have their cases adjudicated.

Allegations about beating persons in custody as punishment or to extract confessions, are also rife. So also are the allegations that those officers who perpetuate such actions are rarely brought to justice. Generally, there is no independent framework to review or scrutinize these unlawful police actions.

African judicial processes, broadly defined, have in general hardly done any better. Prosecuting services suffer crisis from lack of resources, inadequate remuneration, or low morale. In a recent report by David Beresford and Rehana Rossouw,[11] one of South Africa's most respected Attorney Generals, the Transvaal's Jan d'Oliveira, complained bitterly that he was so short of resources that he was unable to prosecute 'the first real Third Force case': "I have simply no-one to allocate to the trial. The case is ready for preparation, indictment and arrests, yet we are unable to proceed", said the AG.

The rapid political changes and the amount of unresolved injustices of the past might have stretched the prosecuting services in this country to their limits. However, the point of this example is that if the indictment of apartheid police generals who authorized and supervised the despicable vandalizing of land and people, obviously high in profile and priority, could stall for lack of resources, how much justice has been denied across the continent for similar reasons?

For those cases that eventually get to court, the type of justice they receive is generally questionable. A constant refrain is that the 'Bench' does not ensure due process and is subject to executive branch influence. At issue here is the independence of the judiciary and their capacity to discharge justice without fear of favor.

Although most African countries have constitutional provisions to protect the judiciary as an independent institution, the reality is that the judiciary generally exercises a modicum of independence in ordinary criminal cases but tends to follow the lead of the executive in national security or politically sensitive cases. With regard to the latter, there are credible reports that those with ties to the opposition are treated more harshly by the judicial system than those with ties to the Government. The process of appointing judges, which in most cases means that they serve at the pleasure of the executive, strongly predisposes judges to bow to political pressure.

In the day to day operations of the judiciary, most courts have unlimited discretion regarding the setting of bail. Bias has been reported in the exercise of

---

[10] For example, during the multiparty elections in October 1995 to February 1996, in Côte d'Ivoire both the Surete (the national police) and the Gendarmerie (a branch of the armed forces) were accused of serious human rights abuses against political opponents.

[11] Internet: http//www.mg.co.za/mg/news/justice-laws.html

this discretion as some courts have deliberately set bail at excessive levels to make it harder for some accused persons to obtain it. Jurisdictions, such as Ghana, in which courts may refuse to release prisoners on bail and instead remand them without charge for an indefinite period, have witnessed judicial bail decisions that were tantamount to injustice.

One result of this bail situation is that as much as 40 percent of the prison population consists of pre-trial detainees. Malawi prisons, for instance, sometimes hold populations, up to 46 percent of which would be pre-trial detainees. Some of these detainees can be held for up to 16 years on remand and then released without proper trial, conviction, explanation, apology or compensation. This sordid state of affairs is compounded by the lack of adequate legal aid. Many defendants who could not afford to supply their own counsel, have also failed to get public defenders (who are most of the time in short supply) to defend them.

Even where legal aid is available, the sizeable backlog of criminal cases means that, to many of these defendants, justice is effectively denied or comes too late to be of any use to their effort to live in harmony in society or as responsible citizens. Where reasons are offered at all, it is generally that the judiciary's budgetary and administrative problems effectively render expeditious trials for many defendants impossible. On closer examination, one would find that most African judicial systems are also handicapped by inappropriate courtroom technology and shortage of trained personnel, resulting in poor record keeping and inefficient case flow management.

Another blight on many African judicial systems is the ease with which ordinary courts of the land can be bypassed by governments who then set up unconventional tribunals to try people accused of even conventional crimes. This has become the hallmark of the judicial systems in countries ruled by military regimes. As the trial and execution of Ken Saro-Wiwa and eight others in Nigeria has shown recently, not only can the ordinary courts be dispossessed of jurisdiction but they can be coerced to legitimize such dispossession. The courts use legal principles such as *locus standi* and *ultra vires* to deny access to litigants or rule themselves out as incompetent to hear cases in which the military juntas have expressed interest. In Ken Saro Wiwa's case, the defendants were denied access to counsel, denied the right to call witnesses of their choice and had no right of appeal. The response from the ordinary courts to this travesty of justice was pathetic.

At the back end of the justice system is correctional intervention, in which the use of imprisonment has become very rampant in Africa. The basis for this over-reliance on jail as a response to crime is extremely questionable for at least two reasons. First, Africa has a very strong history of using community-based corrections to redeem its people from the life of crime. Europeans who colonized the continent did acknowledge this enviable approach. Secondly, modern prisons which have overshadowed indigenous methods have been built upon a philosophy of crime control which entrenches people in criminal careers and perpetuates the enemy in society. On both counts, the dependence on jail to tackle crime is patently misguided.

Even if these prisons are philosophically capable of rehabilitating offenders, their conditions tend to undermine such capability. In most African prisons, conditions are harsh and life threatening, afflicted by problems such as over-crowding, malnutrition, and a high incidence of infectious disease. As the ex-periences of Côte d'Ivoire and Ghana illustrate, these problems have been re-sponsible for the high prisoner death rate. Dabre Brahima, a member of the trade union confederation, Dignite, died recently of an undisclosed illness while incarcerated in the Abidjan prison. In Ghana, the failure of government to provide adequate and timely medical care to prisoners has resulted in deaths.

Reports by the Ivorian Human Rights League and Ghana's Commission for Human Rights and Administrative Justice show that prisons in these countries house together violent and non-violent criminals, adults and minors. A survey of the entire continent reveals that many prisons are in a state of disrepair and thus represent cruel, inhuman, or degrading environments for their populations, contrary to the United Nations minimum standards.

A description of the Jehanam Maximum Security Prison in Kenya, through the eyes of a political prisoner, neatly sums up the general state and conse-quences of imprisonment in that country and applies, *mutatis mutandis*, to other African countries. According to this prisoner,[12] Jehanam is a mere exten-sion of the Kenya Gestapo Services. On the whole, our prisons are destruction centers; they are factories which produce madness, criminality, homosexuality and death.

IS THERE HOPE FOR FUTURE AFRICA?

There is some eternal truth in the saying that where there is no hope, people lose the will to live; they perish. Considering the preceding bleak images of crime and justice in the continent, we Africans need not only hope to make us persist in our determination to live but also conscience to give us the sense of a way and direction out of the quagmire. I shall outline a few bases for hope in this section. This will help us to understand how one can still articulate a vision for a different future, as I shall do in the next section, against the backdrop of a rather sorry state of affairs.

The first basis for hope is the 'law of nature': before every dawn there is darkness. The law of nature is used here to signify that there is some regularity

---

[12] In the article entitled "Koigi wa Wamwere – A Dream of Freedom", which can be found on the internet at: http//www.aschehoug...online/witness20.html, this prisoner is called by the name 'Adungosi'.

in the order of social situations that holds under a stipulated set of conditions, either universally or in a stated proportion of instances. The history of social change shows that when a situation reaches a critical point of saturation, it generates its own antithesis that would lead to mutation. For instance, the barbarity and capriciousness of the European penal system up to the 19th century produced, inter alia, the notions of 'proportionality' and 'certainty' which Cesare Beccaria and Jeremy Bentham articulated as counterpoints. The classical criminology and the penal reforms that arose from this antithetical origin are still with us today and have spread beyond Europe.

Similarly, the decolonization process in Africa followed the high point of untrammeled imperialists, exploitation which generated nationalism and, to some extent, pan-Africanism. While the ensuing independence might have turned out to be more shadow than substance in some of the African countries, there is little doubt that such exploitation could not go on indefinitely. Change, in this regard, became inevitable by the very logic of colonialism generating its own opposite or countervailing process. The liberation struggles in different parts of the world seem to conform to this 'law of social cycles' and can rightly be referred to as 'sociological universals'.

Africa is clearly having its share of dark moments at this point in time. The crimes and injustices are enough to sustain the impression that Africa is frozen in time or, indeed, has regressed when other regions of the world seem to be marching enviably into eternal civility and higher 'humanity'. When these other regions appear to be nurturing their peoples and sending some out as ambassadors or resource seekers for the development of their lands, Africa seems to be destroying its own people inside and spewing out some of them as unwanted elements.

Few other factors have produced such a dark aura around Africa as the 'crime and injustice' factor has done. Among the current adult generations, Africa is not only now considered a high investment risk, but also a high life hazard. The younger generations, especially those living in the cities, have not been spared the uncertainty and social dislocation that crime and injustice cause. The number of street children in Africa is growing rapidly, most of whom are disposed to put their hands to evil.[13] They lose the joy of childhood and grow up as stunted adults with little or no sense of responsible citizenship. The criminal justice system picks them up and entrenches them in criminality into their adulthood. Such a dark reality cannot but portend a bright dawn which conscientious Africans have a duty to hope for and to make happen.

There is also hope in the fact that crime and injustice are not peculiar to Africa (although other regions seem to be handling the problem much more

---

[13] Robert M. Press, "More African Kids Take to the Streets", *The Christian Science Monitor* (February 7, 1994)

effectively), neither are they ingrained in our Africanness. A concerned South African, referring to the wars of the Dutch versus the English, the Xhosa versus government and now, what has been a struggle between the ANC and the IFP/ KwaZulu-Natal, once observed that "it seems as though we in South Africa have a legacy of violence inbred in us. Our society seems forever plagued with some conflict or other". Such observations tend to have a ring of believability around them, but every criminologist worthy of his or her name knows full well that there is a tangible history behind our type of crime and justice situation, a history which is generally littered with legacies of dispossession, alienation, distrust, morbid competition, official corruption, and political acrimony, to mention just a few.

The nations that form Africa may be environmentally, culturally, and economically diverse, but they have all – with few exceptions – shared the experience of neglect and exploitation by former colonial powers. This common history of exploitation has resulted in the extraordinary difficulty in developing the area. Not only did these nations lose control over the management of their vital resources, and hence over their destinies, they also have alien justice systems and their underlying philosophies firmly superimposed on indigenous systems.[14]

For instance, South African law is based on the principles of Roman-Dutch law, although since 1806 it has been influenced by English law as evidenced by the establishment of the law relating to criminal procedure. The Ethiopian Civil Code, promulgated in 1960, and Guinea's criminal code under Sekou Touré, were both based on the French law. Thus, alien powers have reshaped the social realities of once-conquered African countries through use of criminal law and have, in the process, bequeathed to these countries a legacy of criminality and inappropriate justice responses. This history allows us to anticipate that where the foreign law is found to be the problem, something can still be done to find a system more congenial to Africa.

The expressions of hope one finds in academic and non-academic works alike, is another ground for optimism. Keith Somerville notes that there appears to be a new beginning emerging in Africa. He rightly observes that since 1990, there has been slow but steady progress towards freedom and democracy, and then adds: "on this continent where brutal regimes, genocide, and failing economies are the norm, there is reason to hope for the future".[15] Clearly, Botswana enjoying uninterrupted liberal democracy since its independence and having one of the highest economic growth rates in the world, further underpins this hope. Other African countries have an indigenous model to emulate.[16]

---

[14] See Omaji, Paul, "Law and Social Change" in Shariah, *Social Change & Indiscipline in Nigeria*. Kalid Rashid, ed., University of Sokoto, Nigeria, 1987.

[15] Somerville, Keith, "Africa: Is There a Silver Lining?" *The World Today* (November 1994)

[16] Holm, John, "Botswana: One African Success Story". *Current History* (May 1994).

Michael Chege, taking a different approach to the view that Sub-Saharan Africa is collapsing and that it is just a matter of how soon the end will come, believes that from the midst of African chaos something successful will arise. He argues that doomsayers have been wrong before.[17] I could not agree more, Susan Bowman participated in the '95 Sunquest Trip to Kenya. Here is what she had to say afterwards:

> They say that, 'you can leave Africa but it never leaves you and now' I believe it! Perhaps the reason is that Kenya is a destination which is often associated with the threat of disease and potential crime. It is true that precautions are needed by taking the proper medication and being careful when walking about, however we were pleasantly surprised by the North American standards that we encountered ... the surroundings are like nothing you've ever seen! It is as if the world exploded with colour and animals and you're in the cage looking out. I've decided that paradise still exists. It is in Africa![18]

Experiential knowledge can neither be verified nor denied. However, Susan's experience, like many others, points to some hope. In any case, the law of nature and history are on Africa's side. They provide a strong basis for articulating a vision for the future of Africa.

A 'CRIME AND JUSTICE' VISION FOR AFRICA

Appalled by the denigrating poverty of my people, who live in a richly endowed land; distressed by their political marginalization and economic strangulation; angered by the devastation of their land, their ultimate heritage; *anxious to preserve their right to life and a decent living, and determined to usher into this country as a whole a fair and just democratic system which protects everyone and every ethnic group and gives us all a valid claim to human civilization,* I have devoted my intellectual and material resources, my very life, to a cause in which I have total belief and from which I cannot be blackmailed or intimidated (emphasis added).

These are the words with which Ken Saro-Wiwa closed his statement to the Nigerian military court that tried him in 1995. Although these words could not save him from being convicted and executed, they aptly capture the aspiration which I hold very dearly for Africa.[19] Recast in a crime and justice perspective, this aspiration means that I look forward to the reinvention of a safe and secure continent, a continent organized in such a way that every individual or group is afforded maximum opportunity to earn for themselves and their dependents a decent livelihood, the esteem which goes with that capacity and

---

[17] Chege, Michael, "What's Right with Africa?" *Current History* (May 1994).

[18] Bowman, Susan, "Greetings there and home again", Internet: http://www.jwg.com/land/kenya/KThere&Home.html.

[19] Whether Ken is a human rights martyr or a villain is beside the point here. The noble quality of the statement and the vision that it conveys is self-evident.

an equitable chance to fulfill their lawful aspirations of self-development in local and international contexts. Such opportunity is a tested antidote to crime and injustice.

A secure continent is not one without any crimes and injustices whatsoever. That would be an impossible dream to realize. However, it is one where criminality does not continue to escalate and justice does not fail at a rate that holds the people and their land to ransom. I dream of an Africa that will, in future:

– reduce risk factors and/or increase developmental factors in order to minimize criminal tendencies in individuals or groups,

– provide effective protection for life and property and minimize the threat of criminal victimization for the generality of the populace,

– become a place where nationals and visitors alike enjoy professional police services and receive a legitimate and accountable administration of justice which is just, transparent, broad based, and accessible to all irrespective of status,

– reclaim and reintegrate wayward members of its populations from criminality through appropriate correctional methods,

– foster a culture of fundamental rights, and

– attract productive interaction with the international community through mutual respect and social intercourse.

FUTURE DIRECTIONS: HOW TO FULFILL THE VISION

Realizing the vision for the future of Africa as outlined above will require the coming together of at least three very vital factors, namely: visionary leadership in a war against crime and injustice, philosophical shift in criminal Justice, and functional partnership against crime.[20] My investigations reveal that the current leaders of Africa have yet to seriously recognize the potential or, indeed, potency of these factors to counteract criminogeny and legal inequality.

Concerning leadership, Africa needs more than anything else: a new generation of educated or informed leaders able to build on the rubble that it has become, in terms of crime and injustice. These are leaders that are not only impassioned about a safe and secure Africa but also know what it will take to bring safety and security about. With regard to passion, such leaders (a) must be deeply concerned that in our continent, we have a very sick society, (b) must not yield to fatalism or be obsessed with pessimism, and (c) must be persuaded

---

[20] Sociological imagination bequeaths to us the wisdom that the transformation of social framework within which Africans can live, move and enjoy their being is equally, if not more, vital to the realization of our vision for the future of Africa. However, space prevents me from addressing this factor at this stage.

that to surrender the continent to the twin evils of crime and injustice will be an act of consummate betrayal. Fortified in these dispositions, these leaders will then approach the evils with the mind of a general going to war, a war to be planned, resourced and fought with everyone involved, including offenders, victims and whole communities.

In the early 1980s, General Buhari, as Nigeria's Head of State, declared war against indiscipline with some appreciable results, although his motives and methods remained partly questionable. In more recent times, President Mandela has called for war to be declared against violent crimes in South Africa. So, the idea of war against crime and injustice should not be foreign to Africa. Yet, the war for the future must be guided by leaders who have got the necessary heart and head working together. For our present purpose, the kind of leadership required is one that can:

– define a singular aim of building a continent safe to live in for everyone, free of violent crime and fear, and pervaded by a sense of fairness or justice for all,

– formulate a strategic agenda for a right war: i.e. a war that transcends the 'us' and 'them' syndrome in which criminals are on one side and law-abiding citizens are on the other; it should be a war against the forces that turn people against each other or foster deviance over compliance even with just laws and community norms,

– value and mobilize resources (material and human) of all extractions for this war, regardless of class or creed,

– be adept in adapting legislation to meet changing circumstances in a dynamic yet developmental fashion,

– rebuild and modernize judicial systems to facilitate prosecuting and public defense services, to cultivate judicial fearlessness and activism, and to enhance community participation, and

– devise and implement programs to deinstitutionalize corrections and turn prisons into restoration centers.

Even the most extraordinary leadership will fail to deliver all these expectations unless the justice system undergoes a fundamental philosophical shift from adversarial or retributive justice to restorative justice.[21] The former model of justice came with colonialism and supplanted the latter, which had predominated in most of Africa's systems of crime control and dispute resolution. After one century of using retributivism as the official criminal justice policy in Africa, it is evident from the preceding sections of this chapter that the crime and justice situation is nothing but a sorry tale of woes. The continent is littered

---

[21] This point has been fully illustrated in the work that I co-authored with Dr. Quentin Beresford called *Rites of Passage: Aboriginal Youth Crime and Justice*, Fremantle Arts Centre Press, Perth Australia, 1996.

with ruined lives and social relations, morbid fears of criminal victimization, and has become less attractive to positive international engagement.

Retributive justice is primarily negative and backward-looking. It does not consider causes and does not aim at solutions. Instead, it stigmatizes offenders for past actions, making social reintegration near impossible.[22] Its hierarchical, top-down strategy disempowers direct actors in criminal disputations and turns them into dependent entities whose worth consists mainly in their usefulness as witnesses. In these circumstances, it brutalizes individuals, alienates community, and perpetuates divisiveness.

On the other hand, the system that Africa had practiced for centuries prior to colonization was founded upon a 'horizontal method that puts emphasis on community involvement, reconciliation and healing, and is culturally appropriate – one which resonates with popular understanding'.[23] This system, referred to in modern literature as restorative justice, allows families of offenders and victims to bond, encourages community participation, prioritizes interpersonal harmony, applies appropriate denunciatory sanctions, and replaces vengeance with forgiveness, alienation with healing, punishment with education.[24]

As a philosophy of crime control and justice administration, retributive justice is irretrievably bankrupt and can offer next to nothing for the vision of the future Africa outlined in this chapter. In fact, most of the countries in the Western world where it currently predominates have been woefully let down in their fight against crime and injustice, and are now in search of another approach. Australia, Canada and New Zealand, for example, have started experimenting with a system built upon the cultural values of their indigenous populations, namely the Aborigines, American Indians, and Maoris respectively.[25]

The Africa of the future will have no reason to hold onto a crime and justice model that has not only dismally failed its present generations, but is also being jettisoned by those whose ancestors superimposed it on the continent in the first place. What the Western world is now turning to is the system that had served Africa well. Should the Africa of the future seek to re-enthrone the re-

---

[22] This was Howard Zehr's observation in his work, *Justice: the Restorative Vision, Mennonite Central Committee*, US Office of Criminal Justice, 1989.

[23] See Gluckman, Max, "Natural Justice in Africa" in *Comparative Legal Cultures*, Csaba Varga, ed., Aldershot, England, Dartmouth, 1992; Eden, Karen, "Traditional ways and Juvenile Justice: Synergy for a New System in South Africa". Internet: http://www.ac.za/depts/criminology/articles/tradl.htin.

[24] For a comparative analysis which shows the virtues of restorative justice over retributive justice, see Consedine, Jim, *Restorative Justice: Healing the Effects of Crime*, Ploughshares Publications, Lyttelton, New Zealand, 1995.

[25] See Braithwaite, John, *Crime, Shame and Reintegration*, Cambridge University Press, Cambridge, 1989; Hacklar, Jim, *Official Responses to Problem Juveniles: Some International Reflections*, the Onati International Institute for the Sociology of Law, Onati, 1991; Alder, Christine and Wundersitz, Joy, *Family Conferencing and Juvenile Justice: the Way Forward or Misplaced Optimism?*, Australian Institute of Criminology, Canberra, 1994; Hazlehurst, K., *Popular Justice and Community Regeneration: Pathways of Indigenous Reform*, Praeger Publishers, Westport, 1995.

storative justice system, it will not be dismissed as nostalgia for the dead past. Rather, it will be seen for what it is: a strategic diversion towards a system that focuses on solutions. Obviously, the institutional settings in which that system operated in 'traditional' Africa have changed over the years, but the organizing principle remains largely unfaltered. Further, given a long history of practising the system before the colonial interference, Africa will be dexterous in reviving and utilizing the model, and will be in the position to teach those parts of the world that are now searching for a truly effective crime and justice philosophy.

With appropriate leadership and philosophy in place, the next most vital element in translating my criminological vision for Africa into reality is the adoption of a partnership approach in the fight against crime and injustice. Simply put, this means discarding a fetishistic confidence in the criminal justice system as the only instrument to prevent crime and, instead, mobilizing entities that make communities work, such as religious organizations, social clubs, schools, employment agencies, health institutions, business groups, and formal justice agencies, to deal with crime holistically. This approach started gathering momentum in the developed world in the 1990s,[26] and indications are that it offers a viable alternative escape route out of an otherwise vicious circle of ineffective responses to crime.

Being part or a global village, Africa's partnership approach should have local and international dimensions. Let me draw examples from South Africa, a country currently with enormous opportunities for new initiatives, to illustrate this point. At the local level, the rising crime and the resulting distress and fear have led some churches in Johannesburg,[27] the country's business center, to engage in a four-week moral crusade against crime in the region. According to the Methodist Bishop, Peter Storey, the campaign was designed, *inter alia*, to encourage church members to help the police by forming local community policing groups and to 'adopt' police stations for prayer, resource and counseling support.

This program has potential not only to redeem a police force that had acted without accountability under apartheid, but also to mobilize the public to become more active in fighting crime in partnership with the police that they had generally distrusted. For instance, with a redeemed police image, residents would be more eager to alert the police about suspects trying to hide in their communities. Partnerships of this nature and those which focus on other aspects of crime prevention, form part of the way forward for Africa.

On the international plane, the joining of forces by South African and United Kingdom Universities to combat crime provides a useful example. The Univer-

---

[26] This is a trend that I have observed in one of my current research works, entitled "Justice-led Partnerships against Crime in Australia, Canada and New Zealand".

[27] These include the Methodist, Anglican, Roman Catholic, Congregational and Presbyterian Churches.

sity of Cape Town and the University of Newcastle-Upon-Tyne, have embarked on an extensive project for laying the foundations towards restructuring and upgrading the slums in Cape Town. These slums, dubbed as 'townships', were developed at the height of apartheid regime to serve as 'dormitories' for African workers on the peripheral areas of the main urban districts. Deprived of transport and other infrastructural networks, the townships became insular and turned into breeding grounds for violent crimes.

With funds provided by the British Overseas Development Administration (ODA), the project envisages that the townships will be linked with other residential communities and given the economic and social opportunities that they had been denied for so long. This is seen as a strategy for improving the quality of life and reducing the rate of crime in the townships. The implementation process involves the adoption of a multi-sectoral approach, drawing expertise from the public sector, private sector and community-based organizations. It is too early to tell what the outcome will be. Nonetheless, the project bears the hallmarks of a local-foreign partnership par excellence from which the Africa of the future can really benefit.

The essence of partnership at both levels is the pooling of resources, whether they are idea systems, material assets, practical know-how, or personnel, and the involvement of communities to build a broad-based constituency for crime prevention and justice administration. This should occur without creating a dependency syndrome, i.e. with no partner seeking to marginalize or disempower other partners but rather to value and share each other's resources into all phases of the partnership. While current international relations dictate that Africa be wary of would-be foreign benefactors, Africa has given so much (in human and natural resources) to the world community and should legitimately expect to receive some aid in return during its time of need. More significantly, a safe and secure Africa means a less dangerous world. International resourcing of this vision will therefore be well founded. But the miracle has to be home-grown.

CONCLUDING REMARKS

The theme of crime and justice gives joy to no one anywhere in the world. It represents the failure of social systems and reveals the dark side of human beings. As I was writing, this chapter in the lounge room of my house, a young man broke through my house, pulling down the blinds and terrifying my children. He was fleeing from a police officer who tried to stop him because he was driving without wearing his seat belt. Subsequent investigations revealed that this man has a serious criminal record and that he had just come out from jail on 'work release order'. The police officer gave me the opportunity to press charges against my victimizer, but I declined. Instead, based on my assessment of the potential for redemption in this man, I offered to provide support to keep him out of the criminal justice system. Needless to say, both intellectually and experimentally, 'crime and justice' is generally not an edifying subject.

I chose to bring a crime and justice perspective to bear on the subject of the future of Africa because I believe that the fate of Africa in the next century is now inextricably bound with how we deal with the reality and rhetoric of our crime problem and the corresponding systems of injustice. Most African countries seem to have been labeled with a 'crime and justice mark of Cain', throughout the world.

When the leaders in these countries:

- maim and kill each other and use justice agencies to carry out their nasty desires,

- implement policies that generate an army of street children, and

- convert the protection of life and property into a gigantic private security industry,

they unwittingly confirm this mark not only on the continent but also on Africans in the Diaspora. In so doing, they stigmatize the continent as a region of high risk to local and international business or social intercourse. The fact that our current justice system creates people who become a law unto themselves, further tends to alienate those who want to live or do business in Africa. Sadly, the following story is true of many countries:

> I have been sent to Sea Point Police Station, where I was beaten by civil servants. I have been to Polsmoor Prison, where I was sodomized and left bleeding on the cold damp floor. I have been to Places of Safety and Reformatories where I was hardened by warders and fellow inmates, where I learned to hold on to what was mine and take from those who could not fight. I am now the perpetrator of violence and not the victim. On the streets I am a law unto myself.[28]

However, the Africa of the future should not be a breeding ground for lawlessness. There is reason to hope that we can devise crime and justice superstructures that will form effective parts of the process of continent building rather than self-destruction. Africa has got the materials to provide the required leadership. The most effective crime control and justice administration model – the restorative model is part of our indigenous heritage. And the emerging attitude of self-reliance in response to declining development aid means that community mobilization and partnership, rather than dependency on foreign benefactors, will become the dominant paradigms by which we fashion our future. I am hopeful that a safe and secure Africa will come; if only the leaders of tomorrow can begin to take a stand now.

---

[28] Recounted by a young Cape Town shelter worker in Pinnock, Don, Skelton, Ann and Shapiro, Rosemary, "New juvenile justice legislation for South Africa: giving children a chance", Internet: http/www.ac.za/depts/criminology/articles/aart.htin

CHAPTER 14

Africa in the 21st Century: Prospects for Political Development

Hamdy Abdel Rahman

INTRODUCTION

Many researchers strongly believe that African politics is a mystery that is not properly understood because most of the theoretical proposals that attempted to explain political and governance issues in Africa have failed.[1] As a result, Africa is perceived as a continent of black shadows where events are difficult to explain.

There is no doubt that Africa is going through a structural crisis that Sadik Rasheed described as being "development's last frontier". Although other countries are competitive and looking forward to the new millennium, Africa has lagged behind to constitute the fourth world characterized by backwardness and marginalization.[2]

However, preoccupation with the present should not, at any time, blind a nation to its history and its future, since all dynamic nations must focus their attention on planning the future, which is the result of the interaction of its past and present. A nation loses its character if it does not recognize its history. And, it loses its present if it does not focus on its future. Therefore, we Africans must define our own vision of the future based on our culture, existence and our independent history. Unless our vision and the resulting program of reforms are harmonious with our cultures, there will be no development and advancement.[3]

This essay aims to analyze the prospects of African politics as we advance towards the 21st century. It takes the current trends and variables on both the international and African levels into account. The main challenge facing Africans as we approach the new millennium is whether we can overcome the negative attitudes in order to shift from crisis to a new era marked by infinite possibilities.

---

[1] Chabal, Patrick, *Power in Africa: An Essay in Political Interpretation*, St. Martin's Press, New York, 1992, pp. 315.

[2] Rasheed, Sadik, *Africa and Development's Last Frontier: What Prospects*? translated by Mustafa al-Gamaal, Center for Arab Studies, Cairo, 1995, p. 13 (in Arabic).

[3] For more details, see: Abdel-Rahman, Hamdy, *Pluralism and the Crisis of State-building in Africa*, Center for African Future Studies, Cairo, 1996 (in Arabic).

THE ALTERNATIVE PARADIGM AND THE ISSUE
OF UNDERSTANDING

There is no doubt that among Africans there is a crisis in the understanding of the current challenges facing the continent. This has led to a misunderstanding of current events and this is reflected in several publications on the future of Africa which tend to consist of advice and mere speculation and the extrapolation of current trends. The true beginning to creating a new Africa lies in the need to re-examine the history of Africa, its systems and cultures from an internal perspective after about four centuries of external domination.

The Europeans imposed their own vision of African culture on African people. This has made Africans perceive themselves through a European perspective. Europeans became our judges when we have divergent opinions and points of view. Therefore, there is a great need for a new knowledge paradigm that is based on Africa's own vision of its identity and culture. In this new paradigm, different socioeconomic, cultural and political issues should be examined, not in accordance with others' experiences or prejudices, but rather through the lens of history.

According to Chabal, the western analysis of the current situation has been affected by two patterns of studies.[4] The first pattern is represented by the new Malthusian movement that emerged in the 1970s. It attributes the destructive African crisis to the fact that population growth has surpassed its food production. Food production was sacrificed for the sake of export crops which would, in turn, cover the costs of imports, including food. The second viewpoint, although vague, adds an ecological dimension to the crisis. African farming has suffered from both environmental- and human-induced damage, resulting in the inability to achieve self-sufficiency and development.

The major problems linked to the western perception of Africa are manifested by the absence of a holistic analytical vision suitable for the understanding of the current African socio-political reality.

For example, post cold war economic liberalization policies that have become common in Africa have not had any significant success. On the contrary, these have faced strong criticism, represented in an intellectual framework that is known as the African Alternative for development.

DEMOCRATIZATION: FACTORS AND DIMENSIONS

Military systems and one-party rule have resulted in dictatorial political systems that have been characterized by irresponsible and oppressive leadership.

---

[4] Chabal, op. cit., see also: Ayittey, George B.N., *Africa Betrayed*, St. Martin's Press, New York, 1992.

This strengthened negative trends that have greatly damaged the African struggle towards achieving development and democracy. These trends include:[5]

The monopolization of power and the personalization of the political systems: This rendered various power struggles very violent, i.e. military coups, assassinations, and civil wars. African leaders were supposed to play a key role in building nation states. Instead, they sought to maintain their hold on power at any cost. This resulted in the development of the personal rule pattern, in which the leader becomes the center of the political system. Furthermore, one-party domination over the government has, in many areas, led to the emergence of dictatorial systems and personal leaderships that do not permit opposing views. Thus, African parties have relied upon violence and power instead of persuasion in gaining loyalty.

The absence of social justice, and unequal wealth distribution: In pluralistic societies, this led to negative results on the development of political systems after independence. It also led to a system in which loyalties dominated the political process rather than public interest. This resulted in various struggles for power. It is important to note that colonization created a small African elite, which is educated according to western thought. This elite, which later represented the pivot of the petit bourgeoisie in the years after independence, dominates economic and political powers in African societies.

After independence, western countries reinforced dependency on the western capitalist model by penetrating African societies through different methods. These include establishing special relations with the dominant local powers (landowners, business men, politicians, and officers). When necessary, western corporations have not hesitated to bribe local powers.

The deterioration of the economic situation: It has become clear to experts of African development that the crisis of development has started to threaten the very existence of Africa. After the failure of the developmental strategies adopted by the different political systems, some researchers described the 1980s as the lost decade of development in Africa. A review of African economies reveals some key features of the crisis.

The continued state of economic deterioration in the 1990s: According to the United Nations Economic Commission for Africa (ECA), African economies achieved a slight growth of 0.5% in 1990, 2.9% in 1991, -3% in 1992, 0.9% in 1993, and 2.4% in 1994. Average per capita income decreased by 1.6% annually during the first five years of the 1990s, which represents a faster decline than that of the 1980s.[6]

---

[5] See: Abdel-Rahman, Hamdy, *Political Corruption in Africa*, Dar al-Qarie al-Arabi, Cairo, pp. 44–50 (in Arabic).

[6] Rasheed, op. cit., p. 14, see also: Abdel-Rahman, Hamdy, *Democratization in Africa*, al-Siassa al-Dawliya (al-Ahram Foundation, Cairo), No. 113, July, 1993, pp. 8–22 (in Arabic).

The extraordinary increase in foreign indebtedness and the interests on those debts: For example, the analysis of the increase in debt indicates that the total sum of the African debt increased from US$176 billion in 1982 to US$296 billion in 1992.[7]

Most African countries are currently implementing Structural Adjustment Programs (SAP) at the behest of the World Bank and the International Monetary Fund. These programs focus on achieving a financial balance, making prices realistic, and liberalizing the economy. However, the experience of the 1980s and 1990s clearly shows that adjustment programs were not designed for achieving these goals. This has resulted in severe socio-economic damage.[8]

The undemocratic nature of post-colonial African states and the brutality of all-powerful leaders led to severe economic deterioration and deprivation for Africans. The principal concern of these leaders and the ruling class is to maintain their hold on power and to accumulate wealth at the expense of citizens. This has resulted in embezzlement by which billions of dollars were illegally transferred from public coffers to private accounts in foreign banks.

THE SECOND STAGE OF INDEPENDENCE OR OCCUPATION

We understand events by the context in which they occur. In this case, one can state that there is a relationship between the end of the Cold War and a series of developments that came to be called the "democratization wave in Africa".

The effect of political conditionality, including pluralistic democracy, is clear on the democratization process that has been witnessed in many parts of Africa since the 1980s.[9] Nevertheless, the democratization taking place in Africa today is not just a reaction to changes which have been witnessed by the world since the collapse of the USSR. We cannot ignore the yearning and striving of Africans for democracy for over a century. The West, however, did not acknowledge these strivings because they contradicted their imperialistic interests in Africa. It was not uncommon for western powers to describe the strivings for democracy as ethnic conflicts, acts of social violence, or even as a collapse of the political systems. Thus, it is not what is in Africa that has changed, but rather how the world sees and recognizes what happened.

The key question concerning democratization is how suitable liberal democracy is for Africa. Shivgi assumed that liberal democracy is part of the

[7] *Africa at a Glance*, 1995/6, Africa Institute of South Africa, Pretoria, 1995, p. 51. For more details about the debt crisis and its political ramifications in Africa, see, in particular: Onimode, Bade, *A Future for Africa: Beyond the Politics of Adjustment*, Earthscan Publications, London, 1992, Chapter 3.

[8] Uzodike, Ufo Okede, "Democracy and Economic Reforms: Developing Underdeveloped Political Economics", *JAAS*, XXXI, 1–2, 1996, pp. 21–37.

[9] Hamed, Mohammed Bashir, "The African Debate: Democratization and Conditionality", paper presented at the AAPS Biannual Congress: Africa in the Post Cold War Period, Dar-es-Salaam, Tanzania, 18–21 January, 1993.

ideology of domination in Africa, and is primarily to justify the compradory rule and give it a sense of wisdom.[10]

The vision takes African history into account as an integrated whole, imposes the need for congruence between the suggested political system that is to be applied in an African state and the culture, traditions, and ambitions of the African peoples. If this system is not realized, then the political system will be destined to failure, as was the case in Eastern Europe and Africa.

Africans are communal by nature. They have a natural tradition for democracy, and decision-making is based on consensus. The role of the traditional chief was not to arbitrarily make laws. His role was also to unify his people. An African saying states that the president becomes a president through his people, and a people become a people through their president.[11]

The state of flux and change that Africa is witnessing today is not sufficient because democratization is still in its primary stages. O'Donnell and Shmitter believe it is possible to distinguish between two qualitative stages in the democratization process. The first stage is the change to liberalism, and the second is a change towards democracy.[12]

It is safe to state that based on experience, the shifts from dictatorial regimes in many parts of Africa to political liberalism may eventually lead to either a democratic regime or to another form of despotism. Therefore, it should be emphasized that the change towards political liberalism in Africa will not necessarily lead to a full-fledged democracy, which entails the development of three dimensions:

The dimension entailing values and cultures: This dimension views democracy as a higher value that includes liberty, equality, and justice. This suggests the enhancement and spreading of democratic values in society.

The institutional dimension: This is the transformation of values and concepts into institutions, structures, and public facilities. This takes place within the framework of a general consensus on the rules of the political game.

The executive dimension: Political conflicts are resolved through a competitive peaceful approach. Free elections are considered to be the democratic instrument that can achieve political balance and consistency in society.

The aforementioned processes of democratization are different in Africa, form-wise and content-wise. Some countries have followed the national conference approach, whereas other countries such as Zambia under Kenneth

---

[10] A number of African intellectuals believe that the IMF and the West in general are imposing a false and externally dependent form of democracy in Africa. See, for example: Ake, Claude, *Democracy and Development in Africa*, Brookings Institute, Washington DC, 1996, pp. 130–31; and Abdel-Rahman, *Democratization in Africa*, op. cit., pp. 9–10.

[11] Potholm, Christian P., *The Theory and Practice of African Politics*, Prentice-Hall, Englewood Cliffs, NJ, 1972, p. 25.

[12] O'Donnell, Guillermo, et al. (eds), *Transitions from Authoritarian Rule: Prospects for Democracy*, Johns Hopkins University Press, Baltimore and London, 1986.

Kaunda have resorted to conducting political reform through changing the practices of the political center. However, some cases in Africa happened to witness a violent change towards democracy through civil and military disobedience, as in the case of Ethiopia.

Nevertheless, it is important to note that the majority of African states have taken the necessary constitutional and legal measures to enhance political liberalism. Some of these measures include:[13]

- the right to form parties,

- the freedom to join political parties, and

- providing equal opportunities to parties to present their programs to the citizens using the government-owned media.

Despite these measures, some social groups are prohibited from participating in this process of change. For example, Islamic movements were banned from participation in North Africa; this also applies to other movements that are based on regional and tribal interests.

If we examine the Egyptian experience, we find that the political leadership has sought to control the process of political change. This has been occurring since the mid-1970s. There have been several political restrictions on establishing political parties. One prohibits the formation of political parties based on class, religion, or discrimination. Political parties are also prohibited from having links with foreign political groups.

In addition, any new party must obtain permission from the party committee, a semi-governmental authority. Some African states such as Sudan and Uganda have refused political pluralism, since in their view it does not suit the social variation in Africa. These countries conducted elections in the absence of legitimate political parties. Furthermore, other African states limited the number of licensed political parties. For instance, pluralistic elections were conducted in Nigeria with the participation of only two parties in 1993. The results were eventually annulled. The 1992 Djibouti's constitution states that the number of licensed parties should not exceed four.

The previous analysis leads to an important question: Is it possible to achieve political development in Africa in the light of these limitations?

In fact, the exclusion of some social groups from participation weakens the foundations of the state and affects negatively the concept of citizenship. Examples are the Christians in southern Sudan, the Tutsis in Rwanda/Burundi, and the Whites of South Africa.

The experience of the 1980s and 1990s assumes that most political systems have become increasingly open. Nevertheless, a large amount of credibility and

---

[13] See: Abdel-Rahman, Hamdy. "Multiparty Elections in Africa", paper presented at a conference on Parliamentary Elections in the South, Center for Developing Countries, Cairo University, Cairo, 3 July 1995.

good intentions are necessary to build a truly democratic system. This is only possible if political parties participate actively in the political process, guaranteeing a respect for the law which, in turn, will allow a new foundation for citizenship and legitimacy in Africa.

CHALLENGES AND FUTURE PROSPECTS

Africa was one of the most marginalized areas of the world during the Cold War. The changes witnessed since the end of the Cold War and the advent of the New World Order resulted in the further marginalization of Africa.[14] It is clear that despite the unprecedented technological and scientific revolutions (space exploration, the information revolution, and the use of computers), Africa has been absent from the fore. Ali Mazrui best summarized the situation by saying, "while Africa has been marching towards independence, others have walked on the moon".[15]

Africa, which is rich in natural and human resources, suffers today from practical chaos, deteriorating economies, and socio-structural collapse. This has contributed to forming a tragic image of the continent also known as "Afropessimism". If we want to create a realistic vision for the next century we, as Africans should define our vision according to what we want. We should avoid enthusiasm and emotion in explaining events. It is not a disgrace to admit our mistakes. However, we should establish our priorities in a clear manner and stop blaming the West for all our problems. Only lazy societies hold their neighbors responsible for their own mistakes.

The economic challenge

All economic models implemented in Africa have failed to achieve their stated goals. The development policies carried out by African political regimes of various ideological orientations paved the way for policies of structural adjustment.[16] However, it should be known that adjustment programs are not a magical cure. Many of the countries that have applied these programs are faced with economic depressions, political instability, and social conflicts. Poverty, drug use, prostitution, AIDS and crime have all increased in many parts of the continent. Consequently, adjustment programs have been strongly criticized.[17]

---

[14] Callaghy. Thomas, "Africa: Back to the Future?" *Journal of Democracy*, 5, 4 (October 1994), pp. 133–35.

[15] Mazrui, Ali, "Towards the Year 2000", in *General History of Africa VII*, Ali Mazrui. ed., Heinemann, UNESCO, California, 1993, p. 929.

[16] Uzodike, op. cit., pp. 21–24.

[17] Onimode, op. cit., Rasheed, op. cit. See also: Adepoju, Aderanti, *The Impact of Structural Adjustment on the Population of Africa*, James Currey, London, 1993: and Schatz, Sayre, "Structural Adjustment in Africa: A Failing Grade So Far", *Journal of Modern African Studies*, 32, 1994.

The policies of structural adjustment aim to establish economic systems dependent upon a free market by minimizing the role of the state. However, this does not suit Africa. The move towards economic liberalism requires a strong state, an efficient bureaucracy, and an effective banking system. However, African states are presently described as being soft states which are enamored of internal struggles. Therefore, is it possible to compare the African states in this fragile condition to European states when they began to change towards the free market economy?

Although some have attempted to say that structural adjustment policies are not ideological, on the contrary, it is increasingly clear that international financial firms support the creation of a world capitalist system.

It is clear that adjustment policies caused great harm to human development in Africa. The World Bank has recognized this fact and admitted that there is an urgent need to minimize the suffering of poor people who are the losers during adjustment programs.

As we move into the 21st century, it is clear that the African State is the cause of the disease, and not the cure. This condition is best summarized by a traditional leader in Lesotho: "We have two problems: rats and government". All African political regimes have been characterized by placing political and economic power in the hands of the government. This has led to abuse of power, lack of respect for human rights, falsification of elections, and transforming political systems into one-man dictatorships. The fact of the matter is that absolute power leads to corruption.

Therefore, there is no choice for Africa but to achieve self-autonomy. African problems should be resolved in Africa and not in the World Bank.

The intellectual and strategic basis for the African revolution has been available since 1980, when the African leaders approved the Lagos Plan of Action to develop Africa by the year 2000. The implementation of this plan requires a strong political will and a number of political, social and economic actions to confront the marginalization of Africa. Africa could begin the 21st century as a strong partner in the international community if the wherewithal is found by African leaders to implement the Lagos Plan of Action.

The security and stability challenge

Africa suffers from protracted conflicts with devastating effects. There is no doubt that the absence of peace and stability contributes to the marginalization of Africa. We will not be capable of creating a desirable future for Africa in the next century unless Africa is able to achieve security.

---

[18] Abou, Mahmoud, "Africa and Current Changes in the World Order", in *Egypt and Africa: Historical Background of Contemporary African Crises*, Conference book published by the General Egyptian Book Organization, Cairo, 1966, pp. 300–307 (in Arabic).

The starting point for the political resolution of the problems, which are connected to the issue of peace and stability in Africa, is understanding their causes. Conflicts in Africa have been protracted and socially complex.[18] They are also usually connected to the cultural differences of the warring parties. The main characteristic of these conflicts is that they are commonly employed as tools and strategies to resolve disagreements which, for the most part, cannot be resolved militarily. These conflicts are negative zero-sum games because all parties tend to suffer. In this sense, there are no winners in conflicts since all parties lose in one way or another.

The experience of the world order has added new characteristics and dimensions to these conflicts. It tends to increase the chaos and intensity of conflicts. This, in turn, led to the collapse of the state as a central institution, as was the case in Liberia, Somalia, and Rwanda. On the other hand, these conflicts intensified during the wave of democratization witnessed in many African countries. A clear example is Burundi. After the democratic elections, the elected president was assassinated on 21 October 1993.

We can view the situation in the Sudan as a microcosm of Africa in many ways.[19] The Sudan is made up of 579 tribes speaking more than 400 languages and dialects. They practice various religious rituals in the frameworks of Islam, traditional religions, and Christianity.

The Sudan has one of the worst air and land communications systems in the world. Although the Sudan has many human and natural resources such as petroleum, it suffers from a protracted economic crisis to the extent that it is in danger of collapsing.

Since 1955 there has been a long civil war in the south that neither party can win by force. The north cannot govern the south by the use of force, while the south will not give up its desire for autonomy or independence. The real cause of the conflict is related to the issue of organizing relations between the south and the central authority.

Thus, based on historical facts and the characteristics of the Sudan, the correct way to deal with the conflict is through a comprehensive vision for political reform that includes such issues as the form of the state, distribution of resources, and the variety of cultures. This would have to be done without any party trying to resolve any controversial issue unilaterally. Peaceful negotiations within the framework of a national conference would be the best option given the nature of the conflict.

Some might easily conclude that ethnic diversity in Africa is the cause of conflicts in the continent. It is clear that identity and ethnic solidarity contribute to creating a basis for a distinction between groups. The distinction is based

---

[19] For more details, see: Abdel-Rahman, Hamdy, "The Crisis of South Sudan", in *Egypt and Africa*, ibid., pp. 189–229.

on concepts of common interest and the ties of "we", "them", "internal" and "external". These ties restrict the chances of security and life for individuals and ethnic groups in competitive situations. Nevertheless, ethnicity is not an evil in itself, since it can be looked upon as moral competition. The variety of cultures has surely broadened the scope of many Africans and the positive aspect of ethnic diversity can be harnessed for development.

With regard to political interaction, there are several mechanisms available to avoid the negative effects of multi-ethnicity, such as federation and consociational democracy. Switzerland and other multilingual and multicultural countries have appropriate strategies to deal with the complexity of communicating in different languages.

However, the responsibility for confronting this challenge should be borne primarily by the African states. Each state should resolve to remove the major causes of conflict and instability.

THE DECLINE OF CIVIL SOCIETY

In many African states, it is increasingly evident that the institutions of civil society are fragile and ineffective. There is no doubt that these institutions, including labor unions, intellectual groups, student organizations, business societies, and places of worship, play a pivotal role in defending the special interests of their groups and confronting the domination of despots.[20]

The spread of a civil society culture in Africa remains the key factor that could prevent the further rise of despotic leaders. This can only be achieved through interference, representing its members in government, exerting external pressure through demonstration, lobbying and civil disobedience. In addition, these institutions can help spread the values of democracy and citizens sensitize to civil and political rights.

The call to support civil society in Africa should not be perceived as contributing to the weakness of the state. It will actually enhance the state through the improvement of state-society relations. Activating the interest groups and promoting the participation of social groups (especially farmers' groups), are key steps in the strengthening of the state.

Experiences in post-colonial Africa prove that the collapse of the economy and loss of legitimacy of state institutions led to awkwardness in state-society relations. The economic crisis weakens the state, meaning that the state becomes incapable of organizing the society and of executing policies efficiently.

The state apparatus in Africa, with all its administrative inefficiencies and scarce revenue, has helped to create a wide gap between the expectations and

---

[20] Harbeson, John W., et al. (eds), *Civil Society and the State in Africa*, Lynne Rienner Publishers, Boulder and London, 1994; and Woods, Dwayne, "Civil Society in Europe and Africa: Limiting State Power through a Public Sphere", *African Studies Review* 35, 2, September 1992.

the achievements of the political system. It is clear that when society-state relations become tense, the state resorts to the use of suppressive means and transforms itself into a despot. This reduces the state's legitimacy, and thus it becomes an alien institution to the people.

The civil-military relations dilemma

One common occurrence in African politics during the post-independence period is the military coup d'état. African military men became politicized and they represent the most important impediment to democratization. A realistic view ensures feedback between the civil regimes and the military regimes in post-independence Africa.[21]

There are different views with regard to creating an acceptable pattern of civil-military relations that suits the African framework. There have been some voices calling for the need to neutralize the military institution according to the western pattern of development, where the military is looked upon as a pressure group that influences the regime to achieve their group interests. This point of view was expressed in the 1990 Benin national conference when the Chief of the Armed Forces announced the importance of keeping soldiers apolitical.

However, some researchers have suggested the diarchy idea between the military and civilians for the treatment of military interference in authority, since it would be impossible to count the military out of the political forum. This idea seems to be gaining acceptance in a number of African countries. The Nigerian experience during the regime of Ibrahim Babangida (1985–93) is an example.[22]

There is no doubt that legitimizing the state, achieving economic growth, and building confidence in socio-structural relations will represent the foundations of good governance in Africa.

WHAT ARE THE PROSPECTS?

The following question has not yet been answered: Is it possible to transform these challenges into African opportunities? In other words, can we surpass the current crisis and move into the stage of possibilities? In order for Africa to transcend the multiple crises facing the continent, we must democratize, improve our governance structures, encourage unity, cooperation and build integrity. These issues are explored in the following sub-sections.

---

[21] See: Abdel-Rahman, Hamdy, *Military and Government in Africa*, Center for African Future Studies, Cairo, 1997 (in Arabic).

[22] Nyangoro, "Critical Notes on Political Liberalization in Africa", *JAAS*, op. cit., pp. 121–22; and Agbese, Pita Ogaba, "The Military as an Obstacle to the Democratization Enterprise: Towards an Agenda for Permanent Military Disengagement for Politics in Nigeria", *JAAS*, op. cit., pp. 82–83.

Supporting the democracy-development relation

In the post Cold War period, Africa has witnessed a renaissance of democracy, which includes the establishment of stable political regimes and respect for human rights. According to President F. Chiluba of Zambia "The people will learn that democracy is their own creation, and that they don't have to destroy their own baby".[23]

In the light of the absence both of human and social dimensions in the structural adjustment policies that were imposed on many African states since the beginning of the 1980s, success has become something extraordinary in the African experience. Therefore, there is a need to search for an African substitute for structural adjustment that depends on four pillars. These are food self-sufficiency, fulfillment of basic needs which will eradicate poverty, people's participation in the development process in its comprehensive sense to achieve unity, democracy and development, and the realization of African integrity, integration and commonwealth.

The ruling elite holding onto power in some African states fears the outcome of pluralistic democracy. Therefore, the elite gives different insights and explanations that allow them to continue in power as long as possible. In the Ugandan model, President Yoweri Museveni sees no-party democracy as the best model for Africa in this transitional stage. The one-party system has proven to be a failure in Africa, and multi-partyism has been linked to the re-emergence of tribal, ethnic, and geographical loyalties. President Museveni explains his strategic choice by providing a simile where he likens human societies to a butterfly that goes through a metamorphic process in its life cycle. The butterfly starts as an egg, changes to a larva, a pupa, and finally becomes a butterfly. All western societies have gone through these historical changes, whereas African societies are still lagging behind.[24]

No one can argue for the one-party system. However, is it necessary for African states to adopt multi-partyism and free market principles without regard to their own internal circumstances?

Whatever is the case, we need to encourage a debate within African scientific societies to discuss the issues of change and development in Africa. This will eventually lead to the development and application of the African alternative model for a comprehensive development. Nevertheless, there are some basic principles of governance that must be adhered to.

---

[23] Callaghy, Thomas, "Civil Society and Economic Change in Africa: A Dissenting Opinion about Resurgent Societies", in *Civil Society and the State in Africa*, op. cit., p. 238.

[24] Abdel-Fatah, Nermeen, "The African Model of Democracy", *al-Ahram* (Al-Ahram Foundation, Cairo, Egypt), February 25, 1997, p. 5 (in Arabic).

The principles of good governance

The responsibility for the continuity of democratization should be borne by African society, its different sectors and institutions. The three-dimensional equation, which links democracy, accountability and development, pushes towards the establishment of a good pattern for governing systems. This does not mean the imposition of a particular pattern of government, for African society has its own cultural and historical characteristics that must inform any political systems designed to transform Africa in the next century.

Given the diversity of African countries and the history of despotic leaders, governance systems in Africa must emphasize the values of forgiveness and power sharing. In addition, they must be based on the consociational system rather than despotic principles and the Anglo-American model of the "winner takes all".

Besides the theoretical controversy dealing with the best electoral system (i.e. proportional vs. representational), there should be a number of standards in order to suit the pluralism of African societies:[25]

- The electoral system should represent the will of the voters and not just a majority of them.

- The system should encourage the participation of voters in the political process. When voters feel that they can be effective, they usually attempt to act within the framework of the existing system rather than supporting illegal organizations and parties that came into being as a result of social instability.

- Support reconciliation and tolerance instead of arousing existing conflicts. This does not mean to impose a reconciliation policy, but rather it focuses on the mutual recognition of opposing views and accepting the other side.

- Emphasize the principle of accountability. The electoral system must strengthen the principle of accountability.

- Support nationalist parties. It is clear that the ability of the electoral system to achieve peace and stability increases when the political parties depend on nationalism that is linked to societal values and political principles rather than depending on ethnic and regional allegiances.

Therefore, if elections are to help in determining political legitimacy and creating political balance, it is important to have an independent electoral committee to manage the elections, accept international supervision and hand over the role of oversight and monitoring of institutions to civil society organizations. Moreover, it is necessary to encourage ongoing national dialogue between all the parties in order to lay a firm and stable foundation for the political process.

---

[25] Reynolds, Andrew, "Constitutional Engineering in Southern Africa", *Journal of Democracy* 6, 1 April 1995, pp. 97–98.

Supporting unity, cooperation, and integrity

What calls for optimism while we are at the threshold of the 21st century is the fact that the African struggle for liberty, unity, and democracy has succeeded in some cases. With the decolonization of many parts of Africa, particularly in the 1960s, there has been a will to achieve unity at the continental level. This was represented in many instances of the institutionalization of the pan-African movement. Indeed, on 25 May 1963, the Organization of African Unity (OAU) was established. Moreover, the African struggle against colonization and racial discrimination was successful.

In the field of regional economic cooperation, some economic groups have managed to survive. In many cases, they have represented their member states in international and regional negotiations. The most prominent examples are:
- Arab Maghreb Union in North Africa (AMU)
- Economic Community of West African States (ECOWAS)
- Southern African Development Community (SADC)
- Common Market for Eastern and Southern Africa (COMESA)

Because of SADC, it is now possible to make a phone call between Luanda and Maputo without having to go through Portugal. Does this not reflect Africa's ability to achieve, and its determination to depend upon itself? [26]

The most dangerous element that can increase the marginalization of Africa is the collapse of the state as a central institution. The experience of international intervention in Somalia and Rwanda has shown that the achievement of stability and peace in Africa is Africa's concern. Therefore, one of the positive elements in the establishment of pan-African organizations is the possibility for a new conflict resolution mechanism.[27] This is due to renewed interest in preventive diplomacy. It is our belief that Africa has no choice but to activate this mechanism and support it with all the necessary political will.

The dilemma of the internal-external relation

Despite the fact that overcoming the current crisis in Africa and putting an end to its marginalization is Africa's responsibility, this does not rule out the responsibility of the international community. Denial of an international role is utopian thinking. Claude Ake, a distinguished Nigerian intellectual, says:

> The marginalization of Africa in the world economy which we lament is actually an opportunity for putting back development where it belongs, into the hands of Africans... what it calls for is a democratic agenda to press home the need for 'a second

---

[26] *Africa at a Glance*, op. cit., p. 61.

[27] See: Abou, Mahmoud, *African Regional Security*, Institute of African Research and Studies, Cairo University, Cairo, Egypt, 1994 (in Arabic).

[28] Cited in Callaghy, *Africa: Back to the Future*, op. cit., p. 142.

independence' from the autocratic incompetence of the indigenous elite... what is needed now is to create these conditions, seizing as we can the limited opportunities on offer, including the marginalization of Africa.[28]

The main idea in Ake's, as well as other African intellectuals', reasoning is the fact that Africa must take its future into its own hands. This does not exclude the importance of external variables and actors. Africa's and the other southern states' principal demand is the need to establish a New World Order that should depend on collective security and a common fate.

Based on this belief, the West should stop attempting to recolonize Africa by imposing policies and programs that do not take African initiatives into consideration. In this regard, the international community can contribute to ending the marginalization of Africa in various ways by reducing the debts of Africa, encouraging African initiatives that emphasize self-dependence and development, cutting assistance to despotic regimes in Africa, and supporting democratization that ensures genuine public participation.

A VISION FOR THE FUTURE

The prospects of political development in Africa outlined above stem from a realistic and not an ideological vision. The pessimistic scenario that dominates Africa's future exacerbates the current crisis by depriving Africans of their self-confidence. On the other hand, the aim is not to be unnecessarily optimistic, as this might lead into false illusion.

The proposed scenario for Africa is the virtual state model, in which the state reflects the will of the common African. To realize this new vision, Africans should concentrate their resources and strengths on instituting a true, participatory democracy and equitable development.

To be sustainable, this new state system must depend upon the following basic characteristics:

Firstly, the political relationship between the ruler and the ruled should depend upon a democratic foundation in accordance with the principle of power sharing. There is no doubt that Africans will prefer this system of governance which reflects their true belief in the non-validity of conflict and power sharing.

Secondly, the raison d'être of the state should be to serve the interests of the African people and not external ones by aiming at improving the living conditions of the people. By so doing, it will concentrate on developing the human resources and the people.

Thirdly, there must be a real commitment to regional cooperation, which implies the willingness of the state to surrender some amount of sovereignty in social and economic spheres to regional bodies.

This scenario for political development in Africa in the coming decades highlights what might occur if the virtual state model is adopted. It envisions that the international community will respect the African will and also provide the necessary support for transition. Unfortunately, there are still some elements that will resist and pose a challenge to the proposed model. These elements include rebel groups and irresponsible political leaders. However, the outcome of the process is dependent on the commitment to the principle of regional cooperation.

CONCLUSION

This essay reveals that Africa is entering the next century facing many challenges. It can be said that Africa is fighting to survive. If we want to transform these problems into creative energies and possibilities, we must make use of strategic thinking and exploit the available resources. In addition, we must be armed with a clear and motivational vision of what we want Africa to become in the 21st century. The African scientific elite and intellectuals must take up the responsibility for presenting this vision and participating actively in solving the crisis of understanding. Scientific research conducted by African scientists is greatly needed in light of outside misconceptions about the African reality.

The future of Africa will neither be tragic nor a return to the 19th century as predicted by doomsday experts. The crises in countries such as Liberia, Angola, the Sudan, Rwanda, and the Democratic Republic of the Congo (Zaire) led to the existence of the Hobbesian "war of all against all" pattern of sovereignty. The failure of economic reform in many parts of Africa represents nightmare scenarios. Nevertheless, we should view these events as negative trends. We should try to limit their effects and maximize the effects of the positive trends of democracy, unity, and economic integration in Africa. Only this will permit us to transform the multiple crises into possibilities.

CHAPTER 15

Visions of the Future of Africa: A South African Perspective

André Wessels

> *Will the New Century be greeted*
> *by a Golden Dawn or an Endless Night?*
> *Now is the time to ask.*
>
> Clem Sunter, 1992[1]

THE AFRICAN CONTEXT

It is easy to become a victim of Afro-pessimism. One need only examine the situation prevailing in so many parts of our continent: population explosion, drought, food shortages and famine, economic decline, a crumbling infrastructure, war and conflict, the debt burden, the refugee problem, urbanization, crime, and military regimes.[2] Many African countries do not have efficient armed forces capable of defending their countries' sovereignty.[3] To cap it all, there is the scourge of AIDS.[4]

Scott Petersen, the East African correspondent of the Daily Telegraph, stated that Africa "has suffered regular visits of the Four Horsemen of the Apocalypse: War, Famine, Pestilence and Death".[5] According to Petersen, the end of the Cold War heralded an era of optimism with respect to peace and democracy in Africa. Unfortunately, the optimism soon evaporated and more blood-

---

[1] Sunter, Clem, *The New Century: Quest for the High Road*, RA. Gallo and Company (Pty) Limited, s.l., 1992, p. 34. Clem Sunter became head of scenario planning at the Anglo-American Corporation – South Africa's largest company – in the early 1980s. He helped in the development of the classic "high road" and low road" scenarios, has written many books on this subject and related matters, and has addressed a total of more then 100,000 people on numerous lecture tours. Sunter primarily addresses South Africa's problems and future, but in this contribution his ideas are applied to Africa's condition.

[2] As far as the role of the military in Africa is concerned, see e.g. W.F. Gutteridge, *Military Régimes in Africa*, Methuen and Co. Ltd., London, 1975.

[3] As far as Africa's military strength, or lack of it, is concerned, see *The Military Balance 1996/97*, The International Institute for Strategic Studies, London, 1996, pp. 128–131, 139–142, 148, 235–270 and Sharpe, Richard (editor), *Jane's Fighting Ships 1996–97*, Jane's Information Group Ltd., Coulsdon, s.a.

[4] See e.g. Grove, A.T., The Changing Geography of Africa, 2nd edition, Oxford University Press, Oxford, 1993, pp. 206–227.

[5] Petersen, Scott, "Keeping the Four Horsemen at Bay", *The Natal Mercury*, 2.1.1995, p. 7. Article reprinted from *The Telegraph*, London.

shed and pain followed. He identifies "bad leadership, and the growing reluctance of Western donors to attach human rights and good governance conditions to aid" as the roots of Africa's problems.[6]

Small wonder, then, that there are those who refer to Africa as the ghetto of the world.[7] The socioeconomic crisis in Africa is perceived as irreversible and many states are politically disintegrating. In some countries, the rift between the central government and the population is widening; in certain regions, ethnic boundaries are more important than the (often artificial) political borders inherited from the colonial era. After all, there are few, if any, functional nation-states in Africa.

Furthermore, the creation of states seems to have failed in Africa; and there seems to be a total lack of civil responsibility in many countries.[8] But then, of course, one could argue that during the colonial era, societies in Africa were disrupted by foreign intervention, and that in many instances African indigenous traditions were replaced by the alien idea of the nation state. "Africa lost its past and was denied a future".[9] Professor Joseph Maitha's statement made in 1979, that Africans cannot go on blaming the colonialists eternally for all their problems, needs to be kept in mind because the colonialists set up the system, but the Africans were unable to change it.[10]

In the light of the above-mentioned problems, there are academics, politicians and others who are thinking in terms of what many other people regard as the "unthinkable", namely recolonizing Africa. Those individuals place humanitarian needs above national sovereignty, and regard the United Nations (UN) as an important role-player. Over the years, Africa has increasingly come under the tutelage of external powers like the World Bank and the International Monetary Fund (IMF).[11] Could this be the beginning of the third scramble for Africa, after the first scramble for colonies by European powers in the nineteenth century, and the neo-colonial scramble for control over Africa by the superpowers during the Cold War?

As an African, albeit a white African, I cannot agree with everything that the prophets of doom have to say about my continent. After all, my future lies in Africa, and I am attempting to contribute towards the reconstruction, development and transformation of my part of Africa. Luckily, I am not alone in my optimism and my efforts to fight Afro-pessimism and all the negative perceptions that so many people have of my continent and its peoples.

---

[6] Ibid.

[7] Van Rijckevorsel, Rene, "Africa: Getto van de Wereld", *Elsevier*, 16.7.1994, p. 29.

[8] Ibid., pp. 29–30

[9] Colborne, Desmond, "Recolonising Africa: The Right to Intervene?", *South Africa International* 23(4), April 1993, p. 163.

[10] Lamb, David, *The Africans*, Methuen, London, 1987, p. vii.

[11] Colborne. p. 162. See also Paul Johnson, "De Kolonie was zo Gek nog niet: Alleen maar Interveniéren heeft voor Afrika geen Zin", *Elsevier*, 16.7.1994, p. 36.

Take for example the book entitled *The Lie of the Land: Challenging Received Wisdom on the African Environment,* in which the authors challenge many of the stereotypical images associated with the African environment. They argue, *inter alia*, that images of famine and environmental mismanagement in Africa which have helped to shape the attitude of many Westerners towards the continent, "are inaccurate and may actually perpetuate much of the suffering they are meant to alleviate".[12] These thought-provoking findings include the views that the Sahara desert is not advancing relentlessly, but that its boundaries fluctuate naturally; that parts of West Africa are undergoing an increase in the number of trees (in some instances, the higher the population, the more trees are planted, and where trees are felled, this is usually not done to obtain firewood but to clear the land for agriculture). That is not to say that there are no environmental problems in Africa, but the problems must be seen in the right perspective.[13] Even the IMF is cautiously optimistic about future economic growth in Africa, and democracy is gradually being consolidated throughout the continent.[14]

WHAT FUTURE FOR AFRICA?

But how do I see the future of my continent over the course of 30 years, i.e., up to the year 2026? In the light of the dramatic changes that have taken place over the past few years, many South Africans are wrestling to come to terms with their past, but are also keenly debating the future. Planning the future is obviously of the utmost importance in all walks of life, especially in business. The larger the business, the higher the stakes, and the more essential scenario planning becomes.

In my assessment of Africa's future, I shall freely adopt many of Clem Sunter's ideas about scenario planning and the future, as summarized in his publication, "The New Century: Quest for the High Road", applying his ideas to the African situation in general.[15]

According to Sunter, scenario planning sets out from the premise that the future is not what it used to be.[16] He points out that should developing coun-

---

[12] Neale, Greg, "The Lies about Africa", *Sunday Times*, 27.10.1996, p. 16. Article reprinted from *The Telegraph*, London.

[13] Ibid.

[14] Trench, Andrew, "In Africa, things need not always fall apart", *Sunday Times*, 10. 11. 1996. p. 10.

[15] See also the first footnote in this chapter. Those interested in acquiring a more detailed knowledge of and insight into Sunter's ideas, should consult, *inter alia*, the following publications by him: *The Casino Model*, Tafelberg/Human and Rousseau, Cape Town, 1994; *Pretoria will Provide and Other Myths*, Tafelberg/Human and Rousseau, Cape Town, 1994; *South African Environments into the 21st Century* (co-authored by Brian Huntley and Rov Siegfried). Human and Rousseau/Tafelberg, Cape Town, 1989; and *The High Road: Where are we Now?*, Tafelberg/Human and Rousseau, Cape Town, 1996.

[16] Sunter, *The New Century* ..., p. 3.

tries opt for or become the victims of what he calls the "low road" scenario, these countries will remain poor and will continue to mass produce poverty-stricken people; i.e. their economies will continue to grow more slowly than their population.[17] Such countries usually experience political instability, civil unrest, and eventually a descent into a wasteland.[18] Unfortunately, this is already true of certain countries in Africa.

The likelihood that this situation could deteriorate is linked to the possibility that the rich countries of Western Europe, North America, and Japan (countries which belong to and are collectively called the Triad)[19] – could decide to turn their backs on the rest of the world. Should this happen, chaos and disorder may well reign elsewhere in the world. It is possible that Africa and other underdeveloped regions could experience higher crime rates. It is also more than likely that ecological destruction will take place on a scale never witnessed before, because in an effort to survive people will cut down trees and overgraze the land. The Triad will only intervene if their security is threatened, in the form of selective handouts in an attempt to placate the rest of the world.[20]

The Cold War is a thing of the past, and the countries of Africa can no longer play off one ideological block against another. The key variable on which one should build the scenarios of the future is the question of whether the rich nations, i.e. the Triad, will assist the poor nations to become winners in their own right, or whether they will turn their backs on them.[21] As indicated in the previous paragraph, there is a grave possibility that the latter option will be followed – unless, of course, there is a change of attitude amongst the leaders and people of, *inter alia*, the countries of Africa.

Speaking of attitudes, there is a possibility that too many people in Africa actually like to be called "third world", enjoying, the "status" accorded to so-called third world states, instead of working hard in an effort to develop their countries' potential. The concept "third world" is to a large extent, a "first world" invention, and should be discarded by those labeled as being backward.[22] But on the other hand, we, the Africans, must also prove to ourselves and to the world that we deserve our rightful place in the family of nations.

CREATING THE FUTURE: THE RULES OF THE GAME

Clem Sunter has identified four "rules of the game", i.e. trends that will determine future developments in the ever-diminishing global village, and conse-

---

[17] Ibid., p.23.

[18] Ibid., p.29.

[19] Toffler, Alvin, *Power Shift: Knowledge, Wealth, and Violence at the Edge of the 21st Century*, Bantam Books, London, 1991, pp. 430–455, also refers to the idea of this Triad.

[20] Sunter, *The New Century...*, p. 26.

[21] Ibid., p. 10.

[22] Naipaul, Shiva, *An Unfinished Journey*, Hamish Hamilton, London, 1986, pp. 31–41.

quently will also have an impact on Africa and all its peoples.[23] Firstly, there is the unprecedented growth in the population of the poor countries. The Triad has the "rich old millions", i.e. 15 percent of the world's population earning about 70 percent of the world's income, with a per capita income of about $15,000, compared with $1,000 for the rest of the world. It is common knowledge that the richer people become, the fewer children they usually have and the longer their life expectancy becomes, resulting in a geriatric boom.[24]

In the so-called "third world" live the "poor young billions". In 1988, there were about five billion people in the world. By the year 2000, there will be at least six billion, by the year 2012 seven billion and by 2026 probably about 8,5 billion.[25] Africa's population rose from about 220 million in 1950 to about 400 million in 1975 and around 725 million in 1995; and will reach about 850 million by the year 2000. By 2026, the continent's population could reach the 1,75 billion mark. Another factor to consider is the rise of mega-cities that are mushrooming. Cairo, with approximately twelve million people, is the fifteenth largest city in the world, and Lagos has an estimated ten million inhabitants.[26] However, all indications are that by the end of the century, Lagos will be Africa's largest city. At present about 280 million Africans live in cities, almost half of them residing in only 62 urban areas. Thirty cities have a population of well over one million inhabitants each. The Gauteng Province (which can almost be regarded as one sprawling urban area), the Cape Peninsula and the Durban-Pietermaritzburg area (all three in South Africa), as well as the Kinshasa-Brazzaville area, are a few of Africa's largest urban agglomerations.[27]

About 50 percent of the population of most developing countries is fifteen years of age or younger. The challenge facing many countries in Africa is turning the vicious circle of large families and rising poverty into a benign circle of increasing wealth.[28] Although the death rate in Africa has declined over the past decades, the continent's birth rate remains very high. The fertility rate (number of live births per woman) for the years 1995 to 2000 has been projected at 1,7 for Europe, the world average is 2,9, and the African average is 5,4. For the period 1960 to 1970, Africa's population grew at an annual rate of 2,6%, compared with the average world growth rate of 2%. The projected annual African growth rate for 1990 to 2000 is 2,9%, whereas the world average will probably be only 1,7%.[29]

---

[23] Sunter, Clem, *Die Wêreld en Suid-Afrika in die Jare Negentig*, Human and Rousseau/Tafelberg, Pretoria/Cape Town, 1988, pp. 19–55.

[24] Sunter, *The New Century…*, pp.11–12.

[25] Ibid., p.13; Sarre, Philip and John Blunden (editors), *An overcrowded World? Population, Resources and Environment*, Oxford University Press, Oxford, 1995, pp. 62–63.

[26] Sarre and Bluden, p. 63.

[27] Esterhuysen, Pieter (compiler) and Madeline Lass (editor), *Africa at a Glance: Facts and Figures 1995/6*, Africa Institute of South Africa, Pretoria, 1995, pp. 18–22.

[28] Sunter, *The New Century…*, p. 13.

[29] Esterhuysen and Lass, p. 15.

The "poor young billions" and "rich old millions" are locked in an inescapable embrace, linked to one another by, *inter alia*, aid programs, trade, debt, the electronic global village created by the TV mass media, and health problems such as AIDS.[30] After all, AIDS, ebola fever, cholera, etc. do not respect political or class boundaries.

A second "rule of the game" is the revolutionary impact of technology on society.[31] Microelectronics is dispensing people into ever-smaller units of production, and automation is eliminating unskilled jobs in big business. Furthermore, microelectronics is individualizing consumption, as well as individualizing society. Consequently, the computer is not empowering the state against the individual but, on the contrary, is giving knowledge to individuals which is empowering them against the state.[32] Unfortunately, in Africa, where most people do not even have electricity[33] or running water in their homes, most of the inhabitants have not benefited from the worldwide technological revolution, and the state still usually has immense power over individuals.

Technology is revolutionizing transportation and communication. It is reducing the costs and bringing transport and communication to the masses. Technology is also playing a key-role in protecting the environment, e.g. in its quest for ways to conserve energy and to reduce our dependence on fossil fuels. The next wave of technology, according to informed parties, will be biotechnology.[34] However, when, if ever, will all of Africa benefit from this technological revolution? We must guard against the danger of getting lost in the technological world that has been created. It is of the utmost importance that we understand ourselves, our world, and the processes by which our societies were formed, and that can only be done if we see these things (and ourselves) in historical perspective.[35]

The third "rule of the game" is the shift in people's values away from crude materialism to a more balanced approach to life. The way in which people think can change a society. However, certain values do not change. Consequently, language, culture, religion and nationalism are still very strong life forces, because they give an individual his or her identity. In the African context, the question is not how to eliminate nationalism and religious fervor, but how to accommodate these very strong driving forces. Since the late 1980s, there has been a general movement away from ideology and a shift towards systems that work. Ideologues are finding fewer supporters, and people are

---

[30] Sunter, *The New Century...*, pp. 13–14.

[31] Sunter, *Die Wêreld en Suid-Afrika...*, pp.27–34.

[32] Ibid., pp. 30–31; Sunter, *The New Century...*, pp. 15–16.

[33] Esterhuysen and Lass, p. 77. Canada, with a population equal to only 40 percent of that of South Africa, generates more than one-and-a-half times the electricity output of the whole of Africa.

[34] Sunter, *The New Century ...*, pp. 16–18: Toffler, Alvin, Future Shock, Pan Books, London, 1970, pp. 180–189.

[35] *Human Sciences Research Council Newsletter*, 144, Pretoria, s.a.

looking for something more sophisticated.[36] Obviously, my own inclination would be to encourage these trends. It is important to leave future generations an unpolluted, developed environment, but is equally important to provide them with a clear picture of who they are and where they come from. This will give them the self-confidence to build a constructive future.[37]

The fourth "rule of the game" concerns winning and losing nations,[38] but this issue will be dealt with in my discussion of the type of Africa in which I would like to live.

THE AFRICA AND SOUTH AFRICA OF MY DREAMS

We, the people of South Africa, Recognize the injustices of our past; Honor those who suffered for justice and freedom in our land; Respect those who have worked to build and develop our country; and Believe that South Africa belongs to all who live in it, united in our diversity.[39]

In South Africa, we have a new constitution, but we still do not have an elaborate paradigm for development which is a prerequisite for solving problems such as the low level of human development, continuing social conflict, and inadequate economic growth.[40]

In Africa, there is not enough strategic or scenario planning, and we also still have a long road ahead in terms of changing the mentalities of our people regarding certain matters, e.g. racism, tribalism, and developing a new work ethic. However, that is not to say that the people of Africa must lose their identity or become followers of everything that is "Western" and ostensibly "modern".

The "high road" scenario implies a process of closing the gap between the rich and the poor nations, while the "low road" scenario will widen the gap – with dire consequences for the stability of the whole world.[41] In the light of the fact that I, for one, would like to live in a winning nation, which in turn is part of a winning continent, I choose the "high road" as a way out of Africa's doldrums, and I would like to sketch a portrait of such an ideal winning nation.

There are six conditions necessary for a nation to become a winning nation. The most important is education. When the Egyptians built their awe-inspiring pyramids, they were the world's most educated nation. Ideas, rather than armies, conquer the world today. One should always keep in mind that a coun-

---

[36] Sunter, *The New Century* ..., pp. 9, 18–19; Sunter, *Die Wêreld en Suid-Afrika...*, pp. 34–36.

[37] *Human Sciences Research Council Newsletter*, 144, Pretoria, s.a.

[38] Sunter, *Die Wêreld en Suid-Afrika...*, pp. 40–55.

[39] First portion of the "Preamble", *The Constitution of the Republic of South Africa*, 1996, s.l., s.a., p. 1.

[40] As far as the future of development in South Africa is concerned, see e.g. Coetzee, Stef, "Quo Vadis?", paper delivered at a meeting of the Suid-Afrikaanse Akademie vir Wetenskap en Kuns, Bloemfontein, 5.11.1997.

[41] Sunter, *The New Century* ..., p. 10.

try's education system should be designed for the social and economic needs of that particular country.[42] Primary and secondary education is obviously of the utmost importance, but Africa also needs to expand its tertiary education, to produce more scholars of international standing, and to make a bigger contribution towards the international academic debate. A role model in this regard is Professor Cheikh Anta Diop (1923–1986), the great African scholar from Senegal – who has been referred to as the "Pharaoh of Knowledge".[43] Diop not only made a momentous contribution towards the revival of an African historical consciousness, but also propagated a genuine African Renaissance that would guarantee Africa a major role in all disciplines and herald a new humanism.[44]

If we are to avert recolonization (i.e. a third scramble for our continent), if we are to remain free and enjoy the benefits of our continent's enormous wealth, we must take note of what Kwame Nkrumah said many years ago: unite to plan for the full exploitation of our material and our human resources.[45] In this regard, education at the primary, secondary and tertiary levels is obviously of paramount importance. We must cultivate a critical spirit amongst our people. Every individual must take responsibility for his or her future – and for the future of his/her children and their fellow countrymen. Our motto should be: Liberation through education, human development, and the empowerment of individuals.

We must train our people to become champions in all walks of life, both in the public and private sectors. We must have devoted public servants and dynamic entrepreneurs, but we must not forget our music, our arts and culture, our history and our heritage. For obvious reasons, education and culture must not be politicized.

The second condition for a country to be a winning nation is a strong work ethic. The conditions for a work ethic are: a small government (i.e. the government must play its limited role competently, not interfering in the lives of ordinary, law-abiding citizens); low income-tax (so that people will be motivated to work harder); a sound family system (so that children will have a good upbringing); and a competent and accountable government. To ensure that the politicians will be accountable for their actions, there must be a free press and a multiparty system with regular elections.[46] Of Africa's 53 states, 36 have multiparty systems, and since 1990 there have been multiparty elections in

---

[42] Ibid., pp. 20–21.

[43] Mr Abdou Diouf, President of Senegal, in his message in the program of the International Colloquium on Cheikh Anta Diop's Work and on African Renaissance on the Eve of the Third Millennium, Dakar-Caytu, February 26–March 2, 1996, p. 5.

[44] Ibid., p. 3; Abstracts of the Contributors' papers: International Colloquium on the Work of Cheikh Anta Diop – Africa's Renaissance on the Threshold of the Third Millennium, Dakar-Caytu, February 26–March 2, 1996, CNPCAD/X, Dakar, 1996, p. 97.

[45] Lamb, p. 278.

[46] Sunter, *The New Century* .... pp. 21–22.

about 37 states.[47] Progress has been achieved but there is still a lot to be done in the field of democratization.

The third condition for becoming a winning nation is a high savings rate; the fourth is a "dual-logic" economy. On the one hand, a country needs a big business sector with high technology and sufficient financial resources to undertake large projects. However, it is just as important that big business be underpinned by a vibrant small business and informal sector. After all, it is in the small business and informal sector that most of the job-creation takes place, and where the future stars of big business are born. Economic miracles take place when there is a profitable relationship between big business on the one hand, and small business and the informal sector on the other hand.[48] In 1981, the Small Business Development Corporation (SBDC) was launched in South Africa as a joint venture of the public and private sectors. Since its inception, the SBDC has granted loans to about 50,000 entrepreneurs, creating about 400,000 new jobs in the process. The informal business sector in South Africa has an annual turnover which amounts to about 16 percent of the country's GDP.[49] Sustainable economic development is the watchword and, in that regard, South Africa still faces several challenges.[50]

Social harmony is the fifth condition for a winning nation. This implies, *inter alia*, that there must be a strong sense of social justice (i.e. a feeling amongst the inhabitants that the system is fair). Lastly, a winning nation looks outwards and strives to become a global player.[51] Countries must not isolate themselves; and Africa as a marginalized continent must strive to obtain its rightful place in the global village.

In a winning nation, one may conclude, there is a balance between economic development, environmental health, and quality of life.[52] To attain this balance, to become a winning nation, a country (or a whole continent) has to travel the "high road".

Most Africans share a common colonial history, but we must guard against the danger of suffering from historical amnesia. We must know and understand our history so that we can come to terms with our controversial past; and in the process we shall hopefully learn to understand ourselves and those who exploited us. History, after all, enables one to forgive without forgetting. We shall then be able to coexist peacefully, and perhaps even set an example for people in flashpoints across the globe.

---

[47] "Demokrasie vorder wel, word egter steeds bedreig", *Die Volksblad*, 3.1.1996, p. 5; W. Breytenbach, "Die demokrasie op Afrikakontinent bly nog maar steeds wankelrig", *Rapport*, 2.6.1994, p. 21; Esterhuysen and Lass, pp. 102–109.

[48] Sunter, *The New Century...*, p. 22.

[49] *South Africa Yearbook 1994*, South African Communication Service, Pretoria, s.a., p. 193.

[50] Coetzee, p. 12

[51] Sunter, *The New Century...*, pp. 22–23.

[52] Ibid., p. 19.

It is a sobering thought that "nearly all poor countries are potentially rich; they're just badly governed".[53] There are eight requirements for the "high road" scenario: the Triad must share its ideas and technology with the socalled third world (in accordance with the maxim that it is much better to teach a person to fish than to give him or her a fish); where money is forthcoming, it should come from eager investors (e.g. the IMF and World Bank should only assist countries that are dedicated to becoming winning nations); pure aid should be restricted to real hardships and to the provision of infrastructure; there must be equality of opportunity in international trade (i.e. a level playing field, with the Triad eliminating its barriers); there should be a sound international monetary system underpinning the expansion of trade; control should be exercised over the arms trade;[54] peace must be preserved by the UN, backed by the G7 countries;[55] and there must be a balance between economic development and environmental health – once again the UN and the G7 countries have an important role to play in this regard.[56]

Like the rest of Africa, South Africa can either opt for the "low road" (i.e. a passive future in which one simply allows things to happen), or the "high road" (i.e. the active future which one causes to happen). I am in agreement with Clem Sunter that we in South Africa have the potential to become winners, to turn so-called ordinary people into winners – perhaps even becoming role-models for many other people in Africa. South Africa is a microcosm of the world. We have several thousands of the "rich old millions" (about 15 percent of the population, mostly white) and millions of the "poor young billions" (about 85 percent of the population, mostly black) in the country.[57] But we must look beyond Afro-pessimism.

Several great strengths could put South Africa on the "high road" towards developing its full potential in the interest of all its inhabitants – and in the interest of large parts of Africa. Firstly, South Africa's infrastructure is probably the best of its kind in the developing world – from roads, railroads, harbors and airports to our telecommunications system.[58] By the 1990s, 41 percent of all telephones in Africa were to be found in South Africa, as well as 18 percent of all the continent's paved roads, more than 25 percent of its railway tracks,

---

[53] Ibid., p. 24.

[54] Arms worth billions of dollar were pumped into Africa during the Cold War. See e.g. George T. Yu, "Sino-Soviet Rivalry in Africa" in David E. Albright (ed.), *Africa and International Communism*, The Macmillan Press Ltd., London, 1980, pp. 175–177.

[55] As far as UN peacekeeping, operations in Africa are concerned, see e.g. United Nations, *The Blue Helmets: A Review of United Nations Peacekeeping* (2nd edition), s.l., 1990, pp. 213–260, 335–388.

[56] Sunter, *The New Century...*, pp. 24–25.

[57] Ibid., 27.

[58] Ibid.

and no less than half of all the electricity generated. In many African countries, the infrastructural services have been severely disrupted or damaged by lack of maintenance or by war.[59]

A second great strength is the country's mineral resources. South Africa is one of the world's richest mineralized areas, and at the beginning of the 1990s the country was the leading African country in the production of fifteen different minerals. South Africa is the world's largest producer of gold, chromium, alumino-silicates, platinum, vanadium and vermiculite.[60] However, it is necessary to add value to these resources and turn them into semi-manufactured and manufactured products, instead of exporting raw minerals and importing the manufactured products that we need. The natural beauty and mild climate of our country is a third great strength. As stated earlier, South Africa is in fact a world in one country. South Africa has the potential to become the number one tourist attraction in the Southern Hemisphere,[61] and tourism could overtake gold as the chief foreign exchange earner for the country. The number of jobs which could be created is well worth considering. A fourth strength is the people of South Africa. Besides the civil service, there is a vast army of entrepreneurs, and with the deregulation of the economy, more and more small businesses are opening up, changing the face of the South African economy.[62]

Other strengths include the fact that South Africa is situated on the strategic Cape sea-route, has easy access to the African markets, has a sophisticated financial infrastructure, the ability to tackle big projects in a variety of fields; and a very sophisticated medical infrastructure.[63] After all, the world's first-ever heart transplant operation was performed by a South African medical team in Cape Town in 1967.

Notwithstanding all the horrors of apartheid, an ideology and a system that could have terminally damaged or even destroyed the moral fiber of our society, South Africans rose to the occasion when State President F.W. de Klerk ushered in a new era in our history with his epoch-making speech in Parliament on 2 February 1990,[64] unbanning organizations such as the African National Congress (ANC) and the Pan-Africanist Congress (PAC), and freeing Nelson Mandela and other political prisoners. A little more than four years later, South Africa's first-ever democratic elections were held, and on 10 May 1994, Nelson

---

[59] Esterhuysen and Lass, pp. 77–82.

[60] Ibid., pp. 66–68

[61] In 1995, more than two million foreign tourists visited South Africa. Sherrocks, John, "Tourism fears groundless", *The Daily News*, 4.1.1996, p. 14 .

[62] Sunter, *The New Century ....*, p. 28.

[63] Sunter, *Die Wêreld en Suid-Afrika...*, pp. 86–88.

[64] Republic of South Africa. *Debates of Parliament (Hansard), 2 to 9 February 1990*, The Government Printer, Cape Town, s.a., columns 118.

Mandela was sworn in as the country's first democratically elected president.[65] If people believe in miracles, they can happen. It has been a long and bitter struggle for freedom, and there is still a long way to go along the road of reconstruction, development and transformation, but we have proved to ourselves what we can accomplish; i.e. our new national symbols have received wide acceptance,[66] and land reform is underway.[67]

Now that a negotiated political settlement has been reached and implemented, South Africa needs rapid economic growth, because only then will most of the fear that is still to be found in the hearts and minds of many white South Africans be allayed (fear that has already led to too many white professionals leaving the country); and only then will some of the (often farfetched) expectations of many black South Africans be fulfilled. Throughout the history of South Africa, fear has played an important role,[68] and it is imperative that a balance be struck between white fears on the one hand, and black expectations on the other. Just like in the rest of Africa (but especially in the whole global village), the fears of the rich old millions must be balanced with the expectations of the poor young billions.

At the end of the day, South Africa – just like any other country in Africa – is not going to be saved by a black or white messiah, but by turning ordinary people into champions. After all, it is no coincidence that the most successful countries in the world do not have strong leaders in the traditional sense. A country's president, premier or prime minister should be a facilitator between the major interest groups in the country, and not a cult leader or a strong man (or woman, for that matter). The successful modern leader is a person who serves and supports his or her people, bringing out the best in them, liberating their spirit, and making them leaders themselves.[69]

It is imperative that a strong and productive middle class should be created in South Africa, as in the rest of Africa. Africans must accept individual ac-

---

[65] As far as the 1994 general election, its run-up and aftermath is concerned, see e.g. the following articles in a special edition of the *Journal for Contemporary History* 19(2), September 1994: A.H Marais, "Negotiations for a Democratic South Africa, 1985–1992" (pp. 127); J. A. du Pisani, "Negotiating a Democratic South Africa: Bilateral and Multiparty Negotiations, June 1992 to December 1993 (pp. 28–81); J. H. le Roux, "Violence and Intimidation during the Election Campaign – A Review" (pp. 82–112); S. L. Barnard, "The Election Campaign of the General Election in South Africa in 1994" (pp. 113–140); P. W. Coetzer, "Opinion Polls and Opinions on the Results of the Election of 1994" (pp. 219–261); A.C.P Strauss, "Reaction to the 1994 South African General Elections" (pp. 288–322). See also Mandela, Nelson, *Long Walk to Freedom,* Macdonald Purnell (Pty) Ltd., Randburg, 1994, pp. 546–617.

[66] Wessels, André, "In search of acceptable National Symbols for South Africa", *Journal for Contemporary History* 19(2), September 1994, pp. 262–287.

[67] As far as the controversial land issue is concerned, see e.g. Wessels, André, "Die Beleid van die belangrikste Partye in Suid Afrika met betrekking tot herdistribusie" in D.J. Kriek and P. Labuschagne (editors), *Politieke Verandering in Suid-Afrika 4: Herdistribusiefase,* HSRC, Pretoria, 1996, pp. 197–232.

[68] See Du Bruijn, H.J., *Vrees as Faktor in die Regse Blanke Politiek in Suid-Afrika sedert 1948: 'n Historiese Ontleding,* M.A. thesis, University of the Orange Free State, 1994.

[69] Sunter, *The New Century* ...., pp. 29–30.

countability and individual responsibility, including accountability and responsibility towards all other Africans as individuals, as well as towards their community, country, continent and the ever-shrinking global village. Individuals must take the initiative, and must not wait for the government to do for them what they ought to and can do for themselves. The essence of the "high road" lies in the fact that the source of progress is to be found in individual will and individual action. This should not be seen as a call for the promotion of selfishness, but rather for self-fulfilment within the bounds of decent, moral values.[70]

I, for one, am accepting this challenge, because I believe that every person has the potential to make a difference in his or her community, perhaps even beyond the (sometimes ill-defined) borders of that community. If, in years to come, in my small way I have contributed towards the reconstruction, development and transformation of my workplace, my community and perhaps even my country; if I have contributed towards fighting prejudice and racism; if I have striven to heal the wounds of the past; if I have tried to ascertain what the truth is as far as my country's troubled history is concerned; if I have tried to reconcile my people (irrespective of political beliefs, colour, creed or gender) then I will have been a relatively successful (South) African. We still have to build a "new" South Africa. We may never see or experience the "new" South Africa ourselves, but we have a grave responsibility towards ourselves, the future generations, our country and our continent, to follow the "high road" that will lead us to the status of a winning nation.

I fully agree with Clem Sunter that the principal force that will close the gap between the rich and the poor is the natural desire in most human beings to uplift themselves, As long as governments do not intervene unfairly, the "high road" will materialize because the creative genius of ordinary people will ultimately triumph.[71] The world (and especially Africa) is, in fact, at a crossroads. We are the first generation that can irreversibly transform our planet (and specifically our continent, Africa) for the worse; but we are at the same time the last generation that can avert disaster. "We are not at the end of history, as some people believe; we are at the beginning of a new chapter".[72]

In Africa, the clock need not always be at five minutes to twelve. Africans can (and must) become winners in the globalized economic and technological arena. We have been exploited by foreigners for many years and have also done terrible things to fellow Africans, but the vast majority of us are peace-loving and creative people who can contribute towards keeping the Four Horsemen of the Apocalypse at bay and find solutions to problems such as drought, famine, political instability, conflict, urbanization, crime, AIDS, and social and economic decline. Africa need not be the ghetto of the world.

---

[70] Ibid., pp. 30–31, 33.
[71] Ibid., p. 10.
[72] Ibid., p. 27

On the threshold of a new century and a new millennium, I passionately believe in the future of my country, my continent and all its peoples, in the vast human potential that is waiting to be developed, and in our ability to turn ordinary people like ourselves into champions. The golden dawn of the African Renaissance is breaking: *Nkosi Sikelel'i Afrika*, God bless Africa.

REFERENCES

BOOKS

Abstracts of Contributors' Papers: International Colloquium on the Work of Cheikh Anta Diop – Africa's Renaissance on the Threshold of the Third Millennium, Dakar-Caytu, February 26–March 2, 1996, CNPCAD/X, Dakar, 1996.

Esterhuysen, Pieter (compiler) and Madeline Lass (editor), *Africa at a Glance: Facts and Figures 1995/6*, Africa Institute of South Africa, Pretoria, 1995.

Grove, A.T., *The Changing Geography of Africa*, 2nd edition, Oxford University Press, Oxford, 1993.

Gutteridge, W.E, *Military Régimes in Africa*, Methuen and Co. Ltd., London, 1975.

Huntley, Brian, Roy Siegfried and Clem Sunter. *South African Environments in the 21st Century*, Human and Rousseau/Tafelberg, Cape Town, 1990.

Lamb, David, *The Africans*, Methuen, London, 1987.

Mandela, Nelson, *Long Walk to Freedom*, Macdonald Purnell (Pty) Ltd., Randburg, 1994.

The Military Balance 1996/97, The International Institute for Strategic Studies, London, 1996.

Naipaul, Shiva, *An Unfinished Journey*, Hamish Hamilton, London, 1986.

Palmer, Monty, *Dilemmas of Political Development: An Introduction to the Politics of Developing Areas*, 4th edition, F.E. Peacock, Publishers, Itasca, 1989.

Sarre, Philip and John Blunden (editors), *An Overcrowded World? Population, Resources and the Environment*, Oxford University Press. Oxford, 1995.

Sharpe, Richard (editor), *Jane's Fighting Ship 1996–97*, Jane's Information Group Ltd., Coulsdon, s.a.

South African Yearbook 1994, South African Communication Service, Pretoria, s.a.

Sunter, Clem, *The Casino Model*, Human and Rousseau/Tafelberg, Cape Town, 1994.

Sunter, Clem, *The High Road – Where are we Now?*, Human and Rousseau/Tafelberg, Cape Town, 1996.

Sunter, Clem, *The New Century: Quest for the High Road*, RA. Gallo and Company (Pty) Limited, s.l., 1992.

Sunter, Clem, *Pretoria will Provide and Other Myths*, Human and Rousseau/Tafelberg, Cape Town, 1994.

Sunter, Clem, *Die Wêreld en Suid-Afrika in die Jare Negentig*, Human and Rousseau/Tafelberg, Pretoria/Cape Town, 1988.

Toffler, Alvin, *Future Shock*, Pan Books, London, 1970.

Toffler, Alvin, *Power Shift: Knowledge, Wealth, and Violence at the Edge of the 21st Century,* Bantam Books, London, 1991.

United Nations, *The Blue Helmets: A Review of United Nations Peace-keeping,* 2nd edition, s.l., 1990.

CHAPTERS IN BOOKS

Wessels, André, "Die Beleid van die belangrikste Partye in Suid Afrika met betrekking tot Herdistribusie" in D.L Kriek and P. Labuschagne (editors), *Politieke Verandering in SuidAfrika 4: Herdistribusiefäse,* HSRC, Pretoria, 1996, pp. 197–232.

Yu, George T., "Sino-Soviet Rivalry in Africa" in David E. Albright (editor), *Africa and International Communism,* The Macmillan Press Ltd., London, 1980, pp. 168–188.

JOURNAL ARTICLES

Barnard, S.L., "The Election Campaign of the General Election in South Africa in 1994", *Journal for Contemporary History* 19(2), September 1994, pp. 113–140.

Coetzer, P.W., "Opinion Polls and Opinions on the Results of the Election of 1994", *Journal for Contemporary History* 19(2), September 1994, pp. 219–261.

Colborne, Desmond, "Recolonising Africa: The Right to Intervene?, *South Africa International* 23(4), April 1993, pp. 162–163.

Du Pisani, L. A., "Negotiating a Democratic South Africa: Bilateral and Multiparty Negotiations, June 1992 to December 1993", *Journal for Contemporary History* 19(2), September 1994, pp. 28–81.

Johnson, Paul, "De Kolonie was zo Gek nog niet: Alleen maar Interveniëren heeft voor Afrika geen Zin", *Elsevier,* 16.7.1994, pp. 34–36.

Le Roux, J.K., "Violence and Intimidation during the Election Campaign – a Review", *Journal for Contemporary History* 19(2), September 1994, pp. 82–112.

Marais, A.K, "Negotiations for a Democratic South Africa, 1985–1992", *Journal for Contemporary History* 19(2), September 1994, pp. 127.

Strauss, A.C.P., "Reaction to the 1994 South African General Elections", *Journal for Contemporary History* 19(2), September 1994, pp. 288–322.

Van Rijckevorsel, Rene, "Afrika: Getto van de Wereld, *Elsevier,* 16.7.1994, pp. 29–33.

Wessels, André, "In search of acceptable National Symbols for South Africa", *Journal for Contemporary History* 19(2), September 1994, pp. 262–287.

NEWSPAPER ARTICLES

Breytenbach, W., "Die Demokrasie op Afrika-kontinent bly nog maar steeds wankelrig", *Rapport,* 2.6.1994, p. 21.

"Demokrasie vorder wel, word ecter steeds bedreig", *Die Volksblad,* 3.1.1996, p. 5.

Neale, Greg, "The Lies about Africa", *Sunday Times,* 27.10.1996, p. 16. (Article reprinted from *The Telegraph,* London.)

Petersen, Scott, "Keeping the Four Horsemen at Bay", *The Natal Mercury,* 2.1.1995, p. 7. (Article reprinted from *The Telegraph,* London.)

Sherrocks, John, "Tourism fears groundless", *The Daily News,* 4.1.1996, p. 14.

Trench, Andrew, "In Africa, things need not always fall apart", *Sunday Times,* 10. 11. 1996, p. 10.

THESES

Du Bruijn, H.J., *Vrees as Faktor in die Regse Blanke Politiek in Suid-Afrika sedert 1948: 'n Historiese Ontleding,* M.A. thesis, University of the Orange Free State, 1994.

OTHER PUBLICATIONS

Coetzee, Stef, "Ontwikkeling: Quo Vadis?," Paper delivered at a meeting of the Suid-Afrikaanse Akademie vir Wetenskap en Kuns, Bloemfontein, 5.11.1997.

The Constitution of the Republic of South Africa, 1996, s.l., s.a.

Human Sciences Research Council Newsletter 144, Pretoria, s.a.

International Colloquium on Cheikh Anta Diop's Work and on African Renaissance on the Eve of the Third Millennium, Dakar-Caytu, February 26–March 2, 1996 (program).

Republic of South Africa, Debates of Parliament (Hansard), 2–9 February 1990, The Government Printer, Cape Town, s.a.

Summary of the Programme of Action of the International Conference on Population and Development, United Nations, New York, 1995.

CHAPTER 16

The Way Forward

Olugbenga Adesida
Arunma Oteh

The purpose of this book has been to encourage creative thinking by Africans on the future of Africa. The focus was to initiate a dialogue, which would provide answers to three basic questions: what the future could be, what the future should be, and how we might build the preferred future. The publication of the book is the beginning, and not the end, of an ongoing dialogue to build a better future. We Africans must develop the culture of strategic long-term thinking, inquisition and exploration. This is necessary in order to generate alternative images of the future – probable, possible, and preferred. This, we believe, is a required undertaking if we are to be able to create a better future for future generations of Africans.

As noted by Hamdy Abdel Rahman, in his contribution, being preoccupied by present challenges should never "blind a nation to its history and its future". To Rahman, "all dynamic nations must focus their attention to planning the future". Yet, actively thinking about the future of Africa has not been a popular exercise. It tends to be an irregular bureaucratic exercise which does not involve the people. In the words of Admore M. Kambudzi, "Essentially Africa needs a common popular vision. It is the people, the citizens of African states themselves who must visualize the way they wish to live". Therefore, part of this effort is to help in facilitating the process of evolving a popularly shared African vision of the future.

Each essay in this book provides the author's vision for Africa and ideas on how to make this vision a reality. The essays provide new perspectives on the African development challenge and what could be achieved. In short, they all give us new scenarios as to how Africa can build a better future. The optimism of the contributors, given the challenges facing the continent, is remarkable.

The real challenges now are: how do we make this dialogue ongoing and not a one-off exercise? How do we ensure that the process is undertaken at the local, national, subregional and continental levels? And that the process can be undertaken at the local, national, sub-regional and continental levels? This is surely needed because it is only by challenging ourselves, reflecting together, and thinking about the possibilities that we can have the audacity to dream and generate ideas about how to make our dreams a reality. In a sense, we have no choice except to dream of the impossible, given the fact that almost all predictions paint a gloomy picture of the future of the continent.

Africa must not let the enormity of the current challenges blind it to its past and future. For a long time, the continent seemed to have been without a global vision of what we, as Africans, want and how we plan to make our desires a reality. This is a major problem because without a vision of its destiny and a map of the future, Africa will always be reacting to events and will continue to be subjected to other peoples' visions of its future. We must therefore heed the advice of the authors in this compendium that Africa must reclaim its identity and take its future into its own hands.

This is a challenge that all Africans must take seriously. We must commit ourselves to creating a better future for the coming generations. To do this, however, we must begin by reflecting on our past, our unique problems, and our desires, and make proposals on how to move forward. It is quite clear that to create a better future in Africa will require a fundamental shift in thinking and orientation, and not incremental changes. What we need is a paradigm shift in the way we manage our affairs in Africa.

We must, therefore, set up the necessary institutions to facilitate the process of thinking and dialogue about the future in Africa. An independent institute or a foundation that will serve as a think-tank and have the mandate of thinking about the future of the continent is a must, especially in this new world of information and knowledge.

Our hope is that this book project is the beginning of this process. We are planning some follow-up activities. The first agenda is to hold a workshop which will bring together the authors, policy makers, and other interested Africans. The idea will be to propose a continental vision for the 21st century, and thus open up for an African-wide debate and dialogue. Subsequently, we hope to work with others to develop an institutional framework to continue the dialogue, popularize the vision and get Africans actively involved in creating a better future.

This must be an Africa-wide initiative. We need the support of all Africans, particularly the grassroots and other well-wishers to make this happen. We need your ideas and hope you will join us in this endeavor. We are hoping to hear from you all.

Notes on Editors

Olugbenga Adesida (Nigeria) was born in 1965. He is the founder of The Knowledge Network (www.tknonline.com), a futures think-tank and strategy consulting firm. He was previously an expert with African Futures, a regional project of the United Nations Development Program (UNDP) based in Abidjan, Côte d'Ivoire. He is a futurist with particular interests in development and technology futures. He studied economics at the City College of New York and The City University of New York Graduate School.

Arunma Oteh (Nigeria) graduated from the University of Nigeria, Nsukka with a first class honors degree in Computer Science and received a Master in Business Administration from Harvard University. She has worked at the Harvard Institute for International Development and is currently the Division Manager, Investments, Treasury Department, African Development Bank. She was born in 1965 and is particularly interested in the future and socioeconomic development of Africa, national competitiveness and financing technological innovation.

Notes on Contributors

Musa Abutudu (Nigeria) obtained his Ph.D. from the University of Ibadan. He is a Senior Lecturer in Political Science at the University of Benin, Nigeria. Dr. Abutudu is widely published, and has had fellowship stints in Africa and the United States. In 1997–98 he was member of the Institute for Advanced Study, Princeton, USA. He was born in 1958.

Coumba Ndoffène Diouf (Senegal) was born in 1960 in Dakar. He belongs to the Serer group in the Fatick region. He completed his studies at Cheick Anta Diop University in Dakar where he is presently an Assistant Professor of Management in the Economics and Management Department. His areas of interest include strategic management, small and medium enterprise management, and industrial policy.

Godwin Y. Dogbey (Ghana) is a Research Officer in the Policy Analysis and Strategic Studies Division of the Ghana Institute of Management and Public Administration. He was born in 1963 and he holds Master of Philosophy degree in Economics and a Bachelor of Science (Hons) degree in Statistics and Computer Science from the University of Ghana, Legon. He had experience in public service before joining academia.

Admore Mupoki Kambudzi (Zimbabwe) was educated at the University of Zimbabwe and in France where he obtained his Ph.D. in International Relations. He is currently a lecturer in the Department of Political and Administrative Studies at the University of Zimbabwe. He was born 1960.

Geoffrey E. Kiangi (Tanzania) holds a B.Sc. (Eng.), an M.Sc. (Eng.) and a Ph.D. from Leeds, U.K. He has worked as an engineer and a university lecturer in Tanzania and Kenya. He is currently the Dean of the Faculty of Science, University of Namibia. His research interests include software engineering, technology management, and optimization techniques in engineering. He has over 30 publications as books, journal and conference articles. He was born in 1957.

Comfort Lamptey (Ghana) works for the United Nations Development Fund for Women (UNIFEM) in New York, as a Program Specialist within the Africa Division. She also has responsibility for helping to expand the Fund's work in the field of support to women for peace-building activities. Prior to joining UNIFEM, Ms. Lamptey worked with International Alert, a London-based NGO specializing in the field of conflict prevention and resolution. She completed her studies at Sussex University, England, where she obtained both her graduate (Politics) and postgraduate (International Relations) degrees. She was born 1968.

Barbara Mbire-Barungi (Uganda) is an Economist. She is a policy expert with the government of Rwanda. She was previously teaching at the University of the Witswatersrand in South Africa. She is also studying for her Ph.D. in Economics. She was born in 1965 and holds an Mphil. degree in International Finance from Glasgow University, Scotland.

Lawrence Mukuka (Zambia) was born in 1956. He holds a Bachelors (University of Zambia), Masters (Columbia University, New York) and a Ph.D. (University of California, Berkeley) in Social Work. He also received an M.A. degree from the University of California at Berkeley in Political Science, a Postgraduate Diploma in International Law from the University of Zambia and a Diploma in International Economic Relations from the Institute of United Nations Studies (Zambia) in conjunction with the United Nations University in Japan. Since 1991, he has been teaching Social Work at the University of Zambia. Between 1992 and 1996, he was the head of the Department of Social Work. Currently, he is the Director of the Center for Social Policy Studies.

Chika Nwobi (Nigeria) is an undergraduate student at the East Tennessee State University, Johnson City, USA, and was born in 1978.

Levi M. Obijiofor (Nigeria) is a Research Fellow at The Communication Centre, Queensland University of Technology, Brisbane, Australia. Born in 1958, Obijiofor worked at various times as Sub-Editor, Production Editor, and Night Editor in a leading independent English language newspaper – *The Guardian* – in Lagos, Nigeria. Between March 1995 and May 1996, he worked in the Division of Studies and Programming (BPE/BP) in the Paris headquarters of UNESCO, where he coordinated and edited the bulletin and database of future-oriented literature – FUTURESCO.

Bolanle A. Olaniran (Nigeria) was born in 1964. He is currently an Assistant Professor of organizational communication in the Department of Communication Studies at Texas Technology University, Lubbock, Texas. He received his B.B.A. and M.B.A. degrees in Communication at the University of Oklahoma. His areas of interest are computer-mediated communication technology and inter-cultural communication. He has published on these topics in a variety of journals and books.

Paul Omojo Omaji (Nigeria) was born in 1956 in Idah Local Government of Kogi State. Omaji qualified in social sciences and law from Nigerian and Australian universities, culminating in a doctoral degree from the Australian National University, Canberra. He lectured for several years at Ahmadu Bello

University, Zaria and later joined the Edith Cowan University in Western Australia in 1993, where he served as the Coordinator of the Legal Studies Degree Program. He is currently a Senior Lecturer in the Department of Justice Studies. His research and publications have been in areas of law and development issues, indigenous people and the law, human rights law, juvenile justice, crime prevention, and comparative legal systems.

Hamdy Abdel Rahman (Egypt) is an Associate Professor in the Department of Political Science, Faculty of Economics, Cairo University, Egypt. He is also the Founder and Director of the Center for African Futures Studies in Cairo. He received his B.Sc., M.A, and Ph.D. degrees in Political Science from Cairo University. He was born in 1960.

André Wessels (South Africa) was born in Durban in 1956. At the University of the Orange Free State (UOFS) in Bloemfontein he obtained a B.A. degree (*cum laude*) in 1977, a B.A. (Hons) in 1978, a Higher Education Diploma (*cum laude*) in 1979, a Masters degree (*cum laude*) in History in 1982 and a D.Phil degree in History in 1980. After working as a school teacher and then as a historical researcher, he joined the Department of History at UOFS in 1988, where he is at present an Associate Professor. He has published three books and more than eighty articles, book reviews, chapters in books, and other publications, and serves on the editorial board of three academic journals.

Visions of the Future of Africa
(shortened version)

INTRODUCTION

A cursory look at Africa today reveals a continent that is faced with serious challenges. While the population has continued to swell, sluggish economic growth has characterized most countries since the early 1980s. Compared to the sixties and seventies, the quality of life has declined. Poverty, corruption, the debt burden, instability, environmental degradation, illiteracy and unemployment are all increasing. Diseases such as AIDS are spreading exponentially and uncontrollably. These problems are compounded by the "complete disintegration of the State" in countries such as Algeria, Liberia, Sierra Leone, Somalia, Sudan, and Rwanda. The continent appears to have become a laboratory for chaotic social systems and has acquired a reputation for possessing the worst type of dictators. The extent of the pessimism about the future is such that some are already suggesting that recolonization may be the only plausible solution to the challenges facing the continent.

On the other hand, when one examines the current wind of democratic change blowing slowly across the continent, one cannot but see a glimmer of hope on the horizon. The rise of democratic governance, the economic reforms, the attitude of self-reliance that is developing in response to declining development aid, the opportunities presented by recent advances in biotechnology and the information revolution offer hope that Africa may be able to overcome the current development quagmire. Furthermore, the peaceful dismantling of the apartheid regime in the Republic of South Africa under challenging circumstances is evidence that a positive future is plausible for Africa. The possibility that the Republic of South Africa could boost the economic prospects of other African countries if the political situation continues to remain stable, is another reason to be hopeful. We should not lose sight of the fact that it was only about thirty years ago, during the independence era, that Africans and non-Africans alike were sanguine about the future of Africa. From this viewpoint, Africa does have hope.

The above images are only two ends of the spectrum when one considers the wide range of future possibilities that are available to Africa. The aftermath will always be a consequence of the actions or inaction of the stakeholders, particularly Africans. Although futuristic analysis should provide a balanced perspective on the full range of possibilities, a feeling of hopelessness has weighted appraisals of Africa largely towards the pessimistic view with some analysts concluding that the African continent has no future. On the other hand, an examination of the different views of the future of the world reveals several scenarios, including images of an information society, a sustainable society, and a global market place. This is what we desire for Africa, for it is only by revealing the wide range of possibilities that hope can be restored.

We need to do this so that we can begin to lay the foundation for the future that we want. This necessitates a dialogue about the future and particularly about the future of Africa. This dialogue should be about where we are, where we would like to go, and how to get to where we would like to go. This is the reasoning behind the proposed book.

WHY A NEW BOOK ON THE FUTURE OF AFRICA?

Does Africa have a future? What do Africans, particularly the young generation, really think about the future? What are their visions, hopes, fears, ambitions, and goals? How do Africans see the future of the world, the continent, their nation, and their communities? What role do they see themselves playing, not only in their country but in the world of the future? What are their perceptions about the trends that will shape the world, their region, nation, and societies? Which of these trends would they like to encourage and which would they like to discourage? What type of world would they like to live in?

In what forum can these questions be answered? On what accessible platform can the result of a dialogue such as this be presented to the world? Our proposition is a book, a book with contributions from dynamic Africans. The book will take into account a 30-year time frame into the future. Each contributing author will be asked not only to respond to the issues raised above, but to also explore any issue that is important to understanding where we are, where we should be going, and where we might be going. We would be seeking provocative, original and insightful ideas.

Our goal is not to predict the future but to challenge and inspire Africans to explore their desires and empower them to think about the future. What good will this do? It will certainly not lead to an overnight resolution of the African development crisis. Our hope, however, is that it will inspire everyone to think seriously about future possibilities – what future they desire; and to see what individual role they could play in creating such a future. More importantly, we hope that this book will challenge and empower everyone to contribute to the realization of a desirable future. Indeed, creating the future is our shared responsibility.

In engaging in a community soul-searching about the future, an important role must be assigned to the younger generations because they have more at stake. The future belongs to them, their children, and their children's children. They are the leaders of tomorrow. For these reasons, we require that all contributing authors must be 40 years of age or younger. This will ensure that the younger generations can begin to participate in the dialogue on their future.

The book will also provide a platform for them to explore their hopes, visions, ambitions, and fears. We hope that this book will challenge them to start thinking of their roles in creating not only a better Africa but also a better world. To summarize, the objectives of the book are:

- To share with the world alternative visions of the future from the African perspective;
- To generate a debate in Africa, and possibly the world, about the role of younger generations in creating a better future;
- To alert African leaders and the international community on the desires, wishes and fears of the younger generations of Africans; and
- To promote a dialogue on the future, and ensure that Africans, particularly the young, participate in the debate.